Affiliated Identities in Jewish American Literature

Affiliated Identities in Jewish American Literature

David Hadar

BLOOMSBURY ACADEMIC
NEW YORK • LONDON • OXFORD • NEW DELHI • SYDNEY

BLOOMSBURY ACADEMIC
Bloomsbury Publishing Inc
1385 Broadway, New York, NY 10018, USA
50 Bedford Square, London, WC1B 3DP, UK
29 Earlsfort Terrace, Dublin 2, Ireland

BLOOMSBURY, BLOOMSBURY ACADEMIC and the Diana logo
are trademarks of Bloomsbury Publishing Plc

First published in the United States of America 2020
This paperback edition published in 2022

Copyright © David Hadar, 2020

Cover design: Eleanor Rose
Cover illustration © Lilac Hadar

For legal purposes the Acknowledgments on pp. viii–ix constitute
an extension of this copyright page.

All rights reserved. No part of this publication may be reproduced or
transmitted in any form or by any means, electronic or mechanical,
including photocopying, recording, or any information storage or retrieval
system, without prior permission in writing from the publishers.

Bloomsbury Publishing Inc does not have any control over, or responsibility for, any
third-party websites referred to or in this book. All internet addresses given in this
book were correct at the time of going to press. The author and publisher regret any
inconvenience caused if addresses have changed or sites have ceased to exist,
but can accept no responsibility for any such changes.

Library of Congress Cataloging-in-Publication Data
Names: Hadar, David, 1981- author.
Title: Affiliated identities in Jewish American literature / David Hadar.
Description: New York : Bloomsbury Academic, 2020. | Includes
bibliographical references and index.
Identifiers: LCCN 2020001947 | ISBN 9781501360916 (hardback) |
ISBN 9781501360930 (pdf) | ISBN 9781501360923 (ebook)
Subjects: LCSH: American literature–Jewish authors–History and criticism.
| Jewish authors–Biography. | Jews–United States–Identity. | Social networks.
Classification: LCC PS153.J4 H29 2020 | DDC 810.9/3529924–dc23
LC record available at https://lccn.loc.gov/2020001947

ISBN:	HB:	978-1-5013-6091-6
	PB:	978-1-5013-7130-1
	ePDF:	978-1-5013-6093-0
	eBook:	978-1-5013-6092-3

Typeset by Integra Software Services Pvt. Ltd.
Printed and bound in the United States of America

To find out more about our authors and books visit www.bloomsbury.com
and sign up for our newsletters.

In loving memory of Emily Miller Budick

Contents

Acknowledgments	viii
Introduction	1
1 Filiation and Affiliation	23
2 Locating Affiliations	41
3 Jewish American Literary Networks beyond English	61
4 The Jewish Writer as an Old Man	85
5 New Networks with Israeli Writers	105
6 Negotiating Continuity: Writing about Philip Roth in Israel	127
7 Kashua's Complaint: A Palestinian Writer Meets Roth	143
Coda	155
Notes	164
Appendix: An Abridged Map of Author Connections	193
Index	194

Acknowledgments

Somewhere in this book, I will claim that the acknowledgments section is often used to form affiliations and thus shape and maintain the author's public identity. This is probably true of my own acknowledgments as well. However, the section's primary and stated aim is to thank the people and institutions involved in creating the book. I am grateful to many and will use this section primarily to express this gratitude.

This book has its roots in work undertaken at the Hebrew University's English Department. Ruben Borg, Leona Toker, Shuli Barzilai, and Sanford Budick gave me much guidance and support. Fellow students who helped my work include Philip Podolsky, Hannah Landes, Lasse Winther Jensen, Jonathan Stavsky, and members of the research groups "The Critic in Hebrew Literature" and "Local Literature," including Reut Ben Yaakov, Dina Berdichevsky, Amos Noy, Guy Ron Gilboa, and Liron Alon.

The book was developed during two postdoctoral stints. The first was carried out at the Open University in Israel, where my host there was Galia Benziman. My second postdoctoral fellowship was funded by the Minerva Stiftung. I was hosted by the Literature Department of the John F. Kennedy Institute of North American Studies at the Free University of Berlin. My hosts there, Ulla Haselstein, MaryAnn Snyder-Körber, James Dorson, and Birte Wege, gave me good advice about my research as well as navigating life in Berlin. I learned much from other visitors and members of the institute too numerous to mention.

I would like to thank the Philip Roth scholarly community in general and the former president of the Philip Roth Society Aimee Pozorski particularly for creating a gentle and kind environment for discussing a writer whose novels can be abrasive. Brett Kaplan invited me to discuss the material in Chapter 7 at the Jewish Studies Workshop, University of Illinois at Urbana–Champaign. The members of that department and especially Sayed Kashua, who sat patiently while I discussed his own work, were helpful in reworking this material for the book. Other scholars helped shape my thoughts and the text through correspondence, conversation, and editorial work at crucial stages. These include Nir Evron, Milette Shamir, Hana Wirth-Nesher, Michael Kramer, Benjamin Schreier, Josh

Lambert, Jim Phelan, Angelika Zirker, Naomi Mandel, Maya Barzilai, Naomi Sokoloff, Hannah Pollin-Galay, Raanan Eichler, Shimon Fogel, Irene Tucker, Tali Artman, Yael Almog, and many others. In adition, the team at Bloomsbury Academic—Haaris Naqvi, Dana Dimant, Amy Martin, Eleanor Rose, Linsey Hague, Katherine De Chant, and others—did a remarkable and patient job. During the writing of this book, I often asked my network of Facebook friends for help in finding sources and examples and giving feedback on some ideas. I am grateful for the generous help they provided but also for giving me a sense that my questions and ideas are interesting and welcome.

This book would not have been possible without support from my family. I wish to thank my father-in-law and mother-in-law, Avi and Nurit Bar-Joseph, as well as my own parents, Esther and Yitzhak Hadar, for supporting me in every way possible. To my partner, Lilac Hadar, thank you for your support and distractions. Lilac helped me choose the cover image and drew it especially for this book.

Lastly, Emily Miller Budick was a thoughtful, caring, and challenging mentor. She taught me much of what I value about teaching and writing about literature. Emily passed away when I was in the midst of writing this book, which in many ways continues our conversations, correspondence, and work together. Even when our approaches and perspectives are very different, Emily remains always my interlocutor. For these reasons, *Affiliated Identities in Jewish American Literature* is dedicated—with much love—to Emily.

****

Sections of this book are based on papers that appeared in a number of publications:

Material in the Introduction and Chapter 1 appeared in a very different form in "A Course in Ghost Writing: Philip Roth, Authorship, and Death," *Connotations: A Journal for Critical Debate* 26 (2017): 15–39.

Material in Chapters 2 and 4 appeared in "Author-Characters and Authorial Public Image: The Elderly Protagonists in Philip Roth and Nicole Krauss," *Narrative* 26, no. 3 (2018): 282–301.

Chapter 7 first appeared in "Sayed Kashua's Complaint against Philip Roth: Authorial Networking between East Jerusalem and Manhattan's Upper West Side," *Studies in American Jewish Literature* 36, no. 1 (2017): 84–98.

Introduction

Philip Roth's *The Ghost Writer* (1979) is about a young writer, Nathan Zuckerman, visiting an older writer, E. I. Lonoff. In the course of an evening, a night, and a morning, Zuckerman strives to connect with and understand his elder. One method he uses is the discussion of other writers. In order to characterize Lonoff in a college essay, he compares him to Gogol and Chekhov but, later on, other writers, mostly Jewish, are crucial in this process: the fictional Felix Abravanel; Franz Kafka; Isaac Babel; and, most importantly, Anne Frank. Roth, one of the most astute observers of the literary world of his day, shows how links with other writers are pivotal to defining yourself as a writer. In connecting with Lonoff through the medium of other writers, he shows that these are not merely bilateral relations but rather a network of affiliations. One aim of this book is to illustrate that, when discussing literature, we travel from one writer to the next through a network that is not idiosyncratic or random. This network is made up of textual moments created by authors and others as part of an ongoing attempt to define and perform writers' identities. In discussing Babel, Zuckerman performs his literary Jewishness. In choosing to depict this discussion in a novel, Roth performs this same identity. He also teaches us about how writers perform their public personae.

Writers determine much of their public identity—which I define as what people know and feel about them, whether it is true or not—when affiliating with others via works of literature and their accompanying paratexts. These weaker and stronger links are far from free associations or simply the result of self-evident similarities and so-called influences. We think of authors as groups, movements, generations, or members of a national or ethnic tradition, but these containers *do not exist* before they are filled with connected names. These links are forged through labor by authors and other agents, such as editors and critics, to ensure the building and maintenance of a literary network through which readers can understand who authors are and how to read them. *Affiliated*

Identities in Jewish American Literature explores the techniques and vocabulary writers use to perform their identity. As such, it is offered as a contribution to the study of authors' public persona making. The book is concerned, then, with an epistemological and hermeneutic question: How do we know what we know about authors? My answer is that we know them through the networks in which they are a node.

In *The Ghost Writer*, Zuckerman explicitly struggles to define the connection between Lonoff, Abravanel, Babel, and himself. Zuckerman says to Lonoff, "Well, 'connected' of course isn't the right word"—it is too vague, probably, not dramatic enough. "Neither is 'influence,'" which might be too direct and suggest that Lonoff is unoriginal. Zuckerman continues, "It's family resemblance that I'm talking about. It's as though, as I see it, you are Babel's American cousin—and Felix Abravanel is the other."[1] In trying to define Jewish identity for himself and for the other authors, it makes sense for Zuckerman to turn to the vocabulary of filiation, cousinship, family resemblance. Jewish identity, the right to call yourself a Jew, has often been thought of as a matter of family or genetic communality, not only a religious or a national one.[2] Family resemblance suggests a natural, preexisting, essential connection between Jewish writers, one that transcends borders of language and citizenship. It is a very powerful rhetoric and is highly useful for Zuckerman at a moment in his life when he is looking for any kind of affiliation. However, the novel itself, by showing how much work Zuckerman needs to put into forming these ties (and how he sometimes fails), belies the idea that there is any essential filiation. Roth's novel suggests, and this book will show, that any sense of family resemblance between Jewish writers is a result of the kind of networking Zuckerman is carrying out. Thus, I want to move beyond ethnicity defined by family or genetics. Instead, I show how it is constructed alongside many other tropes of affiliation. I seek to redefine Jewish literariness according to bonds with other writers.[3] Looking at authors affiliating with one another allows me to get beyond filiation as the defining feature of Jewish literary identity.

Identity is a fraught subject in general and in Jewish studies in particular. *Affiliated Identities in Jewish American Literature* does not deal with an inherent inner sense that authors may or may not have but rather with what I term *public identity*. To offer a definition, public identities are made up of information, impressions, and associations about and around a person, especially someone famous, whether these are presented by that person or by other people, and whether true or false. This term fits into a frame the sociologist Erving Goffman presents in *Stigma*, a text that deals with the management of identity. Goffman does not deny the existence of an "ego identity," an inner self that is what a person knows themselves to be. However, this aspect of identity is beyond Goffman's sociology. It is also, for the most part, beyond the analysis I propose here. Instead, Goffman discusses social identity and personal identity. Social identity describes the categories in which you may be placed by someone who does not know you.[4] For instance, Hassidic clothes identify a person wearing them as an ultra-Orthodox Jew. On the other hand, personal identity is what makes an individual identifiable as unique. Personal identity markers also anchor a continuous life story;[5] or, in Goffman's words: "Personal identity has to do with the assumption that the individual can be differentiated from all others and that around this means of differentiation a single continuous record of social facts can be attached, entangled, like candy floss, becoming then the sticky substance to which still other biographical facts can be attached."[6] A full name is the most obvious example.

Public identity is that portion of Goffman's "candy floss" that is available to those who are not in everyday contact with the public figure. Goffman's imagery is instructive here because it suggests the stickiness or adhesiveness of identity, which is in sync with the idea that there are strings connecting different people's identities. A variety of lingual, visual, and other texts mediate the information that makes up public identity. These texts are the main way by which such information is available.

Acknowledging that it must be quite different from the image projected in everyday interactions, Goffman, like others, uses the term "public image" to describe public identity.[7] I, however, choose not to lean heavily on terms like public image or persona (although I will, at times, use them) because they make us think of mere surface. They connote falsity and theater—sheer performance, one may say. Public identity, on the other hand, leaves room for the possibility that the identity displayed to the public also represents personal identity. Negotiating aspects of public identity is not necessarily relevant to who the author is in their personal life, but it could be. It is important to make this point as a precaution against the cynicism (my own and others') that accompanies discussions of public image and celebrity. Whenever anyone talks about public image, there is a risk of suggesting that the author is manipulative and dishonest—say, using Jewishness for their own gain. By insisting on identity, I want to acknowledge that personal and everyday identifications are often also resources when authors perform publicly. They do not "manipulate" their readers in the negative sense of the word. Thus, even when I write that the aim of a certain move is to perform an identity, there should be no sense that I am accusing an author of dishonesty or venal motives. Arguably, communicating their nuanced sense of identity is one of the most laudable things writers can do with their talent.

Affiliated Identities in Jewish American Literature presents literary texts and their paratexts in order to show how writers perform their public identities. The French narratologist Gérard Genette helps bridge the gap between text and its extraliterary, by and large nonfictional, thresholds when he introduces the term "paratexts."[8] Paratexts are the texts that surround and present the central texts to the reader. Some examples of paratexts include titles, introductions, and author interviews. Still, while Genette pays encyclopedic attention to the texts at the borders of literature, he always keeps the literary text at the center. The author's life, or what we know about it, does have a role in this solar system of paratexts. According to Genette, what the public knows about the author— in his examples of Marcel Proust being gay and of Jewish descent—functions as a *factual* paratext.[9] I want to turn this idea on its head. Instead of the life or persona only informing the reading of novels, let us start reading novels as paratexts for the author's identity, a cultural narrative in its own right. My readings, even when detailed, have at their core not so much the meaning of the text but rather what the literary work seems to be doing to the author's public identity.[10]

Although this book looks at several aspects of public identity, such as the impression of age, connection with Eastern Europe and Israel, and literariness, it often returns to the question of identifying as Jewish. In Jewish literature studies, the question of who is to be identified as a Jewish writer has been debated for a long time. This issue is difficult because the question of who is a Jew in general has no simple answer. With Judaism variously defined as a nation, a race, an ethnicity, and a religion, many thinkers and scholars show how Jews are not comfortably contained in any of these categories. With literature, the issue is even more complex, because the identification of a Jewish text depends on how one's vision of Jewishness interacts with the text. For example, can a writer who never writes about Jews be said to be a Jewish writer? Perhaps here lies an explanation for why Saul Bellow did not include Kafka in his *Great Jewish Short Stories*.[11] Can a writer obsessed with Christian symbolism be considered Jewish? Ruth Wisse explicitly excludes Bernard Malamud from her *Modern Jewish*

Canon for this reason.¹² Can someone who writes in a non-Jewish language be producing Jewish literature? Perhaps anyone who writes in a Jewish language, like a Palestinian Israeli writing in Hebrew, can be considered a Jewish writer. Over the two centuries of academic study of Jewish literature many answers have been put forward for the question, What is Jewish literature?

In his important essay "Race, Literary History, and the 'Jewish' Question," Michael Kramer offers a compellingly simple, if provocative, answer: "To be considered a Jewish writer … one need not use a 'Jewish' language, or exhibit certain 'Jewish' literary characteristics, or address certain 'Jewish' subjects, or even know how to ask the 'Jewish' question. One need only to be a writer of Jewish extraction, a member of the Jewish race."¹³ Kramer's readers may want to change "race" with "ethnicity" in order not to raise too many essentialist alarms, but Kramer argues that, if you are in any way Jewish in origin and you are a writer, you are also a Jewish writer. If you are not, you simply are not. This answer does not leave much room for gradation and shadings—a sense that Bellow is more of a Jewish writer than Norman Mailer, that both are more Jewish (as writers) than J. D. Salinger is, or that Isaac Bashevis Singer feels more Jewish than all three combined (if I may be allowed some hyperbole). It also does not leave room for the sense that some writers seem Jewish even when they are not ethnically Jewish, as is the case with Sayed Kashua as well as several American writers and intellectuals. In its simplest version, it also leaves out those who have converted to Judaism.

My outlook is much closer to Benjamin Schreier's intervention into Jewish literary studies in *The Impossible Jew: Identity and the Reconstruction of Jewish American Literary History*. Schreier challenges Kramer's assertions and critiques those who share his assumptions. Schreier problematizes identity: "In order to analyze the constitution of a subject [like the Jew] within a historical framework, we cannot assume the existence of such a subject—certainly not in the readily available sociologically, ethnographically or otherwise historiographically instrumental humanist vocabularies. This is the fundamental error of identitarianism that *The Impossible Jew* challenges."¹⁴ Thus, and in step with other post-essentialist thinkers, Schreier argues that, when we study how texts or authors are made to seem Jewish, or part of Jewish literature, we cannot start with the assumption (as Kramer does) that we know what a Jew is. Jewish identity is exactly what these texts and the critics reading them are producing.¹⁵ Taking a cue from Schreier frees up space for exploring the performance of Jewishness (or Jewyness, as he sometimes prefers).¹⁶ It also allows one to legitimately include any writing that seems to be concerned with producing and interrogating Jewishness, even if its writer is not ethnically Jewish. Seeing the networked aspect of the construction of Jewish authorial identity takes us further down this path.

Of course, affiliating with other Jewish writers is not the only means writers have to perform their Jewishness. They can use Jewish identified languages such as Hebrew, Yiddish, Ladino, or Judeo-Arabic, they can quote from Jewish sources like the Talmud or Jewish liturgy, and they can depict Jewish characters and engage with themes that are usually considered Jewish. They can simply proclaim themselves as Jewish. Still, affiliation is a major resource and it has the benefit of performing this identity in a more roundabout manner, one that enables writers to seem Jewish and at the same time not need to say so outright.

For a scholar of Jewish writing, dealing with the issue of filiation and affiliation has the benefit of engaging directly with another central and contested question of the unity (or continuity) of Jewish literature across languages, periods, and nations. This question is entangled with identity because sharing an identity provides unity. In *Letting Go So As to Touch*, or its English version *From Continuity to Contiguity: Toward a New Jewish Literary Thinking*, Dan Miron, who has made his name as one of the foremost scholars of modern Hebrew literature, faces this question of continuity: Can we talk about a continuous Jewish literature, even when we know that it comprises different languages and has been created in different national contexts? Miron's answer is that it would be far-fetched to bring under one roof the variety of languages in which Jews have written for more than 3,000 years. Even modern Hebrew literature and Yiddish literature, which were, at one point, deeply intertwined, have diverged into two independent traditions in the twentieth century.[17] Miron, however, does not give up on a sense that there is some kind of unity in the work produced by Jews. He calls this contiguity and relates it to an underground connection that might remind some readers of Deleuze and Guattari's rhizomatic thinking.[18] How this contiguity takes shape is unclear, and recognizing it is the critic's (Miron's, really) responsibility. I want to argue that many of these recognitions of identity and relevance are based on networks formed by authors. When these networks are not made by the authors (and other agents), they are created by critics and not simply uncovered. *Affiliated Identities in Jewish American Literature* makes explicit how moments of textual ties between authors are a crucial part of what enables readers, lay and academic alike, to identify a writer as being more or less Jewish, as being a certain kind of Jew. Because Jewish identity is complex, as is the status of literary authorship, these relationships are not always straightforward and demand careful reading.

Much of the impetus for looking at the empirical textual evidence for writers affiliating with other writers comes from Bruno Latour's intervention in the field of sociology. In *Reassembling the Social*, Latour exhorts against jumping from local interactions to the abstract contexts that operate behind them. Context is not a different sphere of existence, he tells us. Context does not hide, camouflaged, behind the observable. Instead, it exists on the same level as the places, the processes, or the interactions that seem to require contextualization. These arenas of contextualization link to the observed location, and researchers can follow these links. Latour asks sociologists and other researchers to find the locations in which abstract concepts such as the "Oedipus complex" or "social capital" are assembled and from which they affect other locations. He urges scholars to follow the links between one location to others, just as local, but with more connections.[19] To take one of Latour's examples, economic sociologists should assess the New York Stock Exchange as a central reassembling node in the network of capitalism, instead of talking about capitalism abstractly.[20] In such locations, a researcher can gain an overview of the social world, a panorama, but this overview is only a localized construction. Similar locations for the reassembling of context or the social, as he sometimes calls it, include the social scientist's office—Latour prefers to be specific—where information is sorted, interpreted, repackaged, and then dispatched in the form of knowledge about society.[21]

Latour's perspective stresses not only that these contexts are reassembled but that they are reassembled through connections in networks. Some nodes are more connected, more central. However, this fact does not mean that other nodes do not have the potential for gaining more connections and becoming more central. Arguing for his approach's political potential and against critical sociologists who see themselves as fighting monolithic social forces, Latour writes:

> I think it would be much safer to claim that action is possible only in a territory that has been opened up, flattened down, and cut down to size in a place where formats, structures, globalization, and totalities circulate inside tiny conduits, and where for each of their applications they need to rely on masses of hidden potentialities. If this is not possible, then there is no politics.[22]

So, if we want to avoid automatically following abstract invisible conceptualizations like tradition, ethnicity, or continuity/contiguity, we need to look for the empirical links and networks by which these conceptualizations are enacted. Latour argues that society is not a *sui generis* or self-supporting structure. Societies need constant reestablishment and reconnections by various actors in order to exist; what needs explaining is not why societies change but how they maintain stability.²³ Latour's reorientation of sociological thought motivates me to look for moments of active networking that form the traditions, continuities, and connections (such as the Bellow–Malamud–Roth triangle) literary critics too often take for granted.²⁴

As the above importation of Latour's and Goffman's approaches may suggest, *Affiliated Identities in Jewish American Literature* is deeply influenced by sociological thinking. I view literature as a social activity and believe that sociological tools can help us understand how texts and the people involved with texts function. In this, I am in line with a recent trend in literary studies: the reemergence of the sociology of literature. Some of these new literary sociologists—most prominently Rita Felski—are deeply influenced by Latour's thinking and his involvement of inanimate objects and nonhuman forces into sociology.²⁵ By and large, these sociological critics try to understand how literature as an institution works, without automatically allegorizing texts as having to do with larger social issues (as some earlier forms of the sociology of literature tended to do). On the one hand, my book continues this trend and brings it into contact with Jewish American literary studies where, with some important exceptions, it has not yet made its mark to the extent I would like to see.²⁶ On the other hand, my work differs from much of this trend. While many literary sociology projects focus on the institutions around texts, I focus most of my attention on examining literary texts. My practice of the sociology of literature is one that sees that much of the social interactions take place in and through the written literary texts. Thus, they can be explored through detailed readings. Other scholars focus on what is around the text. Amy Hungerford's *Making Literature Now* is both a good example of this preference and a book I very much admire.²⁷ In her attempt to explain how contemporary fiction is produced and consumed, Hungerford interviews editors and app developers, calls up unknown writers to ask what has happened with their career since their initial publication, analyzes websites dedicated to literature, and describes the innovative design of books. Often (though not constantly) her book is uninterested in what is written on the pages of the literature she examines. The method here is qualitative social science or journalism, not literary. The main social agents Hungerford examines are people and technologies, not texts, even as the technologies carry texts. There is an entire chapter explaining why Hungerford refuses to read David Foster Wallace. In a similar vein, James English's *The Economy of Prestige* examines cultural awards, including literary prizes, but does not really concern itself with the books awarded but rather with the discourse around these prizes, mostly working with media reports.[28]

To be clear, I am not arguing against such methodology or focus. Rather, I am suggesting that additional directions are also worth pursuing. Indeed, a more textually oriented sociology of literature opens it up to those—such as students and adjunct lecturers—without the resources to carry out extensive interviews or archival explorations that are so important to the current sociology of literature.

Continuing to think sociologically, the importance of associations can be discerned from examining how we view ourselves and others in everyday life. When attempting to become acquainted with a new person, especially in relatively small social worlds, one often tries to discover common acquaintances. This information not only provides fodder for small talk but also helps us understand our interlocutor's identity: who they are. The idea that a person's identity is based on the people with whom they are connected has been central to the formation of modern sociology. A pioneer in the field, Charles Horton Cooley, coined "the Looking-glass 'I'" to explain how other people's reactions to us determine our sense of self and identity.[29] We know ourselves through our associations with others; others know us by the same associations. In *Stigma*, Goffman provides us with a catalog of elements that convey social information, paying special attention to "the informing character of the 'with' relationship": "To be 'with' someone is to arrive at a social occasion in his company ... The issue is that in certain circumstances the social identity of those an individual is with can be used as a source of information concerning his own social identity, the assumption being that he is what the others are."[30] Using the example of suspicion of a criminal identity for those associated with known offenders, Goffman highlights how our associates make us legible to others, sometimes far more legible than we might want to be. When writing or presenting their public identities, writers make themselves legible through the association with others or take the occasion to challenge the assumption that they are "what the others are." Our networks make us readable. *Change the network and you change how you are read.*

My assumption is that the way in which we know ourselves and other people in our lives is analogous, if not identical, to how we learn about writers. Social epistemologies run parallel to literary ones. Therefore, insights from everyday wisdom and its codification in sociology can form the basis for our understanding of how readers form their literary knowledge. Some observations from bookish life might illustrate the point. I read an author's work because an author I like mentions her favorably in an interview. Maybe I saw a comparison between them in a review. I hear statements like: "you like Philip Roth, so you probably also like Saul Bellow." On the "big data" scale, online book retailers have developed algorithms to make suggestions to customers about what new authors and books they might like according to their past purchases. When you search for a certain author online, Google often presents you with a list of related authors whose Wikipedia pages you might also want to peruse. The relays between writers are a mode of discovery and a method for the fortification of taste.

It is crucial for any scholar of literature to take note of this network-like aspect of the literary world because it also affects scholarly work. Researchers and critics often organize their studies along lines of already existing associations. When the networks between the authors under discussion do not exist or appear weak, the critic must waste precious space and energy in building up these connections. Eric Hayot presents this lack of association as a problem in project organization and parodies the attempts to justify unlikely connections:

> [Y]ou ... get this problem sometimes with comparative literature dissertations that bring together two writers who don't seem to have much in common—Jorge Luis Borges and Sarah Orne Jewett, or something—thus obligating the writer to begin the whole thing by saying something like, "Everyone thinks that Borges and Jewett have nothing in common, and of course there's no evidence that the former ever knew of the latter. But they are surprisingly connected because both traveled widely, and both had mothers that died young," etc., etc. This is almost always terribly unconvincing.[31]

Thus, when I wrote a paper about Roth and the Canadian author Margaret Atwood, I needed to explain this pairing in detail. Indeed, after a couple of rejections, I ended up cutting most of the Roth material from that paper and publishing it in a journal dedicated to Canadian literature.[32] A paper about Roth and Bellow (whose connection is a critical commonplace) or about Krauss and Foer (who were married) needs much less explaining. Indeed, the latter may need to include an apology for dealing with authors who are too obviously associated.

The matter of the force of inter-author networks in the organization of criticism is observable in both journalistic and academic writing. It is visible in the discussion of established writing and probably even more so in writing about new writers whose place in the literary world is not yet secured. It seems, however, especially relevant for moments in which a relatively forgotten writer is reintroduced. Rediscovery is a reconnection to the network. Let us take Wallace Markfield (1929–2002) as an example. Who? you might ask. In the 1969 *Life* profile that introduced Roth to a larger audience than ever before, Albert Goldman provided a list of writers that help him place Roth. Wallace Markfield is one of the authors mentioned in order to characterize Roth as the culmination of a tradition of Jewish American comic writers. This short list also includes Bellow and Joseph Heller.[33] Since then, Markfield has been largely abandoned by the general readership and rarely championed by academic critics.

Thus, when, in 2012, J. Hoberman tried to introduce *Tablet Magazine*'s readers to Markfield, he needed to connect him to the writers they do know. *Tablet* is a venue that imagines Jewish Americans as its main readership, and it has covered and commented on Roth extensively. Indeed, Roth, here, is of great use: Markfield's "three Jew-obsessed comic novels were eclipsed by the titanic oeuvre of Philip Roth," he tells us, using this statement to define Markfield as well as to explain his minor place in American Jewish letters. Furthermore, Hoberman invokes Roth's mention of Markfield in *Portnoy's Complaint*, as he also does with the rather incidental fact (at least regarding Roth) that they both reviewed films. Hoberman is a film critic, so he thus connects himself to these two novelists. Finally, he reports how "Robert Alter, a long-standing foe of the Jewish American literary renaissance ... used his review [of a Markfield novel] to knock Roth."[34] We see how a central strategy for arguing for Markfield's relevance is to show his many connections to Roth. That Hoberman has not yet been successful in reviving Markfield's reputation does not detract from the fact that he utilizes a very common technique for such endeavors.

This linking rhetoric is so common because readers can characterize authors through the way in which they are connected to other authors. Thus, the Bellow–Malamud–Roth triangle came to suggest that these three authors were a literary voice of Jewish America. Similarly, critics sometimes link Roth with Bellow, Mailer, and John Updike; this grouping is part of the reason Roth is known as a sexist author. To give another, more localized example, in 1975 Alfred Kazin connected Mailer, Gore Vidal, Erica Jong, and Roth to describe how successful authors are expected to be "public figures ... playing the role of confessional prima donnas,"[35] a worrying trend in American fiction—authors being more interested in advertising their prominence than in actually achieving literary greatness. Academic critics utilize this maneuver as well, of course. Daniel L. Medin, for instance, situates Roth in the rather different context of global modernist/postmodernist literature through the affiliation with Kafka that Roth was careful to cultivate. He is able to connect Roth with the South African writer J. M. Coetzee and the German writer W. G. Sebald because the two are also connected to Kafka in various ways.[36] If critics are not aware of the constructedness of the networks they follow and retrace, they risk mistaking roads that already exist for roads they lay themselves. They also risk inadvertently mistaking the roads that have already been laid out by authors for the only paths that we may travel.

That said, exploring the roads laid out or constructed by authors and other agents is what *Affiliated Identities in Jewish American Literature* is about. A consequence of this interest is that, for the most part, the book emphasizes Jewish writers and types of Jews who have already been established as central to Jewish American literature. Thus, I need to acknowledge that many of the writers I consider here are already canonical and, if not canonical, then are certainly acclaimed. The great bulk of the writers I study here are white, Ashkenazi Jews who were born in the United States and write in English. This is the case because my preoccupation is with the mainstream of Jewish American literature. Another project could examine how Jews of color, Sephardi/Mizrahi Jewish Americans, immigrant writers, and writers in languages other than English find ways to affiliate themselves with the mainstream of Ashkenazi Jewish American writers. Furthermore, future research could ask what alternative networks they create in the process of crafting their own brand of Jewish identity. More attention to LGBTQ+ writers would also reveal different paths and emphases (including more attention to poetry and plays). When I come to discuss Israelis reacting to Philip Roth, the issue of Ashkenazi identity comes into play. Chapter 7 also breaks with this Ashkenazi identity by discussing a Palestinian Israeli writer at length, and the Coda examines reactions to Julia Salazar, a Latina Sephardi Jew.

One area in which this study does contain a more balanced representation is gender. Despite the large shadow men such as Bellow, Malamud, and Roth have cast over the field, women from Emma Lazarus to Nicole Krauss have had an impact on Jewish American literature. I believe no account even of the most strictly canonical view of Jewish American literature would be complete without a discussion of women writers, and indeed this book dedicates a large section to their work. That said, I must acknowledge that the issue of gender itself is not central, though I comment on it at various times. I believe that it does affect the ways in which writers network. No doubt, certain rhetorics of affiliation are deeply gendered ("fatherhood," for example); and yet, within the confines of this book, it was impractical to develop this issue at length. Many other studies have examined gendered issues within Jewish and Jewish American literature. A recent example is concerned with filiation and affiliation in the context of women's writing: Zohar Weiman-Kelman's *Queer Expectations: A Genealogy of Jewish Women's Poetry*. Weiman-Kelman creates a new family tree of women poets by grouping Yiddish, Hebrew, and English-language writers and revealing their similarities, especially around queer concerns. Explicitly and with political-cultural intentions, many of the connections Weiman-Kelman exhibits are of her own making. Many were not invited by the writers she discusses, though some were: "Just as lesbian authors [of the 1970s and 1980s], made Yiddish women writers part of their lesbian lineage, I ... make lesbian writers, and Yiddish [and Hebrew] women writers, part of my own queer genealogy."[37] I respect the imperative to create new paths of identification, partly by rearranging past literature, but, in distinguishing my project from others, I explain that, to the best of my power, I have not intervened in the paths created by the authors I examine.

Indeed, distinguishing my project from other critical practices of connecting different authors, among other things, further illustrates how widespread the entangling of authors is in academic writing about literature. First, I am not directly concerned with real-life connections between authors. *Affiliated Identities in Jewish American Literature* is neither a group biography nor an exploration of how interpersonal relationships shape the literary world. Such studies are fascinating and useful but mine is not one of them. I am not interested here in facts but in the discourse about them, in imagined communities rather than the social infrastructure that allows them to be built. So, I can tell you that Roth and Bellow were friends, but this piece of information is beside the point in the context of my argument. What is important is that Roth chooses to publicly narrate this friendship, and other agents publicize it as well.

Some more theoretically inclined papers have also dealt with actual friendships and other social interactions. When the sociologist Charles Kadushin makes an argument for the importance of social network analysis in Jewish studies in general, one of his main examples is literary. He invokes the importance of an interpersonal network around Yosef Brenner, an important writer and editor in fostering the growth of Hebrew literature in the early decades of the twentieth century. He even goes as far as to say that "[t]he relationships provided the emotional and financial support without which there would not have been a revival of Hebrew literature."[38] These connections were often personal and not always advertised—sometimes they were even hidden intentionally. The networks Kadushin wants to explore are social, but my interest lies in their discursive representation.[39]

There are other interventions that review the ways in which authors are connected to one another without tracing face-to-face interactions. These mostly work by connecting the authors to institutions and not directly to one another. Thus, Richard Jean So and Hoyt Long present a sociology of modernist poets through network analysis of publications. In the visual network that they produce through computerized data analysis, "[t]he closer two poets appear, the more likely they were publishing in similar venues and in similar amounts."[40] That is to say, poets are connected in this paradigm because the same venues published their poems, not because they knew each other or because they wrote about each other. These networks are important, but they are not the kind of rhetorically motivated networking that I want to explore. I suspect they have little to do with what the general reader and critics who are not as computer savvy as So and Long can know about authors. That they produce surprising connections is part of the strength of this method, but it makes it less relevant to a project about explicit public identity building.

In this context, Mark McGurl's *The Program Era*, one of the most influential histories of postwar American literature, is relevant. Although McGurl sometimes touches on personal contacts between writers, he mainly works to show how a great variety of writers are connected through the institutions of creative writing (mostly university departments). These institutional networks are not necessarily public knowledge. Therefore, if institutions are used as part of the discourse about writing, they will not serve a part of my project. McGurl, like many other critics, does not altogether ignore moments of literary networking but, again like many other critics, seems to downplay their importance. Thus, he writes about Roth:

> Excepting the "community of writers," familial, ethnic, religious, and especially heterosexual romantic ties are placed under awful pressure in his work. But Roth makes a comparatively effortless identification with, first, the modernist masters (James, Kafka, et al.) whom he learned to appreciate in school, then the Eastern European writers (such as Milan Kundera) ... and finally the warm friendships among writers, mostly male, that make their way (as in *The Ghostwriter* [1979]) into his fictions.[41]

I believe Roth and others put just as much pressure on the community of writers as they do on other ties. McGurl is a little too quick to describe relations between writers as tranquil. *Affiliated Identities in Jewish American Literature* shows how this world of literary affiliations is built and maintained but also how it can be stirred up. In fact, literary relationships are often discussed in the familial, ethnic, and romantic terms that McGurl finds to be more exciting in Roth's work.

It is important not to confuse the active networking I describe here with literary influence. Critics looking for or citing influences make a claim about one writer incorporating styles, themes, ideas, images, or techniques from other writers. Though it is not often theorized, ascribing influence is a vital ingredient in critical practice.[42] Specifically, invoking influence is one of the major means critics have for connecting authors. To many, it seems more legitimate than simple juxtaposition or comparison. In *The Anxiety of Influence*, Harold Bloom—the major theoretician of influence—describes the history of poetry and the shape of specific poems as determined by the poets' struggles with their precursors, the poets who influence them. Poets do not choose their precursors, no more than children choose their parents. "[I]nfluence cannot be willed," Bloom writes.[43] At least since the late eighteenth-century Romantic notion of the individual genius took hold, influence has been something to struggle against and hide from view. Therefore, critics like Bloom are the ones who hold the authority to report on the lineages of influence, not the poets themselves. That a writer actively and explicitly aligns himself with another can be as easily taken as proof that he was not influenced by this writer and therefore found him to be a safe reference. Bloom pronounces that "[c]riticism is the art of knowing the hidden roads that go from poem to poem."[44] However, Latour's thinking can help us see that critics are often the ones who pave these roads rather than uncover them. The brand of criticism I want to promote is concerned with traveling on clearly signposted highways. I want to follow the links that authors create and advertise, not the ones that are either carefully hidden from view or forged by me and my colleagues.

This distinction does not mean the networks examined here are always radically different from those of influence studies. Since I aim to show that critics discern influence with the active encouragement of the author, the networks I find are often similar to the ones usually described by influence. For instance, many have written about the lessons Roth learned from Henry James. For what it is worth, I think Roth did learn from James; and yet, much of this discourse about the influence James has on Roth is surely due to Roth's references to James in his nonfiction and fiction. For instance, in *Letting Go* (1962), Roth's first novel, one character writes a doctoral dissertation on James, while *The Portrait of a Lady* is read by several characters in the novel. Whether or not a critic "discovering" influences seems like a loyal collaborator with the author's project or a victim of the writer's manipulations depends, for the most part, on the rhetoric the critic uses when discussing influence. Does the critic trumpet a new discovery that they have made despite the author's camouflage? Or do they acknowledge that they are cooperating with the writer in placing them on the literary map?

At the same time, looking for how writers affiliate instead of concentrating only on how they influence and are influenced helps us see that the idea of influence is part of a bigger strategy by authors to connect themselves to the literary network that is not restricted to influence. Thus, connections between contemporaries or writers working in different genres would often make the discussion of influence less appealing or convincing, and yet these are affiliations nonetheless. As we will see, Roth is connected with Anne Frank in many crucial ways. However, few critics would want to argue that Frank was a literary influence on Roth because she wrote a nonfictional personal diary as a girl and Roth wrote novels.

Finally, because I discuss references to texts and within texts, I must explain how my interest in inter-author relations differs from intertextuality. The term intertextuality was coined by Julia Kristeva, following in the footsteps of Mikhail Bakhtin, in order to express the idea that no text is original. Instead, a text is always made up of smaller units taken from a variety of sources, creating "an intertextuality in the space of a given text."[45] A text is not created but is rather composed of older material. Since then, intertextuality has also been used as a catchall term to refer to literary practices that incorporate parts or aspects of earlier texts within a new one, for example genre conventions, parody, paraphrase, and quotation.[46] There is no doubt that my study relies on the second definition of the term; yet I will use "intertextuality" sparingly and not only because it has become shopworn and unspecific. I use this term rarely because I want to stress how authors are related, not just their written texts. For example, a study of intertextuality might point out how Roth's *The Ghost Writer* incorporates quotes, plot summaries, and themes from James's "The Middle Years," thus affiliating these two texts. Yet a study of authors' affiliations would stress that these intertexts pour into Roth's attempt to frame himself as a literary author, who, unlike the aloof James, also knows about the pleasures of the body. There is something about the humor and physicality of Zuckerman (as Roth's alter ego) standing on a volume of James's stories in order to listen in on a conversation between another author and his lover that makes the term intertextuality not quite adequate.

Yet one could easily think of life stories and public images as textual and narrative in their nature. This direction is exemplified by the pioneering celebrity scholar Richard Dyer's term "star text."[47] As much as people, and especially celebrities, are texts, my study is indeed about intertextuality even in Kristeva's more radical sense. Identities are built up from fragments drawn from other identities—stuck together like strands of candy floss, to return to Goffman's image. One way in which authors affiliating among themselves could be understood is through drawing on textual material from one persona to another, one star text to another. Nevertheless, my approach reveals exact moments when the sense of connected identities are created rather than a diffuse sense of connectedness and constructedness into which postmodernist intertextuality sometimes falls.

***

Affiliated Identities in Jewish American Literature shows how writers shape this network in order to create and shape their identities and how they attain the authority that comes with these identities. It does so through two chapters that organize and explicate the locations of literary affiliation and the vocabulary used to describe it, and three subsequent chapters that trace how American writers affiliate with writers who are not American. The final two chapters reverse the direction and show Israeli writers affiliating with Jewish American writers, especially Philip Roth. The Coda then returns to the United States to suggest that the idea of affiliated identities is relevant to nonliterary Jews as well.

Chapter 1 elaborates the main trajectory of the book by looking at Philip Roth's *The Ghost Writer*. I argue that this novel plays with the idea that Jewish literary ties are based on a shared filial background exemplified by the idea of family resemblance but that ultimately the novel shows that even family ties are constructed and performed and that every connection is a result of the labor of networking. As part of this reading, I show the variety of means Jewish American writers have for describing their ties to one another. I give special attention to the metaphors of family and the work of turning real family into a literary resource, along with the language of education, social ties, and literary relations such as reading, editing, and interpreting.

Through the examination of a myriad of case studies, Chapter 2 catalogs the main aspects of literary affiliation as it appears in Jewish American literature, thus also proving that this phenomenon is widespread and rich with intriguing examples. In order to maintain coherence, I return several times to Roth affiliating unidirectionally with Kafka and the mutual networking between Roth and Bellow. To paint a fuller picture, I draw on examples of writers who had different methods of affiliation.

The chapter first turns to the issue of affiliation through fiction, which demands extra attention. I discuss the importance of fiction in the creation of an author's public identity. I thus open up an idea that will inform my discussions of works of fiction. As part of this argument, I focus on author-characters as part of the writer's identity network. I show how author-characters can tinge the writer's persona with identities that do not make sense outside of fiction. This method works because readers desire to learn about authors and not only about the fictional worlds they create.

The second half of the chapter covers texts that are usually considered paratexts, those that surround the literary text and work to present it to the outside world. I start by discussing the narration of real-life encounters before moving on to pictorial and photographic depictions of authors sharing real or imagined spaces; I then discuss biographical writing, interviews, and, later, nonfictional texts written by one author about another. Paratexts that appear within the same physical volume as the literary work itself are also discussed; that is, introductions, conclusions, acknowledgments, and blurbs.

In Chapter 3, the toolkit I developed in Chapters 1 and 2 is turned to use in presenting a crucial aspect in the history of Jewish American literature. I argue that an almost consistent trait of literature read as Jewish in the United States is the tendency for authors to network with other Jewish writers from outside of the United States or with non-English-speaking American authors. What changes over this 140-year history is the kind of writers who are the focus of networking. I begin with examining the poetry of Emma Lazarus and James Oppenheim. Both authors affiliate themselves with biblical author-figures. After discussing associations with the Talmud, I move on to the writers of the mass immigration era whose connection with Yiddish writers is almost automatic. I then discuss affiliations with Yiddish writers in the 1950s and 1960s, a time when this alliance does need to be proven. The issue of association with Yiddish writers is explored through a reading of Cynthia Ozick's "Envy, or Yiddish in America," where Ozick both associates herself with Yiddish writers and shows how deeply troubled this connection is.

The next part of the chapter examines the major place Jewish authors writing in European languages hold in the Jewish American repertoire of affiliations. Discussing several writers and works from the 1930s on, I show how they deploy

Kafka and other Jewish European writers to foster a sense of connection to a Jewish literary canon that is not based on Yiddish or Hebrew literature. This connection is crucial for Roth during the years after the publication of the bestselling sexual farce *Portnoy's Complaint*. The final section of the chapter addresses Roth's and others' ambivalence about ties to European writers through a reading of *The Prague Orgy*. This novella is Roth's attempt to come to terms with his attraction to European Jewish writers, especially Bruno Schulz, through a plot that revolves around the retrieval of the missing manuscripts of a forgotten writer. At the same time, *The Prague Orgy* is also a text that enables Roth to distance himself from these Jewish European authors and thus insist on his own originality as an American.

Chapter 4 picks up the idea of networking with European writers and shows how it is involved with a unique way of performing Jewish literariness: writers presenting themselves as old Jewish men. I show how Jewishness is associated with old age both in internal Jewish discourses and in general Western discourse. The chapter also describes how old age is associated with artistic prowess through the idea of late style—the idea that the final period in an artist's oeuvre is distinct in power and form from the rest of their overall creation; that it is a period of innovation despite or even because of old age and the nearness of death. Before presenting a counterintuitive example of a young woman, Nicole Krauss, connecting herself to an old man, Leopold Gursky in *The History of Love*, I offer readings of Roth's 2007 novel *Exit Ghost* and discuss Roth's decision in 2010 to retire from fiction writing. I show how both the novel and the texts that surround his retirement helped form an image of Roth as possessing the authority of late style. I then turn to Krauss to show how she uses novels and paratexts to give her public identity a tinge of lateness and age, even when she is writing in her thirties.

Chapter 5 brings the history told in Chapter 3 into our time and to the Middle East. It does so by analyzing a fairly new development that appeared in the Jewish American literary world in the last two decades. The chapter argues that some important Jewish American writers working in the twenty-first century tend to affiliate themselves with Israeli writers, to tinge their identities with Israeliness. In order to show the novelty of this direction, I look back at how older writers related to Israeli authors. Before the turn of the century, American writers had two main ways to relate to Israeli writers. In the examples I use, Bellow treats Israeli writers as local informants but ignores their literary work, while Roth does engage deeply with an Israeli writer, Aharon Appelfeld, yet fashions him as a Jewish European writer whose living in Israel and writing in Hebrew are far from the most interesting things about his work.

By contrast, Krauss, Nathan Englander, and others engage with Israeli writers such as Yoram Kaniuk and Etgar Keret as writers and as Israelis. They present them as mentors, friends, and even as sources of inspiration. I claim that they do so as a way of gaining the right and authority to write as Jews, especially on the subject of Israel. I conclude with a reading of Krauss's *Forest Dark* (2017) as an imaginative attempt to turn the quintessential European Jewish writer, Kafka, into an Israeli, by imagining that instead of dying in 1924 he immigrated to Mandatory Palestine. Overall, the chapter argues that the idea of Israel has become a useful resource for producing a contemporary version of Jewish literary identity.

Reversing the current of translingual and transnational reception, Chapter 6 presents the relevance of affiliating with Jewish American literature to the understanding of Israeli writing in Hebrew and the shape of contemporary Jewish literature more generally. Here, I engage directly with the question of the continuity of Jewish literature through a study of how Israeli writers and critics negotiate the relevance of Jewish American writers to their identities as Israelis. The chapter examines book reviews and similar texts that appeared in Israeli publications, showing how several Israelis use Roth to perform their identity in its connection to diaspora. Some writers assume or argue for continuity, making a case for learning from the Jewish writer. Other writers use similar opportunities to separate Israel from the alien Americans, thus suggesting a discontinuity in Jewish identity. Between these poles some commentators use Roth to highlight differences between Israelis and American Jews, while assuming that more continuity should exist.

Chapter 7 offers a close reading of the Palestinian Israeli writer Sayed Kashua's engagement with Roth. Kashua is able to assert his identity through playing with the issue of the continuity between Jews from the United States and those from Israel. I show how Kashua, who has been accused by Arab critics of pandering to a Jewish audience, affiliates himself with Roth as a writer whose ethnic group (American Jews) condemned him for self-hatred. At the same time, Kashua also insists on his distance from Roth and on the Jewish Israeli audience's distance from both Roth (as an American) and from Kashua (as an Arab). The chapter also shows how an author who is not Jewish can be entangled in a Jewish literary network but can also choose to subvert easy parallels.

This end point leads to a short coda that tries to establish how relevant my argument of Jewishness as formed by affiliations might be to other social fields. The Coda raises this question by examining the reactions to New York State Senator Julia Salazar in the Jewish American press. Salazar presents herself as Jewish but, for many, she is not entitled to this identity. The range of opinions on the controversy that emerged during Salazar's race for state senate helps us recognize that, for some, if not most, American Jews, affiliation (rather than ethnicity and religion) plays a big role in forming Jewish identities. Finally, the book concludes with some reflection on my own identity as a Jew and as a critic. This conclusion also explains the image on the front cover.

1

Filiation and Affiliation

This chapter unfolds the main argument of the book vis-à-vis Jewish identity by way of a careful reading of *The Ghost Writer*. Indeed, Philip Roth's oeuvre and public image are central to *Affiliated Identities in Jewish American Literature*. This is true not only because he is one of the central figures in Jewish American literature and one whose career spans decades. The main reason I lean heavily on Roth is that I see him as an important theorist-practitioner of the literary world. I believe that, much like an anthropologist wishing to learn about an unknown society, a scholar wishing to understand how the literary world functions should enlist informants. Luckily for me, my informants write comprehensive books. When taking this path, one needs to be careful because their books are works of fiction and they have all kinds of different agendas that might color their reports (the latter is an issue qualitative social scientists also deal with). I read fiction, and Roth's especially, not only as works of affiliation but also as ways to learn about how affiliation works. The connection between fictional characters, you could say, is a kind of allegory for the links available to authors.

To elaborate, Roth is particularly crucial because he is one of the masters of post-1950s American fiction, especially in the art of literary self-awareness. Mark McGurl describes three major strands in contemporary American literature, one of which he dubs "autopoetics," where the drive to "write about what you know" makes writers turn to what they know best: "to represent [their] intimate knowledge of the writing process and its consequence, to address the fact of fiction making."[1] I would add that they also know the process of establishing their identity as authors. Roth is at the core of the formulation of autopoetics. McGurl writes that "Roth can seem by turns endlessly inventive in finding new ways to manipulate [his oeuvre's] few terms, and be without any imagination at all, a nasty narcissist lost in a highly polished hall of mirrors."[2] This hall of mirrors is the literary world that I will explore with Roth's guidance. Roth scholars have long given him much of the power to describe and frame his own work. In an introduction to his book on Roth, Ross Posnock writes, "Perhaps more than any writer, Roth supplies the terms of his own evaluation."[3] This power is exemplified by critics' tendency (granted, not unique) to quote Roth's essays and interviews profusely in analyses of his works. Roth is one of those writers who most often and most complexly writes about what it means to be an author and especially an author in the public eye.[4] Overall, this present book is not preoccupied with intervening in the growing field of Roth criticism but rather offers a reading of Roth's texts in order to better understand some general issues about Jewish American literature and the workings of identity building among writers (no matter their background).

In *The Ghost Writer*, the aspiring writer Nathan Zuckerman invents a story in which Anne Frank survives the Holocaust but still has the world continue to think she is dead. The context for the Anne Frank narrative is a portrait of Zuckerman as a young man. Unlike James Joyce's paradigmatic novel,[5] Roth's text depicts only one episode in the process of its protagonist's coming of age: Zuckerman, a Jewish American writer just starting out, visiting E. I. Lonoff, the experienced but reclusive writer, in his New England home. There, Zuckerman and Lonoff discuss literature, spinning a web that connects a number of Jewish and non-Jewish writers. Marital disputes between the Lonoffs ensue, partly because of Zuckerman and partly because of Amy Bellette, an ex-student of Lonoff's who is also staying over. During the night, Zuckerman discovers that Bellette and Lonoff were lovers. He then imagines or writes a narrative in which Bellette is, in fact, Anne Frank living under a false name. The narration of the story of Anne Frank makes up the "Femme Fatale" section, while the other three sections of the novel are about Zuckerman's evening, night, and morning at the Lonoffs'. The novel as a whole is narrated by Zuckerman in hindsight, roughly twenty years after the events, but the "Femme Fatale" section can be seen as written during his visit to see Lonoff, or soon thereafter.

The context for Zuckerman's rather frantic attempt at affiliation is a crisis in identity and authority. We may say that he is in a crisis of filiation. Zuckerman recently finished college and is embarking on a literary career. "Higher Education," a story in which he depicts Jews fighting over money, based on his family's history, is about to be published. Zuckerman's father, Dr. Zuckerman, is not happy about this turn of events, believing that it will stir up anti-Semitic sentiments that Zuckerman is too Americanized to understand. Dr. Zuckerman enlists the help of Judge Wapter, a Newark Jewish community leader, to help persuade the young author to abstain from publishing his work. Wapter writes a letter to Zuckerman, accusing him of anti-Semitism, attacking his right to write about Jews, and, in a sense, excommunicating him. This letter is a "comic (but probably not much exaggerated) [version] of those angry letters of the sixties,"[6] as Hermione Lee writes in one of the first books about Roth. She is referring to letters by Jews reacting to Roth's short stories. In "Writing about Jews," Roth quotes some of these letters, including one directly threatening to excommunicate him: "What is being done to silence this man? Medieval Jews would have known what to do with him."[7] These reactions, fictional and real, open up a rift with one community that enables Jewishness. These rifts lead to the search for new networks of Jewish identity.

As I am not the first to note, Roth explores literary, ethical, and political issues by transposing them to the family sphere. Roth repeats this typical move in many of his novels. *The Counterlife* (1986) presents some great examples of this move. There, Zuckerman's brother becomes an extremist settler in the West Bank,[8] while Zuckerman's mother-in-law is, as his sister-in-law happily informs him, "terribly anti-Semitic."[9] Both stances are antagonistic to Zuckerman's position. In the case of the mother-in-law, the common, even clichéd, tension with in-laws doubles the tension English "genteel" anti-Semitism exacts on Zuckerman's worldview, while his desire to please his wife forces him to face her mother's hostile sentiments. In the brother's case, the family setting makes Zuckerman face issues (Israeli politics, the Israeli-Palestinian conflict) that otherwise would not enter his consciousness with any real force. In *The Ghost Writer*, Roth juxtaposes family and culture conflicts, sending Zuckerman to affiliate with new peoples in ways mainly drawn in familial terms.

Here, Zuckerman's story reflects the binary of affiliation and filiation, which Edward Said identified as a primary concern for literary critics. In this, Said foreshadows some of the focus on networks that is currently gaining ground in some literary critical circles, especially those influenced by Latour. In his introduction to *The World, the Text, and the Critic*, Said argues that writers and thinkers of the nineteenth and twentieth centuries increasingly mistrusted bonds based on filiation, especially intergeneration bonds. The clearest example he puts forward is Freud's Oedipus complex, "which posits the potentially murderous outcome of bearing children," as Said puts it.[10] Thus, instead of creating relations and continuity through childrearing, writers sought to affiliate in new ways. Discussing T. S. Eliot as an example, Said writes "[t]he only other alternatives seemed to be provided by institutions, associations, and communities whose social existence was not in fact guaranteed by biology, but by affiliation."[11] Thus, there is a move from families to alternative networks, not dissimilar from the move Zuckerman makes when he tries to exchange the ties with his family for those with Lonoff as a spiritual father. Said speaks about affiliating not only with other people but also with political parties and worldviews, though in a manner that is less relevant for my argument. What is relevant is Said's cogent point concerning "the deliberately explicit goal of using that new order to reinstate vestiges of the kind of authority associated in the past with filiative order";[12] or, to put it in a manner that relates to the present argument, new networks are used for the same ends as the old family networks. So, if family has always had a huge role in defining identity—not only for Jews but for Jews in unique ways—then the new forms of affiliation would have a similar role.

Because affiliation replaces filiation, the language used for such affiliation is often based on the vocabulary of the filiation it replaces. This tendency can be seen in a quote from *I Married a Communist* (1998) where Zuckerman discusses the writers and real-life mentors who influenced him as a "genealogy that isn't genetic" (217).[13] The shared root of the words genealogy and genetics helps us sense that family continues to be a ruling metaphor for any kind of affiliation. For Roth, as for other writers, the work of affiliation is often reported in terms of family. My argument here, following Said, is that we must not confuse the rhetoric of family with actual belief in family ties. Critics who try to discern the work of Jewish identity making must negotiate, as Roth does, the usefulness of metaphors based on familial or natural connections and the need to show the labor that such ties are based on. A writer is not born into a family but creates one.

The language of family is absolutely crucial to the way Roth affiliates with others in *The Ghost Writer*. In fact, these constructed networks can truly feel like family resemblances and family ties, even when they are constructed affiliations. Roth concretizes the metaphor of "family resemblance" when describing Anne Frank: "she's like some impassioned little sister of Kafka's, his lost little daughter—a kinship is even there on the face" (170). In critical discourse, "family resemblance" is most often associated with Ludwig Wittgenstein. For him, "family resemblance" is a way to talk about definitions that work as "a complicated network of similarities overlapping and criss-crossing: sometimes overall similarities, sometimes similarities of detail."[14] I do not know if either Roth or Zuckerman are thinking of Wittgenstein when using this term or whether they were just using the same, not altogether rare, metaphor. Interestingly enough, Wittgenstein is mentioned in the novel as an example of a difficult German philosopher who Zuckerman has not yet read but is represented in Lonoff's bookcase (79). It would be possible for Zuckerman to know of Wittgenstein. Still, it would make Zuckerman quite current in philosophical discourse to have known of the Austrian's use of the concept; *Philosophical Investigations* was published a mere decade before the main plot of *The Ghost Writer* takes place. Whether either Zuckerman or Roth is thinking about him, Wittgenstein helps us see how this metaphor is useful when one wants to designate a group to whom one might belong (like Jewish literature or American literature) without insisting on one single common denominator that will unite everyone in the group. Thus, Lonoff (Malamud/Roth) and Abravanel (Bellow/Mailer/Roth) connect despite their differences by resembling some aspect of the Russian Jewish writer Isaac Babel.

Zuckerman can also place himself within this family network. After the mini-lecture about Babel and his American cousins, Lonoff asks him, "Aren't you a New World cousin in the Babel clan, too? What is Zuckerman in all of this?" Lonoff rightly assumes that at least one reason Zuckerman has for describing this network is a wish to carve out a niche for himself. Zuckerman protests: "Why—nothing ... I'm still at the point where my relationship to my *own* work is practically nonexistent" (49). Zuckerman is just starting out and "still" does not have a relationship to anything. However, he is certainly on his way to finding a place in this clan, partly by forging his ties to Old World and New World relatives. Literal genetic ties, literal family resemblance, exist from the moment of birth (even conception for genetic ties). However, Zuckerman expresses his plans to make new family resemblances, literary rather than literal. At the same time that he uses family resemblance so effectively, he reminds us that he is working in order to create it.

Kinship is especially important because it invokes an ethnic or even racial idea of Jewishness that Michael Kramer talks about.[15] Personal appearance is determined partly by our genes, it seems to suggest, and so too is at least some of what preoccupies the literary mind. Most contemporary writers would be loath to make such statements explicitly. However, talking about family resemblance metaphorically can help them to affiliate ethnically without committing to genetic determinism.

"Family resemblance" is an intentionally loose term. This is part of what makes it useful for Wittgenstein and for Zuckerman when he does not want the option of affiliating in a dynamic manner. At other times, Roth and others do not shy away from more concrete family and family-like vocabulary. For Roth (as is the case for Said), the main examples are father–son relationships and romantic ties, including marriage. This means that these networks are highly gendered, with the influencing figures almost always male, while contemporaries, people with whom you have something in common but who do not teach you, are often women. In *The Ghost Writer*, Zuckerman is quite explicit in his desire to have Lonoff as his father, saying that he wants to be "Lonoff's spiritual son" (9). This desire is strengthened by the conflict Zuckerman has with his biological father but is also based on a wider sense that one searches for father figures to guide one's way through life and literature. In *I Married a Communist*, a Zuckerman novel that was published much later but partly recalls a period earlier in Zuckerman's life, this issue is also important and its riskiness described beautifully:

> It is, morally as well as emotionally, a more dangerous game than one knows at the time, getting all those extra fathers like a pretty girl gets beaux. But that was what I was doing. Always making myself eminently adoptable, I discovered the sense of betrayal that comes from trying to find a surrogate father even though you love your own.[16]

Here, Zuckerman describes relations with men who are not writers, but I believe he is also referring to the problematic surrogate parenting that he asks of Lonoff as a man and as a writer a little later in his career. Here, the rhetoric of paternity becomes mixed with a language of sexual courting that is potentially a prelude to the forming of new families. Zuckerman feels like a "pretty girl [who] gets beaux." This passage shows that fathers can be chosen. Zuckerman always tries to find "a surrogate father," suggesting the effort involved in forming family ties. At the same time, it shows that the role of mentor is so deeply gendered as male for Roth that Zuckerman needs to be figured as a girl when performing the role of mentoree.

In Bloom's theory of influence, the competition between father and son—through the mediation of the Oedipus complex—is the central metaphor: "Battle between strong equals, father and son as strong opposites, Laius and Oedipus at the crossroads."[17] Here, Bloom can be read not only as a theoretician but as a Jewish American writer. Like Roth, he is highly invested in father-son relationships. Like Roth and many others in the history of thinking about education, teaching, and parenting, the role of the influencer is constructed as masculine. Women authors can also have literary fathers. Zuckerman's search for a father is paralleled by the relationship Amy Bellette (who he imagines as Anne Frank) has with Lonoff, who is both an older lover and a father figure (she calls him "dad-da" [120]). Again, the mixture of the paternal and the romantic, which

Roth of course did not invent, emphasizes the fluidity of affiliation through filial vocabulary. In Roth, one would rarely find a literary mother. Still, this is possible for others, even if more difficult to create because of sexist preconceptions.

For Zuckerman, desiring a literary father stems partly from dealing with a biological father who tries to interfere with his writing. The issue here, then, is also real parents as literary influences. However, it is important to recognize that even inserting actual family members into the literary network demands literary work. There is no natural filiation when it comes to literary identity. The father and son fight over a story that depicts the family and the Jews in an unflattering manner. This conflict receives extensive treatment only in the second section of the novel, following Zuckerman's evening with Lonoff. Still, Zuckerman (as the older narrator) inserts a reference to the clash with his father into his exposition of Lonoff's character, thus showing that the conflict determines much of what the young Zuckerman is seeking when he visits Lonoff. He is looking for a literary father, but other writers are content with having their parents and other relatives as part of their literary network. The amount of work that importing influences demands emphasizes the constructed nature of literary identity. Part of the reason the trouble over the story is so consequential for Zuckerman is that affiliating with literal family members often has a role in the author's literary identity and not only in their ethnic identity. Literal mothers and grandmothers (and fathers, too) are more often presented as being literary precursors, even (perhaps especially) if they never wrote literature. Two canonical feminist texts can help us see this tendency more clearly. In *A Room of One's Own*, Virginia Woolf writes that the fact that "a very remarkable man has a mother" might signify "a lost novelist, a suppressed poet, of some mute and inglorious Jane Austen," a woman who never wrote because of social circumstance but still influenced the imagination of that "remarkable man."[18] Following Woolf, Alice Walker writes:

> [N]o song or poem will bear my mother's name. Yet so many of the stories that I write, that we all write, are my mother's stories. Only recently did I fully realize this: that through years of listening to my mother's stories of her life, I have absorbed not only the stories themselves, but something of the manner in which she spoke, something of the urgency that involves the knowledge that her stories—like her life—must be recorded.[19]

Walker goes further in pointing to her mother's garden, this feminine, fleeting, and nonverbal artwork, as the main expression of her mother's creative spirit.

Many Jewish writers have echoed this sentiment of actual family members as literary sources.[20] For example, one of Grace Paley's early stories, "Goodbye and Good Luck," is told by an aunt to her niece. Its first sentence, which includes the speech tag "says Aunt Rose," indicates that it is a niece (Lillie) who writes the story. The ending clarifies what Rose expects her niece to do with the story: "So now, darling Lillie, tell this story to your mama from your young mouth."[21] The niece is told the story in order to pass it on. Through this narrative situation, Paley acknowledges in the first story in her first collection that she is indebted to the storytellers in her family. She acknowledges this debt more explicitly in nonfiction. One example is from a short essay about teaching how to write fiction: "This year I want to *tell* stories. I ask my father, now that he's old and not so busy, to tell me stories so I can learn how. I try to remember my grandmother's stories."[22] Parents and grandparents become storytelling teachers. Thus, techniques of literary affiliation (designating a writer as a teacher) bring family members into the network that builds up a writer's identity.

We can see a similar reliance on family stories in *The Ghost Writer*. The story over which Zuckerman and his father are at arms, "Higher Education," never appears in the novel.[23] Instead of the text that he wrote in 1956, the older Zuckerman chooses to give us "the facts" on which he based the story (81)—a choice Roth will make in 1988 when he publishes *The Facts*, an autobiography that revisits events he fictionalized in earlier novels. This choice makes aesthetic sense, sparing the reader 15,000 words of unripe prose and helping us preserve what admiration we have for the young Zuckerman. More importantly, by relating facts, material gleaned from his own experience, Zuckerman justifies the fiction and makes it more authoritative through a claim of real-world knowledge.

However, the value of this knowledge and the right to use it are questioned by Zuckerman's father. It is easy for Dr. Zuckerman to undermine his son's hold over the so-called facts because the facts on which the story is based were never experienced by Zuckerman directly. They were only collected through overhearing his family talking about the subject. Zuckerman, first as a boy and then as a writer, deciphers the family feud from fragments of conversation. The "facts" are stories, fictional to varying degrees. This aspect of how the facts were gathered is dramatized as part of the retelling of Sidney's "mysterious Polish tootsie Annie, whose scandalously florid *shmatas* were much discussed, if never once seen at family weddings, funerals, etc." (104). Annie and her clothes are never seen, never experienced through the senses. Rather, she is talked about.

The use of the derogatory Yiddish *shmatas* instead of "clothes" or even "rags," highlights how strongly this judgment or knowledge of her belongs to the gossipy discourse of a different generation. Roth chose not to use a more obvious Yiddish word when referring to the gentile woman: *shikse*. The reason for this omission might be that many of his readers already know the power, erotic and cultural, that word has for Roth's characters (especially Portnoy); thus, *shikse* would not have the same distancing effect as *shamtas*.[24]

Dr. Zuckerman is aware of how fictitious Zuckerman's "facts" are, especially anything Zuckerman thinks he knows about Sidney. As part of "the facts," Zuckerman presents an anecdote about Sidney: when he was in the Navy, a man called him a "dirty Jew" after losing in a poker game and Sidney threw this anti-Semite overboard (82). The unsuspecting reader might indeed accept it as a true story just as the young Zuckerman did. However, it seems only to have been a tall tale Sidney used to impress his nephews. Dr. Zuckerman insists that this is the case. When Zuckerman brings up this anecdote, he replies "furiously": "Sidney … never threw any redneck off any ship! Sidney threw the bull, Nathan!" (93). Dr. Zuckerman is shocked that Zuckerman still believes Sidney's stories and, more generally, that he accepts Sidney's self-presentation. Dr. Zuckerman's lines, with their near anaphoric use of "Sidney … threw," are rhetorically powerful, even poetic in their own rough way, stressing that even nonwriters can have a gift for words. In *The Ghost Writer*, literary influence is sometimes the choice between a literal uncle and a father.

Roth, though, knows that families are built not only through genetics but also through couplings, an area where the border between filiation and affiliation becomes shady. Eve Kosofsky Sedgwick introduced the term "homosocial" into literary studies as a way to describe how men bond together in ways that support men's power and show how these "homosocial" forms are related to other ways of affiliating, namely homosexual bonds. Influentially, she describes how the role of rivalry over a woman often has more to do with forming ties between men than with consummating romantic ties.[25] Thus, the way Zuckerman desires Amy Bellette, who he discovers is actually Lonoff's lover, also functions to connect him with Lonoff. This triangular structure is at work when one of the men cannot attach himself romantically to the desired woman. Early in the novel, on first seeing Bellette, Zuckerman thinks she might be Lonoff's teenage daughter and is willing, because of her looks and imagined family connections, to wait the seven biblical years to marry her. So, even before he understands Lonoff and Bellette's real relations, Zuckerman fantasizes about becoming not only a spiritual son but also Lonoff's son-in-law. This is similar to the idea in "Looking at Kafka" (1973) that his aunt should marry Kafka, an example of women being used to facilitate ties between men.

Roth can also imagine using marriage (and heterosexual love) for forging ties with women writers. During his night at Lonoff's, he imagines that Bellette is actually Anne Frank and is in love with Lonoff. In the morning, Zuckerman drowsily introduces (in his imagination) Anne Frank as his fiancée to his family. This marriage would affiliate him with the martyred Jewish writer, affecting his image in such a way as to keep him safe from accusations of self-hatred.[26] Affiliating romantically with Anne Frank and through her with Lonoff (as her ex-lover and imaginary father) is a fantasy of reintegrating into the Jewish community. Zuckerman never marries Anne Frank. Nevertheless, the simple attempt, and failure, in a work of fiction connects Roth to Anne Frank and forges a different path not so much for integration into the mainstream Jewish community but into Jewish literary identification.[27]

The Ghost Writer shows us how important family ties are for forming a Jewish literary identity. At the same time, the novel exemplifies how much discursive work is needed for forming these ties. A number of failed attempts to connect make explicit that the work of literary filiation is contingent. The first such failure is an attempt to be adopted by Felix Abravanel, a successful Jewish writer who reminded many readers of Saul Bellow. By the end of the encounter, Zuckerman discovers that "Felix Abravanel was clearly not in the market for a twenty-three-year-old son" (66). This sentence not only expresses the failure to gain a father but also, by using the word "market," suggests that literary filiation is a transaction rather than anything close to a genetic transfer or a natural expression of family resemblance.

Zuckerman relates and contrasts the failure to gain Abravanel's paternity to his bid for Lonoff's patronage. However, the attempt to connect with Lonoff is also a partial failure. By the end of the novel, and despite his need and hope, Zuckerman does not in fact become Lonoff's spiritual son in any sense beyond the most metaphorical. Indeed, it seems like they will not maintain a close relationship. In later Zuckerman novels, it is made quite clear that Zuckerman does not quite continue Lonoff's work in any clear way. In the final scene of the novel, Hope Lonoff exits the house, saying she will never return, and Lonoff goes after her. Preparing to leave for the snowy mountains of New England, he tells Zuckerman: "you must have things to write down. There's paper on my desk ... [for] your feverish notes" (179). Instead of paternity, Lonoff offers stationery. He transforms their relationship from one of potential family to that of writer and potential subject matter: "I'll be curious to see how we all come out someday. It could be an interesting story" (180). The filiation is refused, but the literary bond will endure through the textual connection of the feverish notes and eventually the text of *The Ghost Writer*.

Other moments in this novel and other texts emphasize how relations between authors are constructed and not genetic. A focus on other ways of connecting—other trajectories and avenues—will further my argument about the prevalence of identity making through networks. At the same time, I offer this as a kind of toolkit for finding and analyzing moments of literary networking.

One such relation is an educational one. When awarded the PEN/Saul Bellow Award, Roth's very short statement included this idea almost explicitly: "I began reading Saul Bellow while a graduate student living in Augie March's Chicago in the mid-1950s. I haven't stopped reading and rereading him since. Where Saul Bellow is concerned, I am forever the graduate student."[28] Sometimes this teaching is concretized in the social role of teacher. In "Looking at Kafka," Roth imagines himself as Kafka's Hebrew student.

Indeed, contemporary literature (Jewish or otherwise) exhibits many teacher–student relationships, partially thanks to the flourishing of creative writing programs, where this formal liaison is supported institutionally. We can see this connection of authors in many of the chapters in McGurl's *The Program Era*, where he is able to connect disparate figures like Wallace Stegner, a Midwestern regionalist, and Ken Kesey, the novelist laureate of psychedelia, because Stegner taught Kesey. These ties have been depicted in fiction such as Michael Chabon's *Wonder Boys* (1995). Chabon also makes the teacher–student bond explicitly Jewish when—with some irony—he dubs Roth as "Rav Philip Roth," who becomes the Rabbi of the "nice Jewish boy" who is also "a *mazik*"—a troublemaker. A *Rav* is not only a spiritual leader and expert in Jewish law but also a teacher of the law, the role Chabon gives Roth here and elsewhere.[29]

Education is a major theme in *The Ghost Writer*, where Zuckerman proclaims himself as a "*Bildungsroman* hero" on its first page (3). In the course of the novel, formal education and connection with a professor are presented as a kind of alternative to filiation. Zuckerman describes how, when leaving his parents' home for the University of Chicago, he "was ready as any adolescent could be to fall headlong for Robert Hutchins' Humanities One" (12). To "fall headlong for" belongs to the discourse of love, and Roth shows us how love for a professor or the canon of authors he presents can be a substitute for family. In this introductory course, known as Humanities One, canonical texts, mostly in philosophy but also in literature, would have been discussed as pertinent ethical teachers for the present and the future—"perennial" as the name of Hutchins's approach suggests. Zuckerman contrasts this course with the Jewish education his parents gave him, an education he satirically summarizes as "discussions ... about ... the perils of intermarriage, the problem of Santa Claus, and the injustice of medical school quotas" (12). Their teachings concern the preservation of ethnic uniqueness. "Humanities One" would educate students that cultural particularism is something they should leave behind if they want to be proper citizens of the West.

Education can disentangle Zuckerman from a certain sense of familial Jewishness but can entangle him within a Jewish literary network. Zuckerman first reads and writes about Lonoff in college. There, as part of a creative writing class, Zuckerman meets Abravanel who is willing to be a temporary teacher. In a similar vein, Lonoff teaches creative writing at a women's college. Partly through his role as professor, he is connected with Amy Bellette, who is his former student. Bellette is staying at Lonoff's house and, after a short conversation with her about where Lonoff's role as a teacher is mentioned, Zuckerman contemplates what it would be like to teach. He tells Lonoff, "I don't think I could keep my wits about me, teaching at a school with such beautiful and gifted and fetching girls" (29). He imagines teaching as a path to other contacts, especially to Bellette, with whom the word "fetching" was earlier associated. Lonoff tells him, "Then you shouldn't do it" (29). At first, this sounds like the warning of a responsible adult, but we eventually understand that it is based on Lonoff's own experience of losing his wits over a student.[30]

A less formal set of connections comprise friendship and rivalry. For an example of the former, in interviews around the publication of their jointly edited *New American Haggadah*, Nathan Englander and Jonathan Safran Foer are also depicted as friends. Introducing a conversation between the two of them, Englander mentions "stop[ping] by" almost a decade earlier and informs us how "Jonathan and I usually talk about other things—anything actually— other than the literary, craft-based matters," suggesting an intimacy that is not based on literature alone but that informs their work, at least as editors of their book.[31] The occasion of the interview, the editing of a new *Haggadah*, situates this friendship as Jewish. The *Haggadah*, as many of my readers will know, is the text that is read on the eve of Passover at the *Seder* dinner. The *Seder* is one of the most observed Jewish traditions even among secular Jews, and the *Seder* itself is an occasion for fostering family and social networks.[32] Preparing a text for this occasion solidifies Englander and Foer's joint identity as Jews; producing a revision of these texts enacts their identity as freethinking progressive Jews in the context of friendship.

Rivalry is not quite the opposite of friendship. One example of explicit competition comes from Bellow's foreword to a collection of Isaac Rosenfeld's writings; written long after his death, it reads: "I loved him, but we were rivals, and I was peculiarly touchy, vulnerable, hard to deal with at times, as I can see now, insufferable, and not always a constant friend."[33] Tossing insults and mockery at other writers is a less explicit way to mark a hostile relationship. There are boatloads of such examples, especially from TV talk shows between the 1950s and 1970s. As a scholar looking back at those years, it sometimes seems like authors were brought on almost exclusively to throw witty remarks at the expense of their colleagues. The depiction of rivalry in fiction is also common. For example, in *The Tenants* (1971), Malamud shows a Jewish writer, who might be taken as a version of himself, becoming a bitter enemy, to the point of violence, of his neighbor, an African American writer.

So, as we see, writers find familial and other social ties to be very useful when performing their networks. However, literary connections can be just as useful. By the literary vocabulary of affiliation, I mean such roles as reader, editor, or translator. So, describing yourself as someone's reader is one common approach Roth deploys throughout the collection of essays *Reading Myself and Others*. The collection connects Roth to these others of the title as their reader. The volume is dedicated, with a reference to its title, "[t]o Saul Bellow, / the 'other' I have read from the beginning with the deepest pleasure and admiration."[34] Before setting out to affiliate himself with a whole range of American and European writers, Roth designates himself as someone who has read Bellow from a rather vague but powerful point of "beginning," a point of genesis associated with conception and genetics. In *The Ghost Writer*, Zuckerman is connected to a host of writers (fictional and real) as their reader and as a writer whose work has been read by them. Zuckerman read the works of Lonoff and Lonoff reads his.

Writers can be connected by reading together or by having read the same books and authors. Zuckerman spends the night in Lonoff's study, a crucial site for getting to know any author. Zuckerman examines the study carefully, perusing the bookshelves specifically, eventually listing "everything on the bookshelves I had not read" (78). A fuller understanding of Lonoff and the potential to resemble him can come from reading the same books. Reading all the books seems like "a lifetime of hard labor" (78). In other words, fully affiliating with Lonoff through his reading would require a great deal of work. Zuckerman finds a shortcut to reading together with Lonoff: Henry James's short story "The Middle Years," which Zuckerman reads twice during his night in Lonoff's study. The events of the evening, along with the scene of Lonoff's study, send Zuckerman to read this particular story and shape how he connects not only to James but also to Lonoff and other writers.

Scrutinizing the room, Zuckerman discovers two index cards with quotations typed on them, one of these is from James's story: "We work in the dark—we do what we can—we give what we have. Our doubt is our passion and our passion is our task. The rest is the madness of art" (77). Zuckerman at first says that he "could understand why [Lonoff] might want these three sentences hanging over his head while beneath them he sat turning his own sentences around" (76–7). This observation suggests that these sentences about the task of the artist are important, a kind of motto for Lonoff. At the same time, there is an ominous sense that stems from the way the sentences "hang over his head," the constant danger of the Sword of Damocles. It is clear that Lonoff endowed these words with great authority. The quote makes Zuckerman curious (and I assume many of *The Ghost Writer*'s readers, too). Accordingly, Zuckerman not only informs us that he reads the story but also gives quite a lengthy description of it.

"The Middle Years" deals specifically with the ability to attract and influence readers; or, as one Roth critic puts it, James's story is a "pragmatic allegory about the dangers of literary devotion and overly receptive reading."[35] It is, therefore, a perfect text for thematizing affiliation through reading. Dr. Hugh, a young man like Zuckerman, and a physician who stands to inherit a countess's fortune, diverts his attention from his patron and gives it to Dencombe, an ill novelist he admires. Because of this, the Countess disinherits Hugh and soon after perishes. After the concluding deathbed scene, Dr. Hugh is left with nothing but Dencombe's texts and the memory of his infatuation with their author. Under the influence of Dencombe's novels, Hugh gives up mundane interests and relationships for the love of art and the artist.

Dr. Hugh is not the only one impressed by Dencombe's words. The readers of James's story, Lonoff and Zuckerman, are also moved. Before quoting the final scene verbatim, Zuckerman writes that "down both margins of the final page describing Dencombe's death, Lonoff had penned three vertical lines … the six surgically precise lines seemed to simulate the succession of fine impressions that James's insidious narrative about the novelist's dubious wizardry had scored upon Lonoff's undeluded brain" (115). The lines on the page reflect almost physical impressions on Lonoff's brain. The medical vocabulary, perhaps borrowed from Dr. Hugh's profession—"surgically," "insidious," "brain"—suggests this corporeality but is mixed with the fantastic "wizardry" and aestheticist "fine impressions." This is as though Zuckerman is following Lonoff's reading process. They become co-readers.

Reading the same text can be a powerful force of social cohesion, as anyone who has read aloud to a loved one can attest. This sense appears in Jewish religious rituals, many of which—the *Seder* dinner included—involve reading communally from the scriptures or liturgy. Reverberations of this force resound when Zuckerman's mother wants him to repair his reputation as a good son and a good Jew; she implores him to let his father (and the judge the father recruits to scold Zuckerman) know that he read and liked *The Diary of Anne Frank*, which he, of course, has ("How can you *dis*like it?" he asks [107–8]). She imagines that the admission of this connection to Anne Frank as one of her many readers will diffuse some of the tension around Zuckerman's role as a self-hating Jew. Zuckerman refuses this easy road to being a good Jew at first but will go onto affiliate himself with Anne Frank in much more elaborate ways.

The work of reading can shade into interpreting. This is, of course, the common connection whenever a nonfictional account of a book such as a review or essay is published. Like reading together, exegesis has a great resonance in the Jewish context. For two millennia, the exegesis of the Bible and other texts (like the Mishnah and Talmud) has been a major pillar in Jewish religious creativity and identity. Jewish tradition can be thought of as a continued reinterpretation of texts. This idea of tradition is not unique to Judaism, but it is certainly an attribute that receives much attention in the study of Judaism. This idea of Judaism as a continuous reinterpretation has one secular Jewish manifestation in Harold Bloom's argument that new poems are a misprision, a creative interpretation or misinterpretation, of older poems. In "Looking at Kafka," Roth sets himself up as an interpreter of Kafka, a position he also gives David Kepesh. In *The Breast*, this interpretation is enacted on Kepesh's body (or at least within his delusions), making him an interpreter in the sense used by musicians: enacting a score in real time.

In *The Ghost Writer*, one of the main ways in which Zuckerman connects himself to Lonoff is as his reader-explainer. As part of the exposition of Lonoff's character, the narrating Zuckerman offers two versions of the importance of Lonoff's work for him, both are works of exegesis and both are crucial for

Zuckerman's sense of identity. He writes: "In fact, my own first reading through Lonoff's canon ... had done more to make me realize how much I was still my family's Jewish offspring than anything I had carried forward ... from childhood Hebrew lessons, or mother's kitchen" (12). Zuckerman mentions traditional sites of socialization into the ethnic group, the religious school and family, but presents himself as knowing his Jewishness as a reader. It should be stressed, then, that Zuckerman identifies as Jewish as part of a literary endeavor, not in terms of genetics or nostalgic ties to his home.

He is not just Lonoff's reader but also his interpreter, explaining that Lonoff's "fiction *seemed to me* a response to the same burden of exclusion and confinement that still weighed upon the lives of those who had raised me" (12, my italics). Roth, as someone raised by Jews, has a vantage point from which to explain the burden Lonoff is responding to; but showing himself interpreting Lonoff can also help him perform a different identity: "an orthodox college atheist and highbrow-in-training" (11). He does so by describing the college paper in which he "'analyzed' Lonoff's style," only hinting at his Russian origins by comparing him to writers from a general Western canon who also happen to be Russian: Chekhov and Gogol. Interpreting, explaining, and analyzing someone brings you into contact with them. It also attests to your own identity.

Editing is another important role some writers have vis-à-vis other writers. Roth's role in Penguin's "Writers from the Other Europe," publishing writing from Eastern Europe, connected him to writers such as Schulz and Kundera (the latter he also interviewed). It must be said that editorial work without any further networking is rather weak because it often suggests constraints beyond personal and literary attachment. Thus, when Bellow edited *Great Jewish Short Stories*, a book that as a whole attaches him to Jewish literature, he included writers with whom he would otherwise not associate himself. He was, however, able to use the introduction to distance himself from them.

Julian Levinson describes the dawn of Jewish American literature as a narrative about one author *translating* another's writing. At the beginning of her career, Emma Lazarus (1849–87) was not concerned with Jewish matters. However, later on, she developed an interest in Jewish history and identity. One of the first poetic manifestations of this new interest was a translation of "Donna Clara," a poem about the Jewish past written by Heinrich Heine (1797–1856), the Jewish German poet, two years before his conversion to Christianity.[36] Lazarus not only translated the poem Heine wrote but also used a letter detailing two poems that were to complete a trilogy, to write her own, thus "entering modern

Jewish literature via Heine's abandoned project."[37] Lazarus forms her Jewish identity in correlation with rewriting Heine, who despite his conversion is, for the most part, considered an important Jewish writer.

The word Levinson uses to describe this process is "ghostwriting" (he too places the term in quotation marks because Lazarus is not as invisible as most ghostwriters are expected to be). One way Roth's novel makes itself known as a book about the work of literary affiliation is its title, *The Ghost Writer*. It thus invokes the sense of translating and writing another's story that this term suggests.[38] The role of the ghostwriter suggests a commercial connection between the person who writes (the writer) and also the person whose name is on the title page (the author). The idea of ghostwriting severs the genetic, generative ties between author and text. After all, named authors do not write the book. They only lend their names. As a consequence, ghostwriting tears apart any genetic ties between different authors. The tie between the ghostwritten text and its author is discursively determined: someone must proclaim authorship and ownership of that text without actually producing it. In the same way, writers who want to create networks with others, even family networks, need to perform these ties discursively.

2

Locating Affiliations

The aim of this chapter is to locate the places in which writers perform their identity, especially where they perform their affiliation with others. I look at two main areas for this enquiry: (1) works of literature, focusing on fiction, and (2) paratexts. In order to show how fiction can be a location for networking, I first need to make a more general argument about the role fiction has in the performance of public identity and especially the place characters who are authors (author-characters) have. In essence, fictional characters like Zuckerman and Lonoff should be seen as part of the writer's network as well as instruments used to associate with real writers. After dealing with the role fiction plays, I move on to the second area, paratexts, and explore the myriad places authors and other agents have for forging networks between writers.

Fiction and Public Identity

Since the 1990s (and before to some extent), critics have given more and more attention to the role that public identity, fame, and celebrity play in the literary system and as themes in literary texts. Nevertheless, my sense is that critics working on authors' public identity have not paid enough attention to how fiction affects this image. For example, Timothy Galow notes how "[m]uch of the publicity surrounding [F. Scott] Fitzgerald's early career fashioned the author as both a brilliant writer and *a representative example of the impetuous young adults that populated his early work*. Advertisements, interviews, and Fitzgerald's own autobiographical essays all emphasized his youth, his fast-paced lifestyle, and his literary talents."[1] Galow's statement exemplifies how critics have taken note of authors' interventions. It also shows, though, how fiction is placed on the periphery to their understanding of these interventions. Galow describes Fitzgerald's image by invoking his fiction (he is an "example … of the … young adults that populated his work"); but the fiction, in this account, does not seem to shape his image. There are exceptions to these tendencies, but the emphasis of literary celebrity studies remains on paratexts. Fiction is often read as a representation of fame rather than its manipulation; or, conversely, celebrity is seen as the context through which the critic can better understand the text. In these paradigms, it seems that writers have little use for fiction when they come to engage with their publics.

There are other examples and, in fact, several of them focus on Philip Roth, whose fiction seems to not let readers simply separate it from his public image. The fact that there is a whole volume of essays about Roth and celebrity attests to Roth's resistance to a simple separation between publicity and fiction.[2] In another contribution to the study of Roth as a public figure, scholar of literary celebrity Loren Glass reads the entire range of Roth's Zuckerman books from *The Ghost Writer* to *Exit Ghost*, the final installment when Zuckerman is in his seventies. Glass writes that Zuckerman and the deaths and near deaths he faces in several of the novels were "conceived as a way of managing the conflict between … posthumous fame and the instantaneous contemporaneous celebrity."[3] In imagining the death of an author-character, Roth can supply an image of himself as already dead and therefore eligible for "posthumous fame." Zuckerman adjusts Roth's image. In a similar vein, Stefan Kjerkegaard takes important steps in the direction of creating more room for fiction in this academic discourse by focusing on novels as modes of self-fashioning, even of branding the author as a celebrity. Despite his focus on novels, there are further steps to take. He only discusses autobiographical texts and novels whose protagonists share a name with their writers, sometimes called autofiction.[4] I want to highlight how critics can read other kinds of fictional texts as part of the author's performance. Each and every word has the potential to change or, more likely, fortify the idea of what the writer is like. That is not to say that this is their primary function and certainly not their only one. Novels have many functions, from political propaganda to aesthetic pleasure. Shaping the author's public identity is one such function and the one I will isolate here because it is relevant to authorial networking.

Several other critics within the narratology tradition have recently tackled the role of the author in a head-on manner. Still, they keep their priorities squarely on the author's role in the functioning of the text or the processes of reading. The argument usually proceeds thus: we need to talk about the author (or implied author) because some concept of the author's persona is necessary for interpreting the narrative. One example of this argument is Liesbeth Korthals Altes's engaging work on ethos attribution in narrative fiction. Korthals Altes defines ethos as "a person's or community's character or characterizing spirit, tone, or attitude."[5] What we know about a person's ethos would be included in their public identity. She states that the author's ethos (or what readers can learn about it) "play[s] a central framing role before, and throughout, the reading process."[6] Thus, what readers discover from the text or outside of it about writers' ethos becomes subordinate, at the end, to the hermeneutic process. Knowing that Roth is mischievous and often ironic helps us learn that we should read his text for clues that the text is sarcastic or satirical.[7] A predisposition to the abstract is due, I believe, to Korthals Altes's special attention to issues directly relating to reading strategies. Some room for "author posturing" or performances remains.[8] However, these postures seem to flow back to issues concerning the author's attitudes in a narrower sense. This tendency has a forerunner in Russian Formalism. In "Literature and Biography," Boris Tomaševkij argues that, while the actual facts of life of the author are of no interest to genuine literary scholarship, "the biographical legend"—the public image—is "a *literary fact*" that scholars would be foolish to ignore.[9] He too subsumes the image to the understanding of the text. In her narratological study of the Zuckerman books, Pia Masiero represents this tendency. Explaining how Zuckerman's characterization works across books, she writes: "the portrait of the Rothian artist that emerges cannot but be provisionally coherent because it is the result of a continuing characterization process based on *both* textual *and* extratextual inferences that, as such, are fallible."[10] Part of this extratextual information is surely Roth's own life, but it is important in that it helps us understand the novels. I agree that some sense of the author's attitudes and authority is necessary for reading, but I also believe that the aim of the hermeneutic process is often not only discovering the meaning in the text but learning about its author.

In insisting on this issue, I follow Rita Felski's call in *Uses of Literature* to "engage seriously with ordinary motives for reading—such as the desire for knowledge or the longing for escape—that are either overlooked or undervalued in literary scholarship."[11] Although Felski does not mention it, one common yet undervalued motivation for reading is the wish to know the author. Despite demands from some authors and critics to desist from biographical readings, some people read, at least in part, in order to learn about the person who wrote the text.[12] Joe Moran ties these desires directly to celebrity authorship, that is to say, to the existence of a significant public identity.[13] Some readers wish to know as much as possible about who the author really is as a person. Evidence for the search for the author can be found in writers' complaints about the nosiness of readers. Many critics' favorite example would be Henry James's *The Aspern Papers*. To give a basic summary of a complex text, James's novella presents a ridiculous scholar who not only breaks his ethical code but almost entangles himself in a marriage in order to obtain some love letters by a famous poet.

The tendency to look for the author in the text they produce is related to our everyday experience of communicating: we listen to people not only to learn from them but also to learn about them. This idea is Erving Goffman's basic premise in *The Presentation of Self in Everyday Life*: "When an individual enters the presence of others, they commonly seek to acquire information about him." Though this is not his main interest, Goffman acknowledges that "some of this information seems to be sought almost as an end in itself."[14] In other words, there is an aesthetic, almost literary, dimension to the social process of finding out information about others based on how they behave and what they say. The desire to learn about the author through reading their fiction makes it an opportunity for shaping what people think of the writer. In fiction, self-presentation must be mediated through textual devices. At the same time, fiction allows for manipulations that associate the author with qualities they would find difficult to convincingly perform in face-to-face interactions or other media. In such interactions, an actual body interferes with flights of fancy. If we want to combine literary analysis with an observation about the author's negotiation of the social world, what we need is a reading of the textual devices used by authors in order to shape their public identity.

Identity management is probably not the primary motivation for writing fiction in most cases, though it might be a crucial aspect for certain novels. It is, however, one consideration. I will appeal to my readers' experiences as writers of academic texts. When you write a crucial sentence in an academic paper, you ask yourself if it is true, if it furthers your argument and overall project, maybe if it will be aesthetically pleasing; but you also ask if you want to be known as someone who wrote this and writes like this? Do I want to be known as a witty writer? Do I want to be known as analytical to a fault? Do I want to be known as someone who quotes Derrida or as someone who quotes Foucault? Do too many questions make me seem annoying?

Fictional characters are of special importance for several reasons. First, both public images and characters are representations of human beings but are not actually humans per se. They have an artificial, or "synthetic," component in

James Phelan's words from his book-length discussion of fictional characters.[15] The methods for creating and maintaining characters and public identities are similar. That is to say, characterization is a process that is carried out in fictional as well as nonfictional discourses. Second, because characters seem like people—what Phelan calls their "mimetic" component[16]—it is easy for readers to assume that they are similar to the kind of people the author knows and even the kind of person the author in fact is (or wants to seem like). Minimally, a character is the kind of person the author chooses to invent or represent. Conversely, the character is a kind of person that helps the author make their argument, the character's "thematic" component.[17] Readers are not simply being naive when they suspect Roth, who often chooses sexist men as protagonists, of being guilty of sexism himself. At the very least, we know that Roth is very good at entertaining and presenting sexist attitudes. So, to Phelan's components of character (synthetic, mimetic, and thematic), I could add a fourth component: *authorial*.[18] Characters are not only artificial, imagined people, and carriers of ideas, but also the offshoot of an author who comes to be defined by them.

When character and author are similar in several known ways, readers will find it easier to assume that they are allowed and even encouraged to draw information about the author from the character. These variables would include, but not be restricted to, ethnicity and nationality, age and/or generation, gender, race, class background, and profession. This matrix can include autofiction, fictionalized memoirs, and similar texts, which have had, since the 1970s, an increasingly important role in Roth's writing and Jewish American literature more generally. With autofiction, works like Roth's *Operation Shylock* (1993) or Jonathan Safran Foer's *Everything Is Illuminated* (2002), where one character shares a name (first, last, or full name) with the author, it seems especially tempting to assume that they are the same person or extremely similar. There is no doubt that other facets encourage such conflations.[19]

Few writers have been more susceptible to this confusion and few have been more vocal about their chagrin over it than Roth. This is especially true of the period after the publication of *Portnoy's Complaint*, which is also the period during which Roth most ardently identified with Kafka. For now, all we need to know is that *Portnoy's Complaint* includes several scenes featuring its narrator masturbating. Roth reports an incident starring the bestselling author and Hollywood personality Jacqueline Susann: "discussing her colleagues with Johnny Carson, [Susann] tickled ten million Americans by saying that she'd like to meet me but didn't want to shake my hand. Didn't want to shake my hand—she of all people?"²⁰ Susann's fiction is widely considered to be closely based on her own life and the life of her acquaintances, many of whom were celebrities.²¹ She might have been, therefore, especially inclined to conflate author and character. However, this is one of many such moments of confusion between character and author in Roth's biography but it has become a touchstone (or rather, an I-don't-want-to-touchstone) in Roth criticism. One senses the anger alongside the disdain for mass media over their confusing his novel with an autobiographical confession and thinking that narratives about Portnoy (like his obsessive masturbation) are relevant for determining behavior toward Roth. There were several reasons for the conflation, among them the fact that both Roth and Portnoy were born in the early 1930s and were accordingly about the same age when the book came out, both are Jewish, both are heterosexual men, both grew up in Newark, New Jersey. Along with the confessional tone and coming-of-age narrative of the novel, it is tempting to assume that what is true about Portnoy is probably also true about Roth, especially when conjecturing about private acts and attitudes that cannot be debunked by fact-checking. Indeed, we might learn that, *unlike* Portnoy, Roth has an older brother, not an older sister, and correct our assumptions; but my readers do not need me to spell out what one cannot fact-check about Roth's private activities.

If readers are so prone to relate the character to the authors, why do writers create characters with which they would loathe to be identified? Why would Roth write about Portnoy or, to choose another famous example that will take us away from Jewish literature, Vladimir Nabokov about Humbert Humbert, the hebephiliac kidnapper-rapist? There might be other answers, but I will offer two mutually supporting ones. First, it stands to reason that authors do not always expect the strength of this identification or how unpleasant it might be. Both Roth and Nabokov were much less famous before these novels came out. They could not have fully foretold the cultural impact the novels would have. Additionally, authors may reason that risking the connection with a dubious character is worthwhile when it opens doors to new ways of expression or opportunities for achieving artistic and worldly goals. *Lolita* and *Portnoy's Complaint* are widely considered classics of twentieth-century American literature, were crucial for securing their authors' reputations, and made them a lot of money. They are unimaginable without their problematic protagonists.

Most professional critics would not conflate Portnoy and Roth in their writings (though some associations probably linger). This is, however, not the case with Nathan Zuckerman, who is often seen as Roth's other self. Zuckerman, indeed, has been used to discern, if not biographical facts about Roth, then certainly his attitudes. Zuckerman shares many biographical details with both Roth and Portnoy. Yet, contrary to Portnoy, who is a lawyer, Zuckerman is a writer. His vocation and role as a creator of fiction bring him closer to Roth than any other character (with the exceptions of characters named Philip or Philip Roth). This trend has been apparent ever since the reception of the first Zuckerman novel, *The Ghost Writer*. A reviewer for the *New York Times* mentions parenthetically that Zuckerman was already used as one of a number of "fictional stand-ins" in an earlier Roth book, *My Life As a Man*.[22] This comment is made so offhandedly that it positions the idea that Zuckerman is an alter ego to seem self-evident and routine. Similarly, the *New York Review of Books* reviewer asks, "Is Nathan really the Philip of twenty years ago?"[23] The reviewer dismisses this question as one of a series of uninteresting ones but does so in a way that suggests that an affirmative answer needs little proof.[24]

Book reviewers are useful in the study of author-character conflation for three reasons. First, they represent a certain segment of the reading public that shares these tendencies. We can think of reviewers as a sampling of readers' responses even if they represent a highly skewed sampling. Second, we can look at reviewers as opinion leaders. Such reviewers shape how some readers see the link between Roth and Zuckerman. Lastly, if the public had no to little tolerance for conflating and affiliating authors with characters, reviewers would likely not dare publish such suggestions. Thus, the fact that these ideas are expressed in public by men and women whose profession is writing about books shows that it is a viable option in our culture. Reviews both indicate and mold how readers link a character with its author.

A character's vocation as an author seems to encourage readers to conflate and confuse author for character. First, the situation itself conveys that whoever wrote the text is a writer. Even if we know nothing about them, we can be sure that the text was written by someone who is, having written the text, a writer. This is a tautology, but it is here to show that the role of author is self-evident in most cases. We might not know the writer's age, ethnicity, or gender. We might not know if they are a successful author or a failed one. But an author they must be. Even in cases where readers know more, the point still stands that one of the most basic facts about the author will still remain their profession or role. The second reason is that the existence of author-characters themselves may make readers ask questions about the actual author and what they are like. This is similar to when the appearance of Jewish characters in a novel brings up questions about the author's Jewishness and right to depict

Jews. Thus, author-characters remind readers of the existence of authors and of one specific author in particular.

All this is crucial for understanding that fictional authors are part of the network that helps characterize real authors. Since much of what readers know about writers comes from authorial affiliations and groupings, not direct characterizing, readers not only confuse or conflate authors with their characters but also relate them to their characters. Zuckerman is an author worth thinking about when contemplating Roth, just as much as Bellow is. This point about networking is especially important when the author-character is very different from the writer but still affects their public image. For instance, Nicole Krauss identifies with a writer in his eighties even when she was in her early thirties.[25]

To take the next step, author-characters are not only tied to the writer who invented them, they are also nodes by which to network with other real writers. There are a number of ways in which affiliating with actual authors can be carried out via fiction.

One such path is fictionalized biographies or biofiction, novels in which at least one main character is a fictionalized author. Cases in which Jewish American literary authors use another real Jewish author as the protagonist seem to be quite rare. Or rather, cases of plausible versions of historical authors are rare. Still, two examples are Dara Horn's A *Guide for the Perplexed* (2013), which contains a chapter fictionalizing an episode from the life of the great philosopher Maimonides (and takes its title from Maimonides's philosophical masterpiece), and her earlier novel *The World to Come* (2006), which features Der Nister (a nom de plume that translates as "the Hidden"), a Yiddish writer. Jewish American writers seem much more likely to use writers in floutingly fictional ways. Roth's use of Anne Frank in *The Ghost Writer* is the most prominent example but far from the only one. In *Hope: A Tragedy* (2012), Shalom Auslander also imagines Anne Frank who survived the Holocaust. This time around, she is an old writer hiding in a New England attic for decades, trying to finish her first novel. This novel affiliates Auslander not only with Frank but also with Roth through Roth's more well-known use of her image. Roth himself is also mentioned. One character says: "You know who I saw the other day? ... Philip Roth," while another eventually answers, "I thought he was dead."[26] This remark is offhanded, and the idea that Roth might be dead suggests his irrelevance but it still encourages anyone that looks for debts and influences. Since the tone of the novel is often humorous and ironic, it is easy to see this remark as a sly acknowledgment rather than a serious attack on Roth's relevance.

Autofiction—fiction in which the protagonist is a fictional version of the author (and shares their name)—may offer many opportunities for author networking. In the second part of "Looking at Kafka" (1973), Roth bridges the gap between Kafka's death and his own birth. The second section is an autofictional and counterfactual narrative where, instead of dying in 1924, Kafka immigrates to the United States and works as a Hebrew schoolteacher in Newark. There he encounters the young Philip, who, prompted by his father, invites the lonely refugee teacher for a family dinner. Kafka, believe it or not, dates Roth's aunt, but this relationship ends abruptly. Even in fiction, the attempt to invite Kafka into a familial relationship with Roth fails. Still, the literary relays between Roth, the fictionalized young Roth, the fictionalized Kafka, and the historical Kafka remain strong.

Another method of networking through fiction is to include characters who stand for or represent an author or group of authors. The degree to which a writer is recognizable as a veiled representation of a real person varies a great deal. It seems, for instance, that there is broad agreement that the titular character of Bellow's *Humboldt's Gift* (1975) is Delmore Schwartz, who was also a real-life friend and rival, the poet who is best remembered today for his short story "In Dreams Begin Responsibilities" and for dying middle-aged, alone, and broke. In such cases, the novel would be described as a *roman à clef* and even accused of revealing too much about the real person behind the different name, as was the case with Bellow's *Ravelstein* (2000), which was based on philosopher Allan Bloom's life. In the middle ground, there are characters that seem to be inspired by real writers or a mixture of real writers but who are not straightforward depictions of any single recognizable person. This is the case with Roth's E. I. Lonoff, who, in *The Ghost Writer*, resembles Malamud but also Isaac Bashevis Singer and Roth himself, and, in the same book, Abravanel is a cocktail of Bellow and Mailer (and more than a dash of Roth). At times, the character seems to represent a category of writers and not specific ones. For instance, Malamud's *The Tenants* (1971) depicts a Jewish writer, Harry Lesser, who fails to sustain a connection with Willie Spearmint, an aspiring African American writer. Spearmint comes to stand for the entire (at least male) tradition of African American writing from Frederick Douglass on. Apparently, many critics see an especially strong link with Amiri Baraka.[27] However, reading Spearmint's manuscript, Lesser muses, "The Life he writes, whatever he calls it, moves, pains, inspires, even though it's been written before, and better, by Richard Wright, Claude Brown, Malcolm X, and in his way, Eldridge Cleaver."[28] Lesser is moved, but he is moved by Spearmint as another representative of a story he already thinks he knows. Arguably, Lesser's failing to maintain the friendship comes from his inability to see the African American writer as anything but a representative. Whether Malamud meant for it to do so or not, *The Tenants* works as much at disengaging its author from African American writers as it does engaging with them.[29]

Still, one must avoid too easy generalizations about fictional characters as sources for affiliating with specific writers or specific groups of writers. I want to stress that claims for obviousness of certain veiled portraits need to be accepted with a certain reservation and checked against early reception. To return to *Humboldt's Gift*, a 1990s reference book entry about the novel pronounces that "the visionary poet Von Humboldt Fleisher [was] *obviously* modeled on Delmore Schwartz";[30] but was this fact so obvious to early readers of the novel? Some reviewers indeed do describe the Schwartz connection as a well-known fact, with one writing that "By now everyone knows that the poet Von Humboldt Fleisher is closely modeled on Delmore Schwartz";[31] and yet, it seems not everyone knew back in 1975. The reviews for the *Wall Street Journal* and *Studies in American Jewish Literature* do not mention Schwartz at all, out of either a lack of knowledge or a sense of propriety.[32] Some examples fall in between these extremes of not knowing and assuming "everybody" knows. In the *New York Review of Books*, the reviewer notes that "something unassimilated about this larger-than-life character [Humboldt] intimates that he is based too closely on a real person or persons" but does not provide any guesses as to who this person is, apart from suggesting that he is one of two "alter egos" for Bellow.[33] Certain features of the novel (and Bellow's reputation) suggest that characters are drawn from real life, but this does not mean that readers will always automatically see the obvious connection. Another reviewer heard of the Schwartz connection but refuses to accept it fully, suggesting a list of other poets: "Supposedly modeled on Delmore Schwartz, Humboldt also suggests shades of Jarrell, Lowell, Berryman, Roethke, all the incorrigible, sensitive wild men who've risked (and sometimes given) their lives for insight."[34] Here, Schwartz's crucial role is a rumor, a supposition made by other people, not the reviewer. At the same time, she makes the case that the character is a mix of several figures and not a connection just to the one Schwartz. Though in the know, this critic chooses to refine the common supposition into a less strictly one-to-one correlation. Thus, it seems important to point out that, whenever we use a character to talk about affiliation, we must realize that these are less automatic than a few decades of hindsight and critical consensus might make it seem. While the tie between a character and the writer who wrote about him is automatic even if complex, the tie between that character and any other real person is often open to debate.

More often, other authors will not be characters in the novel. Instead, they are discussed and mentioned by narrators and characters. Examples are numerous, but sometimes they are more clearly the labor of connection than in other cases. Roth's *The Breast* (1972) features the literature professor David Kepesh metamorphosing—Gregor Samsa-style—into a giant female breast. One possible explanation offered by Kepesh for his metamorphosis (or delusion) is reading and teaching: "I'm grasping at straws, you see. I thought 'I got it from fiction.' The books I've been teaching inspired it. They put the idea in my head … Teaching Gogol and Kafka every year—teaching 'The Nose' and 'Metamorphosis.'"[35] In *The Breast*, the character is so entangled with other texts and authors that he reenacts them on his body. Through this plot, readers might sense how entangled Roth's imagination is with such writers. In a prequel to *The Breast*, *The Professor of Desire* (1977), Kepesh travels to Prague to learn more about Kafka and has a dream in which he is introduced to a sex worker Kafka visited (again we see a woman as an instrument for male networking). When the character discussing other authors is a writer who readers tend to connect with the real author, the connections are stronger (as I argued earlier in this section). Thus, I would predict that most readers will tend to take the ties created in *The Ghost Writer* as better indications of Roth's network than Portnoy's or Kepesh's preferences. Still, these different kinds of references within fiction are crucial for the creation and maintenance of authorial networks, especially when these are combined with efforts in the paratexts.

Paratexts

Fiction has a crucial role in forming literary networks, but a critic interested in public image must recall that this public image operates even for those who have not read a word of the writer's literary works. This is possible because of paratexts, the (usually) much shorter texts that surround literary works and present these works and their authors to the public. Alongside the paratexts that lie closer to the text, such as acknowledgments and introductions, which would usually only be read by people who also intend to read the main text or have already read it, we find media coverage or more distant paratexts such as interviews, photos, and reviews that are likely to be encountered by a larger swath of the public. All these are relevant and will now be discussed as locations in which writers and other agents carry out the work of affiliation.

I will not have much to say about real-life encounters save to note that they are often an impetus for creating textual connections and can fortify the impression that authors are indeed strongly connected. Authors will often represent personal encounters in texts in order to make textual attachments. Our knowledge of such connections comes from biographical writing, which might be authorized explicitly, implicitly, or not at all in print (periodicals and books) and other media (like radio shows, podcasts, documentaries). Some of the information about Roth's attempt to form a personal connection with Kafka comes from Claudia Roth Pierpont's *Roth Unbound: A Writer and His Books* (2013). This book, part biography, part literary appreciation, draws much of its material from conversations Pierpont conducted with Roth. The extent to which *Roth Unbound* was controlled by Roth has been contested, but, though it is not his official biography, it certainly bears the stamp of his influence and at many points defends him. One reviewer writes: "The reader of *Roth Unbound* often has the sense of Roth looking over the author's shoulder, authorizing or at least advocating certain interpretations. Pierpont's evident pleasure at being in Roth's inner circle … seems to make her want him to be a likable person";[36] another writes: "Behind Pierpont's narrative is Roth's ur-narrative, the charismatic author's voice often more definitive than the voice of his critic and biographer."[37] Pierpont's book, perhaps more than most biographical texts, lies on the borderline between self-presentation and presentation by others.

Materials within it, then, can be assimilated, with some care, into a discussion of Roth deliberately affiliating with Kafka. Pierpont tells us that, when visiting Prague, Roth proposed marriage to Kafka's youngest niece in order to help her exit Czechoslovakia. She declined the proposal so Roth never becomes literally related to Kafka. However, the fact that he tried to create this attachment, especially since he told Pierpont about his proposal, is telling.[38] In another direction, we can also see this proposal as a gambit that did not quite pan out to publicly and permanently link himself with Kafka.

A joint photograph can also link people captured within its frame. These visual representations seem uncontestable records of two authors meeting and having real contact. Making this idea the essence of photography, Roland Barthes writes: "I call 'photographic referent' not the *optionally* real thing to which an image or a sign refers but the *necessarily* real thing which has been placed before the lens, without which there would be no photograph."³⁹ Despite many reservations about this idea, some of the sense that the photographs are objective remains and shapes how we "read" photographs as more real and more referential than other texts. Some examples of the power of joint photographs can be found on Nathan Englander's Twitter account. This account is not overly active, but it does contain several pictures of Englander with other authors, including an old photo with several famous contemporary authors such as David Foster Wallace, Jonathan Franzen, and Zadie Smith. In this photo, Englander looks out of place, being the only one before the row of writers. Smith seems to be drawing back from him. I can guess that this was not his intention in posting the photo, but it makes Englander look like he does not belong on the top rung of contemporary fiction writers. In another, much warmer photo, a fake mustached Englander seems friendly with two authors identified with Jewishness: Gary Shteyngart and Aleksandar Hemon.⁴⁰ The juxtaposing of these two photos seems to prove that Jewish American writers are connected in real life as a group and this common denominator is an important part of Englander's identity.

A joint photo should be *impossible* in the case of Kafka and Roth. Nevertheless, the *Life* photographer Bob Peterson found a way to produce such a joint portrait when Roth was photographed alongside a poster of Kafka, creating an image where, at first glance, it seems as if they share the same space.⁴¹ Utilizing the referential assumptions of reading photos, Peterson actually puts them together. This photograph first appeared as a two-page spread in *Life Magazine*. There, the two men occupy different pages, the fissure between them perhaps suggesting some separation but also blurring signs that show that they do not share the same space. From a certain perspective, it even seems that Kafka is physically in front and not behind Roth. This photo was used just before the publication of *Portnoy's Complaint*. The "shade of … Kafka," as the caption puts it, appearing as part of one of the first introductions of Roth to the very wide audience of *Life*, says much about the extent to which Roth affiliated himself with Kafka circa 1969.⁴² Let me stress that *Life* was heavily reliant on its visual aspects and that, for many readers, the ones who mostly flip through the magazine, this photograph could be their major and even sole contact with Philip Roth.

This kind of photographic affiliation requires many mediators, as is the case with other examples: Roth, the photographer, and the writers and editors who decided to use the photo in such a prominent place. Just as in the case of Pierpont's book, we see how the author and other agents work together to create a network of affiliations. Lorraine York's *Margaret Atwood and the*

Figure 1 1969 *Life Magazine* spread featuring a photo by Bob Peterson of Roth with Kafka in the background. The fold of the paper fosters the illusion that Roth and Kafka share the same space. Photographed by David Hadar.

Labour of Literary Celebrity argues that authorial public image or celebrity is produced by many agents' cooperation. This monograph presents in great detail the mediations around the Canadian writer's public image and even her fiction.[43] More generally, this point about many mediators sits well with Felski's adaptation of Latour. For Felski, "If [texts] make a difference, they do so only as co-actors and codependents, enmeshed in a motley array of attachments and associations." Literature is a web, part of a larger social web, which enables text to connect and act on other actors, including, and most importantly for Felski, readers. So, too, are the public identities of authors, which Felski does not explicitly include (or exclude) from her analysis. "Artworks can only survive and thrive by making friends [and] creating allies," she writes.[44] The same is just as true of authors. Therefore, it is important to remember the other mediators or agents that participate in the process.

To return to visual representations, one in which writers usually do not have control and that offers less of a sense of a real-life encounter than the photograph is the group painting. The most famous example of this would probably be Raphael's *The School of Athens*, which represents an impossible picture of many of the major philosophers of the Greek world in one space.[45] On an adjacent wall in the room that functioned as private library, Raphael painted an image dedicated to famous poets from Sappho to Virgil to Dante, imagining them all together on

Mount Parnassus, the dwelling place of the Muses.⁴⁶ Not surprisingly, there is nothing quite similar in Jewish American literature. Still, I mention this medium because it shows the power of juxtaposing images of authors as a means of creating literary networks. Unlike photography, paintings and drawings do not suggest an actual coming together but rather a purely idealized one. One illustration shows contemporary Jewish American literature as a group in one space. This image illustrates "The New Yiddishists," a 2009 *Vanity Fair* article about a new wave of Jewish American writers. Done in rough black lines by Tim Sheaffer, it shows Roth frowning top and center with other writers around him. Roth's head is significantly larger than that of most of his younger Jewish colleagues, suggesting his importance and perhaps greater brainpower. While Roth's arms are crossed, suggesting anger but also a sense that his work is done, the others (Chabon, Englander, Foer, Horn, and, least easy to recognize, Krauss) all have writing tools and look like they have something to prove. The image illustrates what the journalistic report and the interviewed therein say with words: a new generation of Jewish writers is busy entering into the field Roth dominates.⁴⁷

Staying with a genre closely associated with journalism, another case of cooperation between authors and other agents is the interview.⁴⁸ Interviews present many opportunities for self-presentation by way of other figures. The most obvious of such opportunities are moments when authors are asked about their influences or favorite authors. These moments can be seized on for explicitly affiliating with others, even if often the results are lists of authors, which are a rather weak form of networking. One often-cited example in Roth criticism occurred soon after the publication of *Portnoy's Complaint*. When George Plimpton asks Roth to what extent *"stand-up comics"* like Lenny Bruce influenced the novel, Roth denies significant influence from these masters of entertainment, nevertheless maintaining a tie through disaffiliating. Presumably, he could have convinced Plimpton to drop the question by not giving an interesting answer. Instead, Roth claims a debt to "a sit-down comic," Kafka, thus also half connecting him to the standup comics.⁴⁹ We can also see how affiliating with one writer enables disaffiliating from other writers, in this case comedy writer-performers.

Sometimes the significance is not only in what is said in the interview but the very fact that one author interviews or has a public conversation with another author. This is a favorite method of Roth's, as attested by the interviews he conducted with others and collected in *Shop Talk: A Writer and His Colleagues and Their Work* (2001). Two of the interviewees are Czech and thus connected for us with Kafka, and several others include references and discussions of him. Thus, the interviews act to create a triangular affiliation, Roth–Interviewer–Kafka. An especially curious case is an interview with the Yiddish writer I. B. Singer about the Jewish Polish writer Bruno Schulz. In this interview, Roth explicitly uses one writer, to whom he does not express a special connection, to understand and connect to a third. In fact, there's a fourth writer in the wings: Schulz translated Kafka into Polish and his short stories are often described as Kafkaesque.

At other moments, the writer shows more independence when creating ties, working with fewer mediators. An important way to connect is through nonfiction writing about other authors. The very fact that Roth, who over his long career did not write many essays, chose to write ones about Kafka, Malamud, and Bellow ties him especially to those three. Naturally, when an author writes reviews, biographies, or critical essays as a common practice, the impact of the very choice to write is less significant. Such is the case with authors-critics like, most prominently among Jewish American writers of the last half-century, Cynthia Ozick. Even then, writing an essay that turns out to be an especially vital moment in the reception of a certain writer makes the tie more significant.

The essay itself can have, and often has, moments of explicit affiliation. This direct networking is visible in the first, less fictional, part of Roth's "'I Always Wanted You to Admire My Fasting'; or, Looking at Kafka." This high point in the Roth–Kafka liaison was first published in *American Review*, a widely circulated literary journal in the form of a mass-market paperback that earlier had published excerpts from *Portnoy's Complaint*. The Kafka essay was later republished as the final essay—a kind of final word—in Roth's *Reading Myself and Others*; in *Why Write? Collected Nonfiction 1960–2013*, it is the first essay, a kind of introduction to the entirety of Roth's body of essays and interviews. The Kafka essay is made up of two distinct parts: the first is a nonfictional (yet embellished) account of Kafka's final year, including readings of some of his texts; the second is fictional about Kafka moving to Newark and becoming Roth's Hebrew teacher. In the nonfictional section, a link between Roth and Kafka is also important. For instance, Roth describes looking at "a photograph taken of him at the age of forty (my age)."[50] He thus presents himself in close proximity to Kafka's image and resembling him in age, and perhaps in other facets as well like his nose, "the nose of half the Jewish boys who were my friends in high school."[51] Roth continues to describe the final year of Kafka's life with detail and some fancy, in the process making it clear that he has dedicated much time and attention not only to reading his writing but also to thinking about Kafka's character and Kafka as a character.

Beyond the direct control of writers, critical writing like essays, reviews, literary commentary, and academic journal papers and books are of course also opportunities for critics to connect writers or to strengthen existing bonds. Every time someone writes an essay about Roth and mentions Bellow or vice versa, for instance, the bond between them is strengthened and maintained.

All of the texts that I have described thus far can be entered under the rubric of paratexts, even if they are not published in the same book as works of literature. Yet students of authorial networking should give special attention to the genres of nonfiction that operate as an immediate paratext for books. These include introductions, afterwords, blurbs, and acknowledgments. These are part of authorial identity management exactly at the crucial moment when readers are about to engage with the writer for long periods or just after they have done so. These paratexts might be written by authors for their own work or ones they produce for the works of others.

Bharati Mukherjee (1940–2017) was born in India but spent most of her adult life in Canada and the United States. In the brief introduction to her short story collection *Darkness* (1985), she explicitly affiliates herself with Jewish American authors, conceiving them as immigrants or the offspring of immigrants. She writes: "I see myself as an American writer in the tradition of other American writers whose parents or grandparents had passed through Ellis Island."[52] Though descendants of immigrants must include non-Jews as well as Jews, she fortifies her tie to this tradition and her performance of immigrant identity through affiliating herself and her writing with two Jewish writers. First she explains that "[t]he book I dream of updating is no longer *A Passage to India*" by British cosmopolitan E. M. Forster (1879–1970); "it's *Call It Sleep*" by Henry Roth (1906–95), a Galicia-born Jew. She goes on to highlight the fact that the book is dedicated to Malamud. She ties her current identity as an almost Jewish immigrant writer to a new ability to read Malamud, who is "a man I have known for over twenty years as a close friend, but Bernard Malamud the writer is a man I have known only for these past two years, after I learned to read his stories as part of the same celebration" of immigrant life in the United States.[53] The ability to read is tied to the shifting identity as a writer, just before we start reading her stories.

This example also shows that affiliations can create impressions that cannot be admitted outright. Mukherjee cannot come out and say I am a Jewish American writer. That proposition would be both false and politically incorrect, not so much because of appropriating Jewish culture but being too ready to give up her own Indian identity. However, she can say that she can rewrite and embody Henry Roth and Malamud, two central figures of Jewish American literary history. Jonathan Freedman discusses Mukherjee's "Gestures of literary affiliation,"[54] as he calls them. He uses these gestures as a starting point in discussing how Mukherjee's work is actually significantly different from her Jewish precursors. He concludes that she is a case of transcending influence (invoking Bloom's anxiety of influence).[55] This is one example, by the way, of a critic who follows tracks that the writer has laid out at least up until a certain point. Freedman is careful enough about laying out Mukherjee's own affiliation with Malamud so that it is made clear that the connections he makes are their joint venture.

Writing the paratexts for others enables different trajectories. This is often an opportunity to define relations vis-à-vis the writers being introduced. At the same time, the writer of the introduction models how readers should approach that writer. Delmore Schwartz received an enthusiastic introduction from the singer-songwriter and—why not?—rock poet, Lou Reed (1942–2013). Reed presents Schwartz as a teacher, source of inspiration, and as the greatest genius he had ever met. Thus, he makes himself out to be someone who was uplifted and shaped by the great, but doomed, man. One can take note that, for readers encountering Schwartz through his relationship with Reed, the collection can become a way to decipher what the writer has meant for the singer. What readers learn about Schwartz from the texts is colored by what they know about Reed and his art.

In introductions to anthologies or collections, writers can place themselves vis-à-vis a number of writers at once. Bellow's introduction to *Great Jewish Short Stories* (1964), well known for his presentation of laughter and trembling as the core of Jewish literature, also does much work in the way of affiliation and disaffiliation. Bellow actively disaffiliates himself from the Yiddish writer I. L. Peretz (1852–1915), writing that his stories "depend too much on a kind of Talmudic sophistication which the modern reader, and I along with him, knows very little of." Bellow identifies himself as a modern secular Jewish reader by describing his lack of appreciation for—even inability to properly read—Peretz and by implication the Talmud and the edifice of Jewish religious creativity that was built on it. No less importantly, he affiliates himself with the younger writer Philip Roth, and at the same time disaffiliates himself from Leon Uris (1924–2003), whose *Exodus* (1958)

Bellow sees as kind of advertisement for Israel. Bellow mimics those who say, "posters are needed more urgently than masterpieces" as those same kinds of people who exalt *Exodus* and disparage Roth's 1959 *Goodbye, Columbus*, a book which, unlike Uris's, is represented in the anthology. He then attacks these people as no better than the Soviet oligarchy that persecuted Boris Pasternak. Thus, Bellow lands on the side of art and on Roth's team. In this early 1960s text, we see how Bellow actively solidifies the ties between himself and Roth.[56] Before our eyes, Bellow shapes the network of literary Jewish America some critics take for granted. No less important, for a reader who took the introduction to heart, the different writers in the anthology are read in their relations to Bellow.

The acknowledgments are often more important for affiliating with nonwriters or for showing a more mundane connection with writers (such as those who were one's editors or teachers as well). Yet, as when Englander thanks the Israeli writer Etgar Keret for being his "hairiest muse," it is sometimes the ground for more complex affiliations.[57] Gérard Genette writes about dedication what is also true of acknowledgments: "Whoever the official addressee, there is always an ambiguity in the destination of a dedication, which is always intended for at least two addressees: the dedicatee, of course, but also the reader, for dedicating a work is a public act that the reader is, as it were, called on to witness."[58] Genette here talks about the work and not the author's image, but it seems to me obvious that the decision to dedicate a work says as much about the author as about the work. A similar point can be made about the blurb, which has become ubiquitous in American book publishing.[59] The person who writes the blurb is often more important than what the blurb actually says. When one sees a quote from Roth on the front cover of Krauss's *Forest Dark* (2017), it matters little that he writes that it is "A brilliant novel"—such superlatives mean little in what is after all advertising copy (I think this is a moment when a little cynicism is warranted). What is significant is that Roth's name is up there affirming Krauss's identity as a serious Jewish American fiction writer.

So, to sum up, there is a great variety of textual junctions for writers to create their networks with others. These can be very long, like an entire novel, or very short, like a "brilliant novel" blurb on the title page. Like the photographs we looked at, they might not be verbal, though mostly there is some linguistic aspect. It is now time to move from the synchronic description to a more diachronic narrative about the changes in the sources of networking employed by Jewish American writers. The toolkit of locations and vocabulary for literary networks developed in the first two chapters will be of great use moving forward.

3

Jewish American Literary Networks beyond English

This chapter begins a three-chapter arc that describes and analyzes the history of Jewish American writers affiliating with other, non-American, Jewish writers. Jewish American writers moved from biblical and other religious or ancient precursors to affiliation with writers in Yiddish, first almost automatically and then more artificially, and then moved to writers in European languages, often Holocaust victims and survivors. I present the story of dominant choices. Once an option is opened up, it continues to be available, even if it is used less than in its most dominant moment. I focus on Jewish writers affiliating with other Jewish writers. This focus is not intended to devalue the ways in which affiliating with non-Jewish authors (mostly European and American) was crucial for the writers under discussion. In fact, these ties are often essential for the performance of their identities as literary writers or as Americans. Julian Levinson shows that connections to Americans like Ralph Waldo Emerson and Walt Whitman could even help mediate connections with Jewish writers.[1] Similarly, Jennifer Glaser presents how racialized others, among them many writers, have been useful for Jewish writers in negotiating their shifting position as Jews in the United States.[2] For instance, Philip Roth's encounter with Ralph Ellison is critical for how he dealt with Jews who opposed him.[3] I deal here, however, with how Jews identify themselves as Jews through links with other Jewish writers. Some of this history has already been written, though not in these terms. Because my precursors have been comprehensive, I give more attention to recent developments and less space to the late nineteenth-century and early twentieth-century writers.

Histories of Jewish American literature often progress from a strong connection to Jewishness (sometimes expressed in writing in Jewish languages) to greater assimilation to a disappearance of any dominant Jewish identity. Instead, I want to tell a history of the changing ways of identifying as a Jew and the different ways to be a Jewish writer. In focusing on languages other than English, my approach follows a somewhat different path from the history Hana Wirth-Nesher presents in *Call It English*, where she charts a move from a dominance of idiomatic Yiddish in Jewish writing from the beginning of the twentieth century to around the 1960s to a dominance of liturgical Hebrew as a second, somewhat less important, language for Jewish American writing in the second part of the century.[4] My history starts with Hebrew and ends with Hebrew again, but a very different kind of Hebrew, not liturgical, but the one spoken and written by Israelis. Our histories differ not only because of different start and end points (I will start with Emma Lazarus and end with writings that were produced after the publication of Wirth-Nesher's book) but also because I focus on connections between authors rather than on the use of languages.

That said, in looking at Jewish American networking beyond American literature, I also focus on languages other than English. The center of the Anglophone Jewish republic of letters is the United States. Canadian or British Jewish writers might be actively connected to American Jews, but the reverse is rare. Howard Jacobson may be described as an English Roth, but Roth is never the American Jacobson.[5] An obituary for Mordecai Richler, a Canadian, reports that "When he began to publish, in the mid-fifties, he was often grouped with the great generation of American Jewish writers, as a slightly lesser, northern version of Roth and Bellow and Malamud,"[6] but writings about either three almost never bring up Richler, certainly not in a manner that belittles Roth, Saul Bellow, or even Bernard Malamud. No less important to my choice to move beyond English is that American Jewish literature, as Wirth-Nesher and others have shown, is deeply if not uniquely multilingual. It is not only multilingual in including Yiddish and Hebrew. Beyond these Jewish languages, it is also receptive to authors who wrote in other, mostly European, languages and traditions.

Ancient Hebrew (and Aramaic)

Many critics have posited Emma Lazarus at the inception of Jewish American literature in English, Lazarus's turn to Jewish themes in the 1880s being the crucial moment. Coming from a largely Americanized home (and a mix of German and Sephardi parentage), she started her poetic career, under some guidance from Emerson, without any overt interest in her Jewish identity. Indeed, much of her engagement with Jewishness hinges on identification with a Hebraic tradition, not the languages spoken in the everyday lives of the Jews who were her contemporaries. She even studied Hebrew and translated poets from the Golden Age of Hebrew poetry in Muslim Iberia. Around the same time, she reshaped her poetic persona to connect to biblical author-figures.[7] In "The New Ezekiel" (1883), Lazarus works explicitly to associate herself with a biblical prophet, who as such is also a figure of literary strength. The poem opens with a series of questions, the first of which is "What, can these dead bones live, whose sap is dried / By twenty scorching centuries of wrong?" bringing to mind Ezekiel's Vision of the Valley of Dry Bones (chap. 37), where the prophet sees bones come back to life as people, an image that functions as a national allegory for the return of the exiled to the Land of Israel. The line also adds a time marker, "twenty scorching centuries," placing the speaker of the poem at least two millennia after the original Ezekiel and close to the historical Emma Lazarus. The second stanza opens with a resounding "Yea" to the questions of the first stanza and ends with a promise: "I ope your graves, my people, saith the Lord / And I shall place you living in your land." This poem offers the renewal of prophecy along with the renewal of Israel. It thus renders the poet as a new prophet, specifically a new Ezekiel. Ezekiel and the other "Literary Prophets" are known as authors of their books, but Lazarus secures the association between prophecy and poetry when she describes the dry bones as those of "psalmist, priest, and prophet."[8] In this list, joined together by a 'p' at the beginning of each word (the 'p' in psalmist may or may not be sounded), the role of a vehicle of God's word and worshiper (priest) is aligned with that of the writer of poems of worship, the Psalms. In writing this poem of national revival, Lazarus places herself in Ezekiel's sandals, creating a literary affiliation that sustains her role as a Jewish writer and one of prophet-like importance and resonance.

Staying with the biblical authors, I jump ahead three decades to a discussion of a mostly forgotten poet, James Oppenheim (1882–1932), who was a member of the Young Americans group and edited *The Seven Arts*, a modernist little magazine. Oppenheim not only connects himself to this biblical tradition but also provides an example of how a non-Jewish critic connects a Jewish writer with the Hebrew Bible. In an essay titled, "The New Poetry Movement," first published in the *New York Times* in 1917 and in book form in 1919, H. L. Mencken (1880–1956), the critic and intellectual, writes rather approvingly: "Oppenheim, equally eloquent [as Carl Sandburg], is more conventional. He stands, as to one leg, on the shoulders of Walt Whitman, and, as to the other, on a stack of Old Testaments."[9] In order to describe this new poet, Mencken combines, in one comical image, an American reference and a reference that is associated with Jews. Note that he writes "Old Testaments" rather than Bibles (which, from the Christian or Western point of view, would always include the New Testament). He continues in what reads as exclusionary Orientalizing and anti-Semitic language:[10]

> The stuff he writes, despite his belief to the contrary, is not American at all; it is absolutely Jewish, Levantine, almost Asiatic. But here is something criticism too often forgets: the Jew, intrinsically, is the greatest of poets. Beside his gorgeous rhapsodies the highest flights of any western bard seem feeble and cerebral. ... his dithyrambs ... are often inchoate and feverish, but at their best, they have the gigantic gusto of Solomon's Song.[11]

He finishes this assessment of the Jewishness of Oppenheim's poetry with a reference to *Shir haShirim*, a biblical book of love poetry, often attributed to King Solomon. Mencken connects Oppenheim not only to Whitman but also more fancifully to the ancient Hebrew poet king.

Oppenheim is not passive in this connection with mythical Hebrew poets. In what is his central poetic work, *Songs, for the New Age* (1914), he aligns himself explicitly with "David, of Asia," a phrase he uses twice in that book.[12] Furthermore, in the poem "The Morning Stars," Oppenheim attributes the sentiment that "the morning stars sing together, / He said the rocks do sing and that the hills rejoice" to "the psalmist," who is traditionally thought of as King David.[13] Though there are similar ideas in Psalms, the most direct source of the first line is Job 38:7,[14] which is not usually attributed to the King of Israel. So it is curious that Oppenheim insists on attributing these ideas to one poet, whom he later names as David. After this initial idea, the speaker complains that he cannot hear these celestial sounds; he ends up turning to "David, of Asia" and saying that once he stepped out into the "desert of Loneliness," referring to David's time in the literal desert of Judea, he can hear the same music David hears. The combination of the star theme and the call on David may remind us of the Star of David, a traditional symbol of Judaism and Jews. This poem offers an example of a Jewish writer positioning himself as an heir to David.

Some may argue against the relevance of David and Ezekiel and Jeremiah to the story of Jewish identity building because the Hebrew Bible is a resource for all Western writers, especially American ones because of the Protestant and Puritan roots of much of American culture. For instance, Jeremiah lends his name to an important genre in American literature, the Jeremiad. However, as we see in Lazarus and in Mencken's opinion about Oppenheim, biblical references are sometimes figured in specifically Jewish ways, especially if combined with reference to more narrowly Jewish sources like the Hebrew poetry of Muslim Spain or the Talmud.

Moving forward, I will turn to prose and especially prose fiction. Still, one can posit that poets perhaps more easily identify with biblical authors since most books with traditionally ascribed authors are either clearly in verse like Psalms and Song of Songs or are presented in an oracular mode like Ezekiel. If I were to stay with Jewish poets—think of Allen Ginsberg—perhaps the biblical author-figures would have kept their central place well into the twenty-first century.

Moving forward in the history of Jewish literature, we reach the Talmud. The Talmud is a collection of laws, biblical interpretations, wisdom, and narratives from late antiquity and written mostly in the Semitic language of Aramaic. It is the anchor text of Judaism. One of the premier American scholars on the Talmud, Daniel Boyarin, has called it a "traveling homeland" and posited it as an alternative to a territorial centering of Jewishness. That is to say, it has the same power of identity building that territory has for other nations.[15] One cannot exaggerate its importance for religious Jews, but it does not fit easily into my story about the formation of authorial Jewish identity. This is so not only because many of the authors I write about are by and large secular (we saw Bellow disowning the Talmud when he distanced himself from Peretz) but because the Talmud was not written or authored in the way we understand those ideas today. It was rather discussed, related orally, memorized, collected, edited, and compiled. Known in Hebrew as *Torah she-be-'al peh*, the Oral Tradition, the men (and very few women), the rabbis whose words are quoted, are presented as speaking rather than writing their narratives, polemics, and interpretations. Thus, figures like Rabbi Akiva can be invoked as wise men but not usually as writers or scribes. That said, and because it is so central, I can mention that American writers, not only scholars, did connect themselves to this complex text.

In Abraham Cahan's (1860–1951) epic novel of immigration to America *The Rise of David Levinsky* (1917), the titular character starts out as a *yeshiva bocher*, a Talmud scholar and a good one at that. I could make the argument that the titular character is easily taken for an alter ego for Cahan, including in his role as a former scholar; but, in this context, it would be better to assert that, because he is writing for an American audience, Cahan must explain what the Talmud is and how it is studied by the devout students. He thus connects himself to this text as someone preparing an introduction for it.[16] Levinsky eventually immigrates to the United States, leaving his studies behind, but this pursuit remains part of his character and part of Cahan's image.

Furthermore, literary critics have sometimes linked Jewish writers with the Talmudic tradition. One of the most explicit examples is Ezra Cappell's *American Talmud: The Cultural Work of Jewish American Fiction* (2007). In this book, Cappell invokes the multiauthored status of the Talmud to make a claim that many Jewish American writers are working together on a body of work that can be read together and one that forms what he calls a "moral center."[17] The Talmud is used as a rhetoric that affiliates several twentieth-century writers and also connects them to more distant figures in the tradition. All of this is done under the aegis of Judaism and Jewishness, blurring the lines between these concepts.

Yiddish

Cahan should be more easily connected with another, more secular and more recent, aspect of Jewish culture, Yiddish literature. Yiddish developed during the Middle Ages as the language of Jews living in German-speaking areas and later in Slavic areas as well. By the nineteenth century, different dialects of Yiddish, all combining Semitic, Germanic, and Slavic components, were spoken by the Jews of Eastern Europe. Yiddish, with some twentieth-century exceptions, uses a variation on the Hebrew alphabet and, like Hebrew, is written from right to left. What is known as modern Yiddish literature developed in the mid-nineteenth century as part of the secularization of Jewish life. This literature included such figures as Mendele Mocher Sforim, I. L. Peretz, and Sholem Aleichem. For Cahan and other immigrants who produced literature in English in the early twentieth century, the connection to authors writing in their mother tongue must have been natural and almost inescapable. Cahan was probably more important as the Yiddish journalist and editor of *Forverts* (*The Forward*) than he was as an English fiction writer. In this former role, he published works by the best and best-known Yiddish authors, affiliating with them in editorial as well as economic ties. No additional work needs to be done if the reader has even the slightest knowledge of the Yiddish world. For a writer like Anzia Yezierska (1880–1970), whose subject matter (like Cahan's) is Yiddish-speaking immigrants, the connection with Yiddish authors is also easily made. Overall, the first-generation immigrants seem not to need to focus on affiliating with Jewish writers but rather with American or other gentile writers in order to gain their American rather than, quite secure, Jewish credentials. Eminent Jewish man of letters Irving Howe (1920–93), who in *World of Our Fathers* places himself as a son looking back, makes a similar point when he writes: "Cahan was not one of the sons turning back on the Yiddish world, he was completely in and of it, a major intellectual of the East Side."[18]

With this quote, we may indeed turn our sights to the sons and daughters who try to connect themselves as editors, readers, translators, and indeed offspring of the Yiddish writers. So, the connection with Yiddish becomes more work for second- and third-generation writers, especially after the Holocaust. Levinson places Howe at the center of such efforts. He describes Howe as recovering Yiddish literature and culture for postwar American audiences, mostly through the project of translating and anthologizing Yiddish literature. The first anthology was the 1954 *A Treasury of Yiddish Stories*, edited by the Yiddish poet Eliezer Greenberg and Howe, who supplied a ninety-three-page introduction. Levinson credits the book as a whole with "creating a detailed portrait of East European Jewry,"[19] and I would add, positioned Howe as the editor and interpreter of the authors in the modern Yiddish tradition, a position he used not only to foster his own identity as a member of the Jewish literati but also to arbitrate which English-language fiction writers have a right to connect to these authors.

Levinson sees Howe's editorial projects as a nexus through which fiction writers also connected themselves with Yiddish literature, though perhaps via more ambiguous roads than those traversed by Howe. Bellow did so through his role as translator and editor. The translation of Singer's "Gimpel, the Fool" in fact was invited by Howe for his anthology.[20] Levinson points out that the translation "coincides with and may very well have caused Bellow's shift to a new model of Jewish hero."[21] Thus, Levinson uses his own authority as a critic in conjecture with the fact that Bellow translated Singer to form a Yiddish affiliation for the major Jewish writer of the 1950s and 1960s. Levinson also associates Malamud, and even Philip Roth, with this trend. Furthermore, he describes how "Cynthia Ozick's substantial work for Howe on *A Treasury of Yiddish Poetry* (1969) coincides with the period in her career when she was beginning to identify more and more as a *Jewish* writer."[22] He hints that translation caused the strengthening of her Jewish identity, but I read her willingness to affiliate herself with Yiddish poets as a strategy of identifying as Jewish.

In order to elaborate this point regarding Ozick, I now offer a reading of her "Envy, or Yiddish in America" (1969), which explicitly associates her with Yiddish writers. This reading will show how, while connection with Yiddish writers can be accepted as valuable, it is finally conceived of as problematic and unsustainable. "Envy"—like *The Ghost Writer*—is a text that is both about affiliation and is actively performing it. Ozick's story follows Edelshtein, a Yiddish poet living in 1960s New York, who publishes his poems in an obscure journal called *Bitterer Yam* (Bitter Sea) and is read by a handful of aging Jews. To an American eye, the journal's name may suggest a sweet potato gone bad. It is a bitter yam. These kinds of ridiculous failed communications are at the heart of Edelshtein's isolation as a writer in a mortally wounded if not dead language. Nevertheless, and only to a certain extent, Ozick's story is an act of connection. It is clear that the person who could have written this story must be quite knowledgeable about Yiddish and its literary canon. Numerous real Yiddish writers and poets are mentioned (a list of Yiddish poets takes up ten lines of prose),[23] Yiddish words are often used, and the story exhibits knowledge of Yiddish literary styles and real-world Yiddish institutions. From the evidence of the story, one can surmise that the author of this story has either an intimate knowledge of Yiddish writing or else she has thought that it is important enough to research it in depth. In writing this story, Ozick not only shows herself as an expert in Yiddish writers but also as someone who is willing to put thought and sympathy into imagining what it is like to be one. Focalized through Edelshtein's eyes, it shows its author as entering the mind of a Yiddish poet.

At the same time, the content of the story bodes ill for such a connection between English-speaking American authors and Yiddishists. Edelshtein concerns himself with the potential for networks. The central figure of this frustration is Yankel Ostrover, a writer of Yiddish stories who has been widely translated into English and other languages and seems to be universally adored.[24] The text describes his public image: "Though he writes only in Yiddish, his fame was American, national, international" (47). This figure, most likely based on and satirizing I. B. Singer, is connected to Edelshtein through a common language as well as personal ties. The New York Yiddish literary scene is a very small world. Nevertheless, Ostrover is part of the larger American–international literary network. Ostrover seems to be the main target of the "Envy" of the title, but there is another target that is less prominent in the story but no less important for my argument: Jews writing in English. The story opens with describing Edelshtein as "a ravenous reader of novels by writers 'of'—he said this with a snarl—'Jewish extraction.'" In a clear case of protesting too much, the narrative states, "He was certain he did not envy them, but he read them like a sickness. They were reviewed and praised, and meanwhile they were considered Jews, and knew nothing" (42). He is entangled by envy but is also connected as their reader. His obsession shows his sense that he, indeed, should be connected to them and that perhaps they should have an interest in him as well. At the same time, his sense that they are not Jewish and certainly not Yiddish enough (Yiddish is the Yiddish word for Jewish) shows that he is disconnected from them: "Spawned in America, pogroms a rumor, *Mamaloshen* [mother tongue, but always meaning Yiddish] a stranger, history a vacuum" (42). Calling them boys and girls (52), and comparing them to *cheder-yinglach* (boys learning how to read Hebrew), shows that he wishes to be a teacher and a fatherly figure to them. He has no children of his own, an issue the story returns to several times. The bad grades he gives them show that he fails at assuming this role and that they fail (never really trying) at taking the role of students, remaining ignorant of what Edelshtein sees as the basics of Jewishness. The story seems to be about how Jewish American writers will not associate with Yiddish writers, unless this Yiddishist is Ostrover/Singer.

Edelshtein's idea is that the main obstacle that stands between him and literary success is the fact that he has no translator. He lacks a literary connection that is close enough to save him from obscurity. In a letter to Ostrover's publishers, he implores them to furnish him with a translator but is answered that "reputation must precede translation" (53), creating what he sees as a kind of catch-22: you need a translator in order to gain a reputation, but you can't have a translator if you do not have a reputation. On the night of the main events of the story, he meets a niece of a fellow Yiddishist, a young American-born woman, and tries to navigate around the reputation–translation catch. Hannah reads Yiddish despite her American upbringing. She has even read some of Edelshtein's poems. He believes that, as a niece of a friend and a lover of literature, she should be the perfect translator. A gendered dynamic is also at work here: the woman is meant to serve as a vessel for transferring the man's legacy, in a way that runs parallel to patriarchal expectations of the family structure. It is easy to connect Ozick and Hannah as both are literary people, American-born, female, and, as of the story's publication, young. Once one learns that Ozick actually translated Yiddish poetry, the connection is almost inescapable (if you are at all inclined to making such connections).

After a night of walking the streets, Edelshtein finds Hannah in his colleague's apartment and implores her to be his translator. She refuses and the altercation gets so bad that he slaps her. She says to him things like "Die now, … all you old men, what are you waiting for? Hanging on my neck … parasites, hurry up and die" (97). Echoing the anti-Semitic rhetoric of the Jew as parasite, Hannah sees Yiddish writers as old bloodsuckers trying to feed off of her. It is clearly a connection to be severed and grown out of. Even when spirits are calmer she explains that she will not translate his poems, even for pay, because "You don't interest me" (99). The "you" can be read as singular, referring only to Edelshtein, but it can just as easily be a plural you, referring to the entire Yiddish literary community. From the evidence of the story alone, it might not be such a great loss to be disconnected from this kind of Yiddish writing. And yet, this story, along with other texts by Ozick, places her as a writer especially in tune with the Yiddish and more broadly the Jewish tradition.[25]

The story also shows how Jewish American writers, including Ozick herself, cannot fully align themselves with the Yiddish tradition because of the dangers of falling into obscurity together with the old Jews or seeming to be merely their translators (and therefore only of secondary importance in the eyes of the world). This tension between the need to connect to Jewish writers and the dangers of Yiddish can lead to the next step in the history I am tracing: that of relating to Jewish writers in non-Jewish European languages. In fact, about two decades after publishing "Envy," Ozick will write a novel, *The Messiah of Stockholm* (1987), depicting a man who fantasizes that Bruno Schulz is his father, presenting a new network of Jewish identification. This novel is dedicated to the writer I most identify with this new direction, Philip Roth.

"Envy" was published at the end of the 1960s, a time when Roth was under siege about his Jewish identity and his right to write about Jews. The story seems to satirize Roth and other contemporary writers. These writers' poor to nonexistent Yiddish does not prevent them from using it in their prose: "One word here, one word there. *Shikseh* on one page, *putz* on the other, and that's the whole vocabulary! ... They know ten words for, excuse me, penis, and when it comes to a word for learning they're impotent!" Edelshtein writes to Hannah (79–80). As Edelshtein knows, Roth and others like him did not choose to affiliate themselves with Yiddishists; and yet, they did form affiliations in order to highlight and negotiate their Jewish identities. A moment of such marked disinterest is Roth's interview with Singer. This interview makes it clear that Roth is not concerned with one of the most well-known Yiddish writers but instead speaks with Singer as a way of looking for Schulz. Having discovered that Singer reviewed one of Schulz's collections, Roth "telephoned Singer, whom I had met socially once or twice before, and asked if we might get together to talk about Schulz and about what life had been like for a Jewish writer in Poland during the decades when they were both coming of age there as artists."[26] It seems important for Roth to describe their ties as fleeting social ones—he met Singer "once or twice." In the course of the interview, they come to be connected by reading Schulz (and Kafka) together, but Roth asks Singer very little about his life and almost nothing about his work. What Roth wants to know about is Jews writing in Polish—the non-Jewish European language. This must be what fascinated Roth because he also writes in a non-Jewish European language, English.

With some exceptions, ignoring Yiddish writers continues into the twenty-first century. Even when younger Jewish American writers do find the Yiddish language fascinating, they do not connect to Yiddish writers as much as one would expect. A later example of this trend can be found in Michael Chabon's essay about how he came to write a novel set in an alternative reality where Israel does not exist but instead the Jews have a homeland in Alaska. In this homeland depicted in *The Yiddish Policemen's Union* (2007), secular Jews speak Yiddish as their native language. This language is clearly important to Chabon and yet he does not reach it through Sholem Aleichem or Singer or any other Yiddish writer. As he reports in "Imaginary Homelands," his imagination was not set on fire by the idea of a land where Mendele Mocher Sforim was the national writer. Rather it is a phrasebook, *Say it in Yiddish*, a long list of basic words and sentences, that makes him imagine a land where Yiddish is still spoken.[27] Through an anecdote about an uproar he created among Yiddishists on a listserv called Mendele, Chabon redefines himself as akin to Philip Roth as a writer who is known for creating an uproar among Jews. So, even when Yiddish is at the center, contemporary American writers will not often associate themselves with its writers.[28]

Other European Languages

From the 1960s on, Jewish American writers became dissatisfied with Yiddish writers for reasons about which I can offer an educated guess: most are not well known enough beyond the world of Yiddish speakers; they often assume a religious knowledge; and they were identified too much with earlier generations. Importantly, Yiddish writers did not share Jewish American writers' predicament of writing in a non-Jewish language for a non-Jewish audience. Jewish American writers were in need of different directions if they wanted to have any use for Jewish writers from outside the United States and beyond the English language. This new direction was not invented in the 1960s, of course. A precursor for this move can be found in Lazarus's use of Heine, described in Chapter 1.[29]

Despite this important precedent, before the 1960s American Jewish writers did not spend much energy connecting with writers in European languages as Jews. Some connections surely exist, but they seem to rarely emphasize Jewishness. For an example, we can return to Delmore Schwartz, this time as a writer and not as someone written about. Schwartz is well known for affiliating with modernist writers, among them were Jews but also anti-Semites.[30] Consider his autobiographical closet drama *Shenandoah*. There, an older Shenandoah Fish looks back at the day he was given his incongruent name, the day of his bris, the ritual circumcision that enters a young baby into a bond with the Jewish God. The trauma is not found in the circumcision but in the name he was given, a name that comes from the American landscape—the Shenandoah Valley located in Virginia and West Virginia—and has Native American roots. This first name clashes with the Jewish-sounding Fish to form a ridiculous handle. The older Shenandoah contextualizes his entry into Judaism within the modernist canon:

> Let us consider where the great men are
> Who will obsess this child when he can read
> Joyce is in Trieste in a Berlitz school,
> Teaching himself the puns of *Finnegans Wake*
> Eliot works in a bank …[31] (212–13)

This goes on to include Pound, Rilke, Yeats, Thomas Mann, and others. Somewhere in the middle we find Kafka:

> Kafka in Prague works in an office, learns
> How bureaucratic Life, how far-off God,
> A white-collar class' theology[32]

Kafka is mentioned here as part of a long list of modernists and is associated with the idea of him as a bureaucrat. He is *not* someone who shares facial features with classmates (as he is in Philip Roth), nor is he someone who underwent a bris, even though the context might suggest this connection may be important. Even when theology is brought up, it is not a Jewish theology but a white-collar worker's, a clerk's, theology. There's a connection to a Jewish writer but it is not performed as a connection to Jewishness.

Similarly, Bellow, who is older than Roth, does not show anything like the level of interest in Jewish writers that Roth does. Even when he invents a Holocaust survivor in *Mr. Sammler's Planet* (1970), he presents him as a biographer of one very English novelist, H. G. Wells. This is a move that seems to be carried out in order to distance Sammler and his creator from an overtly Jewish canon.[33]

I am sure some counterexamples for this trend could be found. Yet there are few examples that have the prominence that this move has from the end of the 1960s on. It is worth, then, looking at one of the most prominent and recurring examples: the connection Roth built with Kafka.

Here, I want to approach the Kafka–Roth liaison via a reading of one of the most searing attacks on Roth, taking it as an opportunity to answer the question of why Roth (and writers like him) need the connection to Jewish writers. To understand one aspect of the public relations work that the tie with Kafka must carry out for Roth, it is worthwhile drawing a spotlight on how many of the references to Kafka come just before or just after the 1969 publication of *Portnoy's Complaint*. This novel made Roth rich and famous far beyond what was possible with the literary readership he had for his first three books. It is also very funny and deals with provocative sexual matters. It, therefore, had the potential of overwhelming Roth's image as a literary author and making him seem like a writer of light entertainment, the kind of public image that, arguably, stuck to John Irving after the publication of *The World According to Garp* in 1978, even though he was known as a literary postmodernist before the publication of his bestseller.[34]

Reenter Irving Howe, formerly a protagonist in the story of affiliation with Yiddish authors and now Roth's antagonist. Howe's "Philip Roth Reconsidered," which includes lines such as "The cruelest thing anyone can do with *Portnoy's Complaint* is to read it twice," informed its readers that Roth should not be regarded as a literary author.[35] Howe not only attacks Roth's merit as a literary author but actively works to readjust and even disconnect him from the network of literary authors. This is most clear when Howe invokes "the tradition of Jewish self-criticism and satire." Howe writes:

> reviewers [of *Goodbye, Columbus*], including myself, ... assume[d] that this gifted new writer was working in the tradition of Jewish self-criticism and satire—a substantial tradition extending in Yiddish from Mendele to Isaac Bashevis Singer and in English from Abraham Cahan to Malamud and Bellow ... Beside Mendele, Roth seems soft; beside Cahan, imprecise. (73)

At first, Howe offers a tradition to which Roth can be connected but later he will snatch it away. This tradition hinges on names of established Yiddish and American authors, all older than Roth though some still active when Howe was writing (two, Singer and Bellow, soon to receive Nobel Prizes). Then, he makes a move that keeps Roth in that network or tradition, though placed unfavorably compared to the founders of this tradition: softer than Mendele Mocher Sforim and less precise than Cahan. It is important to note that, even when ranked low in the tradition, any rank still keeps an author as part of the network. This seems especially crucial because Howe discusses a first book, suggesting that Roth seemed to have had the potential to occupy a higher rank in that tradition and become a node in the network he describes. I think it is true that Roth does not connect to Jewish literature through the tradition of Yiddish writing, but that does not mean that he does not find other paths to literary Jewish identity.

At this point in Howe's argument, Roth is still affiliated with Yiddish and Jewish American writers so Howe cannot stop here. He goes on to disconnect Roth from this network altogether (or at least connects him to the network as someone who does not belong to it), snatching away the tradition that was offered earlier: "But now, from the vantage point of additional years, I think it clear that Roth … has not really been involved in this tradition." Severing Roth's tie with Jewish writers is not enough for Howe because he wishes to make readers reconsider Roth's place in the literary network as a whole. Thus, his next paragraph opens: "This deficiency [in sustenance form a Jewish tradition], if deficiency it be, need not be a fatal one for a Jewish writer, provided he can find sustenance elsewhere, in other cultures, in other traditions," or in my terms find other affiliations, latch on to other segments of the network. Using his authority as a critic he is able to say, "But I do not see that Roth has [found sustenance elsewhere] … his relation to the mainstream of American culture"—meaning highbrow culture—"is decidedly meager" (73). Roth is connectionless according to Howe and this is one reason why his work lacks literary worth.

This discussion of meager connection to the literary tradition is the context for Howe's accusation—often unfavorably quoted by Roth critics—that Roth has "thin personal culture." Let us look at what Howe says is *not* important for personal culture. Immediately after the first use of "personal culture" he writes: "That [Roth] can quote Yeats and Rilke is hardly to the point" (73). Howe does not choose those authors haphazardly. First, we will notice that they are not Jewish; but, second, Roth does have characters quote them. Rilke's "Archaic Torso of Apollo" is quoted at the end of *The Breast*, as a symbol for Kepesh's continued commitment to culture, literature, and education.[36] Portnoy quotes Yeats in a rather more scandalous context: he recites "Leda and the Swan" as part of sexual contact and describes it as a poem "about fucking. A swan fucks a beautiful girl."[37] No wonder, then, that Howe did not see this quote as saving Roth from vulgarity. Reading Howe not especially generously, I see this declaration of the irrelevance of quotations as an insistence that it will be the professional critic who will determine where and to whom the writing is connected, not the writer himself. We may imagine him pronouncing, *Roth may namedrop and quote as much as he wants, I, the critic, will be the one to establish his affiliations or lack thereof.*

It is fascinating, in this context, that Howe refuses to mention Kafka throughout the article, even in his dismissive one-paragraph discussion of *The Breast*, a novella that makes much more sense as a reimagining of Kafka's *The Metamorphosis* than it does without this intertext. This is the entirety of the prickly discussion:

> *The Breast*, extravagantly praised by my literary betters, is a work to which, as students would say, "I cannot relate." Well-enough written and reasonably ingenious, it is finally boring—tame, neither shocking nor outrageous, and tasteless in both senses of the word. Discussions will no doubt persist as to its "meaning," but first it might be better to ask whether, as a work of literature, it exists. For simply on the plane of narrative it cannot, or ought not, hold the interest of a reasonably mature reader. (77)

Howe's sense that the work does not exist and his insistence on remaining on "the plane of narrative" suggest this suppression of literary allusion and affiliation. Howe seems to willfully suppress how this is a novel about somebody who connects himself too much with Gogol and Kafka. Howe is on a mission to disaffiliate Roth. Howe therefore refuses Roth's solicitations that he be integrated into a different network.

Howe does not leave Roth without any relation but rather connects him to the mass audience. He, furthermore, establishes links between Roth and the stand-up comedy world and that of sentimental Jewish writing, everything in short that Roth has been trying to escape. Linking and unlinking is a crucial tool for Howe's attempt to discredit Roth's worth as a writer. The essay draws attention to how Roth, at that point, was fighting to establish and maintain that he has not only skill and vision but also a legitimate connection to what Howe calls tradition. Roth's success in establishing himself as a major literary writer, in making that role part of his public identity, has to do with his insistence on a connection to Kafka and other literary writers, gentile and Jewish, American and European. However, Kafka's Jewishness also plays a part in legitimizing Roth's Jewishness and thus also connects him in a roundabout way to exactly the tradition Howe wants to deny him. This victory of the writer over the critic is not only the story of Roth's career but also a high point in this strategy of Jewish American literary networking. This strategy is identification and connection with secular Jewish writers who write in non-Jewish European languages.

Not all European Jewish writers are as useful in this strategy as others. Roth and his peers needed to turn to writers connected to a central component of Jewish American identity, Jewish suffering and the memory of the Holocaust. Thus, in *The Ghost Writer*, Roth ties himself, through Zuckerman, to Anne Frank, who at one point he describes as "the most famous" of all "Jewish writers" (152). In the novel itself, Zuckerman imagines marrying Anne Frank as a kind of legitimization of his writing about Jews, of being a Jewish writer. Though the connection of Roth and Anne Frank is complicated by questions of the legitimacy of this kind of representation, as that debate remains open, the tie remains as a feature of Roth's public image.

Still, the Holocaust is not the only Jewish story, even if it does seem to be the predominant one. Grace Paley—and this is perhaps one reason among many that she is not as central to Jewish American literature as I think she deserves to be—chose a different path for affiliation with Jewish writers (when she did so at all). In one introduction about Isaac Babel, republished in a volume of her nonfiction, she associates herself and her family with Jewish suffering in Tsarist and Soviet Russia. She writes: "Perhaps I feel [sorrow upon reading some Babel stories] because it is so close to my parents' story of their own town's drowning in the 1905 manufactured wave of pogroms."[38] Paley connects the way in which some of Babel's stories overwhelm her with her identity as a descendant of immigrants who fled Russia because of anti-Semitic violence. Furthermore, she associates her family's storytelling ("the picture given to me") with Babel's literary writing. Similarly, in *The Ghost Writer*, Zuckerman discusses Babel as a figure that helps him understand how the Malamud-like Lonoff and the Bellow-like Abravanel share a "family resemblance" (47–50). In *The History of Love*, Nicole Krauss has her protagonist Leopold Gursky (who will survive the Holocaust) write a magical-realist obituary for Babel who was murdered in the Stalinist Purges. This obituary opens a series of such poetic eulogies that ends with a piece about "The Death of Leopold Gursky."[39] She thus connects Gursky (and herself) to a group of suffering Jewish writers starting with Babel.

Paley does not need the extreme violence of pogroms, purges, and genocide to connect her identity as a second-generation immigrant Jew with the Jewish writers beyond the English language. In an essay that was first published as an introduction to a volume of short stories, she connects herself in those terms to the Brazilian writer Clarice Lispector. Lispector's family immigrated from the Ukraine to Brazil when she was two months old, Paley reports. As "an American immigrant Jew," this destination is baffling, but the bafflement is overcome through the memory of "a South African cousin" and her "mother's best friend [who] immigrated to Argentina." Paley thus situates herself and Lispector as part of a history of Jewish migration from Europe outward. One outcome of this immigration, growing up with two languages, also implicitly joins them together as writers: "It's not unusual for writers to be the children of foreigners. There's something about the two languages engaging one another in the child's ears that makes her want to write things down."[40] The immediate context here indicates that these sentences are just about Lispector. However, the "not unusual" generalization makes it seem like Paley is also talking about the child of immigrants she knows best.

So, we saw how writers like Heine, Kafka, Babel, and Lispector, who are not directly connected to the Holocaust, are useful for identity building; and yet, the Holocaust looms large in how Americans think of the Jews of Europe. At least for this reason, writers who were victims of the Holocaust are crucial for the phase of affiliation I am describing. For example, Emily Budick shows how Bruno Schulz "became something of an obsession" among Jewish writers.[41] Schulz was a painter and writer of strange short stories in Polish. It is said that he was murdered by one Nazi officer as a way to seek revenge against another Nazi officer who protected Schulz.[42] The story of his murder became a much-repeated exemplar of the precocity of Jewish life during the war years and the loss of great writers and intellectuals.

As part of his work in the "Writers from the Other Europe" series for Penguin, Roth brought out Schulz's uncanny and poetic short stories in English. These efforts are probably what earned Roth the dedication, mentioned earlier in the chapter, in Ozick's *The Messiah of Stockholm*. On most matters of Jewish identity, Ozick and Roth are diametrically opposed but, on Schulz, they agree.[43] Here, we have a moment where ties with European writers help consolidate intra-American bonds that would be difficult to form in other ways. Though he did not discover the manuscripts themselves, as an editor and literary promoter Roth took on the role of medium or ghost writer, producing a dead author's text for the English-speaking public. Since then, Schulz has become both influential and iconic for several Jewish writers, including Ozick, Krauss, Chabon, Foer, and the Israeli writer David Grossman, all of whom incorporate Schulz into their fiction.[44] Emily Budick, working from a psychoanalytic perspective, finds in the many novels that refer to Schulz in different ways an "obsessive, compulsive whirl of repetitions and fixations" and indeed this is one effect when all these texts are considered together.[45] However, the Schulz obsession, much like interest in other European writers, is also a way to affiliate with an iconic Jewish writer and through his image even connect a writer to other contemporary Jewish writers.

I would never argue that this kind of affiliation is easy or always satisfactory. On the contrary, representing victims, even writer victims, is highly problematic. In offering a close analysis of Roth's *The Prague Orgy* (1985), I will show how it problematizes Roth's role vis-à-vis Schulz and other European writers who suffered and even died in the Holocaust. I will address this ambivalence over committing to ties through the image of the writer as a messenger from the dead. In a nonfiction book about writing, Margaret Atwood suggests the "hypothesis ... that not just some, but *all* writing of the narrative kind, and perhaps all writing, is motivated ... by a desire to make the risky trip to the Underworld, and to bring something or someone back from the dead."[46] This idea has received more theoretical perspectives, such as French intellectual Maurice Blanchot's dense rewritings of the Orpheus myth as an allegory for the writing process.[47] It also comes up in fictional representations of writing such as Atwood's *Lady Oracle*, where the protagonist channels her dead mother through a Spiritualist practice of automatic writing, literarily becoming a medium.[48] Roth does not present the living author as a medium for the dead in general but specifically for dead authors, Jewish ones in particular. In *The Prague Orgy*, Zuckerman explicitly wishes to give a new voice to a dead author. In this novella, Zuckerman travels to Communist Czechoslovakia with the mission of retrieving the manuscript of an author who was murdered by a Nazi officer. Zuckerman eventually fails at his task, but the novella should be read as a meditation on how and why an American author can make himself into a vehicle for a European one. Like *The Ghost Writer*, *The Prague Orgy* is a text about a partly successful effort to affiliate with another Jewish author. The failure to become a medium is not quite a failure but rather an experiment in becoming an author who is affiliated with others and at the same time is known for much more than these affiliations.

Zuckerman arrives at his mission to the dead in the midst of another crisis of authority and identity. The novella begins with a visit from a Czech émigré writer, named Sisovsky. Leading up to his enormous request that Zuckerman travels to Europe in order to smuggle out the stories Sisovsky's father—again, a father—wrote in Yiddish, he analyzes Zuckerman's position as an author in America. Sisovsky is aware of the infamy Zuckerman earned by publishing *Carnovsky*, the *Portnoy's Complaint* of Zuckerman's oeuvre, and he makes sure to push the right buttons in order to remind Zuckerman that he is in a crisis. As part of his initial flattery, Sisovsky points out "that it [*Carnovsky*, or more widely, Zuckerman's writings] had a scandalous response."⁴⁹ He compares the misreading and perversion of Zuckerman's work at the hands of critics to "the fate of [Kafka's] books in the hands of Kafkologists" (9).⁵⁰ After this aggrandizing of Zuckerman, Sisovsky tries to unsettle Zuckerman's position, or at least to show he knows Zuckerman is feeling unsteady. Sisovsky commiserates with Zuckerman: "You come to belittle the meaning of your vocation … There is a definite existential weakening of your position" (9). Sisovsky argues that controversy and inadequate criticism have destabilized Zuckerman's literary status and his sense of what he does. The short time frame that elapses between this exposition of Zuckerman's existential plight and the request to retrieve the stories marks the trip to Prague as a potential cure. In sync with my overall argument, Mark Shechner frames this trip as a search for the "personal culture" that Howe had found to be "thin" in his acidic reassessment of Roth. Prague and especially Kafka should lend Zuckerman this "culture" that, according to his critics, he is lacking.⁵¹ Sisovsky wants Zuckerman to believe that a voyage to Europe in quest of a treasure trove of stories by a dead author will help reconnect Zuckerman to some literary network. As several Roth critics argue, Sisovsky's father's status as a victim of the Nazis cannot be ignored.⁵² In creating for himself a Jewish literary father who was murdered in the Holocaust, Zuckerman is attracted to the same absolving power that marrying Anne Frank in *The Ghost Writer* would have had. If his literary father is a victim of anti-Semitism, how could anyone claim that Zuckerman's fiction betrays the Jews?

Olga, Sisovsky's abandoned wife, states her own interpretations of Zuckerman's fantasies when she meets him in Prague: "The marvelous Zuckerman brings back from behind the Iron Curtain two hundred unpublished Yiddish stories written by the victim of a Nazi bullet. You will be a hero to the Jews and to literature and to all the free world" (75). Olga's sardonically presented script is likely to have been on Zuckerman's mind all along. At any rate, it comes from Roth's imagination. He hopes that resurrecting this author (or his reputation at least) will connect him to a Jewish literary tradition in a way that will make him if not a "hero" then not a villain either. Bringing back a dead author should enable him to write with less fear of Jewish subversion and with more authority, an authority that is based on the Jewish past and literary history. Zuckerman will be known as the one able to connect to the past.

For the mission to succeed, it has to be figured as a voyage to a land of the dead. Zuckerman at first seems to be able to create such somber images and associations. Europe has long been a trope for death and the past in American literature, as can be seen in James's *The Aspern Papers*, which is a precursor text for *The Prague Orgy*.[53] In James's novella, an American critic travels to Venice to retrieve some papers—written by a long-deceased American poet—from a woman the world was sure must have died many years earlier. In a Jewish context, the link between Europe—especially Eastern and Central Europe—and death is pronounced. Eastern Europe can be seen as the land of dead Jews, not living ones, even though there are Jews living there. When Zuckerman visits Prague, the idea that Europe is the site of the dead Jewish past becomes almost explicit. During his first evening in Prague, "the capsized tombstones of ... the oldest Jewish cemetery left in Europe" are pointed out to Zuckerman. Europe as an entity is associated in this passage not only with a Jewish cemetery but with a rundown Jewish cemetery, one in which there is no living person to take care of the "capsized tombstones." Zuckerman goes on to describe the cemetery: "Twelve thousand Jews buried in layers," invoking centuries of Jewish life that is no longer visible but now only archeological (30). Though this set of images is not the only view of Prague the novella offers, it is the view that has to do with the city's past and seems to interest Zuckerman the most.

Prague is associated not just with the Jewish dead but especially with dead Jewish authors. Prague is inevitably known to literati as Kafka's city and its buildings are often depicted as the backdrop to Kafka's fiction. The inhabitants of Prague are aware that Westerners come to their city because of the great author. As we have seen, Sisovsky, trying to influence Zuckerman to accept the mission to Prague, uses the enthralling power of Kafka and is sure to mention him several times in their conversation, at times flattering Zuckerman, at times aggrandizing his father. Olga, Sisovsky's wife who still lives in Prague, and who is crucial to the mission because she holds the manuscripts, asks Zuckerman when she first meets him, "Why are you in Prague? Are you looking for Kafka? The intellectuals all come here looking for Kafka. Kafka is dead. They should be looking for Olga" (33). While Zuckerman, unlike David Kepesh in Roth's *The Professor of Desire* or Roth himself on his first visit to Prague, is not, in fact, looking for Kafka, Olga senses that he is looking for a dead author and not a living one like herself.[54]

To sum up this part of the argument, tempted by Sisovsky, Zuckerman travels to what looks like a land of the dead, indeed the land of the dead Jewish authors, with the aim of retrieving the texts of one such author. He and others think that, by accomplishing this mission, he can stabilize and fortify his position as an author. Zuckerman is, for a time, to become a medium for a dead author's messages. If the mission succeeds, Zuckerman's own literary authority will be fortified through an association with the dead Jewish writer.

Zuckerman, however, does not complete his mission. Olga's statement, "Kafka is dead. They should be looking for Olga," is a crucial moment in the narrative. With this statement, it is made clear that Prague will not yield its dead authors so easily. Though the literal reason for Zuckerman's failure is that the secret police confiscate the manuscripts for political reasons, in my scheme it is more important to relate the failure to the way that Prague, especially as it is represented through Olga, refuses to be perceived as a netherworld. Zuckerman's failure is due to the way Prague is shown to be a lively city, especially in the semi-secret life of its intellectuals and artists. Despite the way the novella sets up Europe and specifically Prague as a site of death, and despite Prague offering some locations to justify this designation, the city shows itself to be a bustling one, with people who are unquestionably alive. Zuckerman mostly interacts with certain segments of the Prague intelligentsia whose intellectual pursuits are thwarted by the communist regime but who present themselves as making up for this lack of freedom with hyperactive sexuality. On his first night in Prague, Zuckerman is taken by his guide, Bolotka, to a mansion where an orgy is underway. Indeed, as both the title of the novella and the sexual mores of some of its citizens suggest, Prague is orgiastic; its god is Dionysus, not Hades.

As a Eurydice figure, Olga exemplifies Prague's lust for life in the shadow of death in her own flesh. She is the romantic interest of an author (Sisovsky) who has been left behind in a figural underworld, in Sisovsky's European past. She is also connected with the dead as the keeper of Sisovsky's father's manuscripts. Her physical appearance seems to support claims that she is symbolically dead: "Heavy white makeup encases her … face" (31). The white face suggests the paleness of death, while the heavy makeup might suggest the work of a mortician. A fair complexion is hardly rare in Central Europe, but the way Zuckerman takes note of Olga's whiteness suggests the role he expects her to assume. As an agent of Sisovsky, Zuckerman travels to the netherworld to contact Olga, making him an Orpheus by proxy.

Yet, soon enough, Olga puts herself clearly on the side of the living. She will not play Eurydice for Zuckerman's pleasure. Apart from making aggressive sexual advances toward Zuckerman, Olga also contrasts herself as a living author with the dead author. To requote: "Kafka is dead. They should be looking for Olga" (33). Olga wants intellectuals to come to Prague to see her, a living author, and not the dead Kafka. Her living flesh, not Kafka's ghost, should be the main attraction. She, representing the city, refuses to be considered dead. She desires, like Tita Bordereau toward the end of James's *The Aspern Papers*, to marry the protagonist, in Olga's case Zuckerman, and thus escape. Instead of guardian of the treasures of the dead, Olga wants to be saved, like Eurydice might have been, by the love of, or at least a marriage of convenience with, an author. She is disappointed when Zuckerman has no desire to affiliate himself with her. All he really wants from her are the writings of the Jewish victim. At first, she refuses to give him these stories. When she does hand them over, the manuscripts are inside a candy box—a traditional gift during early courtship—suggesting that she has not wholly given up on the possibility of a romantic tie with Zuckerman.

On the literal level, Zuckerman fails. He is not able to convey a message from the dead Jewish writer to those Jews living in the United States. He never becomes a medium and never quite finds any dead spirits with whom to communicate. So, it might be claimed that this novella is merely an exploration of the failure to come into contact with the literary dead. It could be assimilated into my narrative about American writers forsaking the Yiddish tradition. Yet I believe there is more to the story than that. Zuckerman is a medium for the dead insofar as he attempts to become one and the crucial fact about the journey is that it produces the text of *The Prague Orgy*. He can tell a story of trying to bring back a message from the dead. Like many before him, from Orpheus to the narrator of *The Aspern Papers*, he falls short, but he has inhabited the role of medium and sojourner in the realm of the dead. At the same time, the failure assures that he is not seen as merely a medium. He does not have a message from the dead; he only has the story of looking for that text. He is both associated with them and known to have failed in creating the relationship.

There can be little doubt that Roth is thinking of Schulz as he is writing *The Prague Orgy* (a reason why this novella is not really about Yiddish literature or the Yiddish language).[55] This is obvious through some biographical parallels between Sisovsky's father and Schulz: both were teachers, both were "horribly shy of people" (23), and both, of course, were European Jewish writers. The most striking parallel is the story of their deaths: as Sisovsky tells it, his father was under the patronage of a Gestapo officer. When this officer kills a Jew who was useful to another officer, he kills Sisovsky as revenge, later explaining "He shot my Jew, so I shot his" (24). This is almost exactly the story, much repeated, and possibly false, of Schulz's murder. Later on, Olga will say that Sisovsky's story is a lie and that "it happened to another writer." One of the functions of Olga's debunking of her husband's story is to make sure readers think of Roth's success in Schulz's revival before Zuckerman fails at his own attempt to publish Sisovsky.

After being so successful at presenting Schulz to the public, Roth needs a story that is parallel to his story with Schulz story but one with a different ending. Zuckerman's fiasco reflects on Roth, giving him the failure he needs in order to protect himself from his success of bringing to life the powerful, perhaps too powerful, voice of Schulz. As I said, Jewish American writers find much power in associating with dead European ones, in being literary mediums; but, at the same time, living writers must be incomplete, distorting mediums in order to be perceived as authorities and not merely transmitters of other voices. If they don't want to disappear as mere mediums, they need to fail. Roth devised the story of failing to transmit and translate Sisovsky in order to subvert his success as Schulz's editor but simultaneously keeps the connection useful. Even without thinking of Schulz, the failed connection to the European writer helps Roth designate his identity as both American and Jewish, both in touch with a Jewish tradition and not quite fitting into it. Moments of affiliation can signify an identity as a restless wandering author just as much as they can give a sense of being grounded in a tradition.

4

The Jewish Writer as an Old Man

Long sections of Nicole Krauss's 2005 *The History of Love*, a novel about creating affiliations, are narrated by Leopold Gursky, an obscure writer and Holocaust survivor in his eighties. Krauss was in her early thirties when the book was published; and yet, I will argue that this association with a writer who was born and raised in Europe and is also an old Jewish man tinges Krauss's public identity with the shade of age and through it Jewishness and literariness. Krauss and other authors have an interest in seeming older than they are for at least two reasons. First, they are interested in the strong association between Jewishness and old age. Second, there is a degree of literary authority to be gained from the position of an older writer in possession of what may be interpreted as a late style. Here, I provide an extended example of how the connection with fictional and real European writers can help form a public identity with rich shadings.

Roth's Image as an Old Man

Writers build the association with old age through connections to author-characters and to real writers who come to be associated with late style. Before presenting the counterintuitive example of Krauss identifying with/as an old Jewish man, I want to explain the concept of late style though the lens of a more standard case: a writer who as an old man uses fiction and paratexts to emphasize this position. During the last decade or so before his retirement, critics tried to identify a shift in themes but also in the style of Roth's later novels and especially *Exit Ghost* (2007). Providing an example from a widely circulating magazine is important because I am arguing that these ideas have some cachet with the general reader outside of literary studies. James Wood combines thematic and formal considerations in one sentence from his *New Yorker* review of *Exit Ghost*: "The fantasy of endlessness," the desire to keep living forever that Wood identifies as a thematic core of Philip Roth's novels in the last third of his career, "has found its form in *late* Roth—in a spare, pragmatic prose, apparently unconcerned with literary effects, focused only on its subject."[1]

Late style and late period are important terms for art, music, and, to a lesser extent, literary criticism. Thinkers and critics use lateness to describe the final period in an artist's oeuvre as distinct in power and form from the rest of their overall creation, a period of innovation despite or even because of old age and the nearness of death. The most influential commentaries on this subject have come in Theodor Adorno's essay on Beethoven and in Edward Said's posthumous *On Late Style*.[2] However, late style as an aspect of reception is more relevant to the argument here. In this direction, Gordon McMullan's *Shakespeare and the Idea of Late Writing* convincingly argues that late style developed as a critical construct and is not inherent to many of the works and authors who have been said to exhibit it. He argues Shakespeare's oeuvre does *not* truly show a distinguishable late style. Lateness is a matter of reception and interpretation rather than a quality inherent in authors or texts. Still, once critics and other readers have established a pattern of reception, authors can invite it. They can manipulate their literary texts and paratexts in order to seem to be late stylists.

As for the nonacademic and semi-academic reception of lateness, some readers would be familiar with Adorno's formulations about late style, even if they have not read Adorno directly, because it has been repeated and refracted in various texts.[3] For example, some ideas from Adorno's essay were available to many readers through Thomas Mann's admitted appropriation of them, at times in almost the same words, in his 1947 *Doctor Faustus*. Edward Said's "Thoughts on Late Style," in which he takes up Adorno's conception, was published in the *London Review of Books* in 2004 (a year before *The History of Love* and three years before *Exit Ghost*). Said's *On Late Style*, edited by James Wood, appeared posthumously in 2006 and was reviewed in major newspapers and magazines. Returning to the *New Yorker*, in 2006 John Updike, also an aging writer by then, published "Late Works."[4] Updike's piece begins as a review of Said's book but continues as a rumination on writing in old age. Clearly, late style and similar terms circulate beyond purely academic theoretical discourse. This realization is important for understanding the identity-building process Krauss undertakes.

Over the last decade or so, late style has become a recurring theme in literary criticism concerning Roth. Peter Boxall points to a general trend—writers of Roth's generation and even slightly younger ones engaging with this idea—and includes Roth and *Exit Ghost* in this discussion. One early example of such engagement is Matthew Shipe's reading of *Exit Ghost*. Shipe connects Zuckerman's aging body and failing mind to his disengagement from American politics (the novel takes place around the 2004 election, which Zuckerman largely ignores). Shipe uses these preoccupations, along with an analysis of the style and intricate structure of the novel, to argue that *Exit Ghost* exhibits Roth's late style, comparing sections to the sparseness of Richard Strauss's late songs and the whole to Beethoven's final compositions, which were the subject of Adorno's contemplation of late style.[5]

With due respect to Boxall's or Shipe's readings, the thing to remember, in my context, is that the identification with late style was not invented by critics but rather invited by Roth through a series of textual devices. Most important among these features is the identification between Roth and Zuckerman, the aging protagonist of *Exit Ghost*. This novel is in many ways a mirror image of the earlier *The Ghost Writer*. Zuckerman is now seventy-one years old and living in rural New England close to where Lonoff's home was located. As readers of *American Pastoral, I Married a Communist,* and *The Human Stain* already know, he has been more or less secluded there for the last twelve years. Just before the presidential election of 2004, he travels back to New York where he is to have an operation to mitigate his incontinence (brought on by a prostate operation—there is no cure for the impotence caused by the same operation). In New York, he meets Amy Bellette, the woman he once thought might be Anne Frank, who has in the meantime married Lonoff and is now suffering from brain cancer; Billy Davidoff, an aspiring Jewish writer who is married to Jamie Logan—yet another aspirant who becomes Zuckerman's object of love or lust; and Richard Kliman, a Jewish journalist who plans to write Lonoff's biography and reveal an incestuous affair Lonoff had with his sister when he was fourteen—a detail that was likely inspired by information Henry Roth revealed about himself in a series of autobiographical novels he wrote toward the end of his life. Here, Lonoff is associated with an author who was born in Eastern Europe and who lived to be an old American Jew. Henry Roth also had a very clear late period that came after many decades of silence.

Lonoff here signals Jewishness and literariness. In fact, Lonoff, unlike Henry Roth, never publishes a final novel (even though there is a manuscript, Zuckerman refuses to read it). More important to the description of Roth as a late stylist is the figure of Zuckerman as an old writer himself. The old protagonist reminds readers of Roth's own old age. Seeing Zuckerman write texts that are affected by his age, his loss of memory, and his impotence makes readers notice that Roth's writing was also carried out by an old man. Since Zuckerman is from the same generation as Roth, it is easy to imagine that they also share some of the effects of aging and the sense of obsolescence. Intertextual references form one path for Roth to encourage this reading. Thus, *Exit Ghost* references pieces by a number of artists, most prominently *The Shadow-Line* by Joseph Conrad and Richard Strauss's *Four Last Songs*.[6] These references align Zuckerman (and through him Roth) with predecessor late-work practitioners and thus invite readers to place him in this category.

As we know, fiction does not shape public images on its own but rather interacts with paratexts and facts to do so. Indeed, the paratexts that surround *Exit Ghost* make the case that Roth should be appreciated as a late stylist. In the context of this novel, emphasizing lateness has to do with the insistence that, after almost three decades in which Roth's Zuckerman has appeared in novels (and an autobiography), Roth intends for *Exit Ghost* to stand as the last novel that features Zuckerman. The first sentence of the plot summary on the back of my copy runs thus: "Nathan Zuckerman returns to New York in the long-awaited final installment of Philip Roth's renowned Zuckerman series."[7] This paratext, probably not written by Roth but present on the threshold of his text, not only entices readers to buy and read the book but also frames the interpretation of its content. Similarly, when the novel came out, Roth asserted that he would not be publishing any more Zuckerman books.[8] Indeed, *Exit Ghost* stands as the last Zuckerman novel. The parallels with *The Ghost Writer* and the revisiting of its themes and characters, along with the recurrence of the word "ghost" in the titles, make the newer novel a fitting counterweight or bookend to the first novel in the series. With its stage direction of "exit," the title suggests a conclusiveness that, if the ghost is Zuckerman, then the novel is his curtain call.[9]

Zuckerman's retirement prefigures Roth's own retirement, an event that certifies the novels from this period as late even before Roth's actual death in 2018. In *The Counterlife*, Zuckerman's brother, Henry, discovers that Zuckerman wrote his own eulogy. *Exit Ghost* can be read and has been read as a kind of eulogy for Zuckerman and even for Roth. His uncommon decision to retire contributes to this idea. In an interview with a French magazine that was published in October 2012, Roth admitted that he had not written any fiction since *Nemesis* (2010) and that, in fact, he no longer wrote.[10] A month later, the news reached the English-speaking world through a short piece in the online magazine *Salon*.[11] It spread widely, was corroborated by Roth's representative, and elicited many responses. One of these responses carries a title that is highly resonant with my argument: "Philip Roth: A Eulogy for a Living Man."[12] What the author of that title—not always the same person as the writer of the article—registered here is how Roth's retirement is also a way for him to proclaim the end of Philip Roth as an author.[13]

Roth was determined to separate the end of his career from the end of his life, much like he did in *Exit Ghost*. He could thus supervise the cultural work that takes place after his death as author. Roth was involved in the celebrations of his eightieth birthday, which some also saw as a farewell to Roth the author. Adam Gopnik, for one, discerned a "touch of the elegiac" in Roth's birthday celebrations, while David Remnick drew attention to the sense of an ending in his report of the main event at the Newark Museum.[14] Roth saw his complete works published through the Library of America and made sure that everybody knew his works were complete and that there would be no more fiction after the last novel included in the final volume. In an interview with the *New York Times*, we learn that Roth is writing notes for his biographer, Blake Bailey. Though, presumably, Bailey will have the final say over the shape of the book, it seems that Roth is writing his own autobiography through these notes, which are so lengthy and numerous that the biographer fears he will not have time to read all of them.[15] His retirement, alongside the publication of his death-obsessed novels in the last decade of his career, of which *Exit Ghost* is the example most directly related to authorship, created the situation whereby Roth's old age, lateness, and impending death (which came in May 2018) were an important part of his public image. While Strauss's *Four Last Songs*, which Zuckerman listens to in the novel, were named thus by his friend and music publisher Ernst Roth, Philip Roth takes the trouble to present some of his books, especially *Exit Ghost* and the four short novels that make up *Nemeses*, as late. Thus, affiliating with old writers was part of an overall strategy for creating a controlled and yet grand finale to Roth's career.

Late Style in *The History of Love*

It makes sense that an old writer would be able to emphasize the fact that he is old, but can a young writer like Krauss take on old age? *The History of Love* presents a convoluted plot that revolves around two protagonist-narrators: Leopold Gursky, an elderly Holocaust survivor and retired locksmith living alone in a junk-filled Manhattan apartment, and Alma Singer, a fourteen-year-old girl, named after the woman, Alma Mereminski, for whom Gursky wrote

The History of Love as a young man in Poland. Gursky's *The History of Love* was published in Spanish under another man's name (Zvi Litvinoff, whose story is told in the third person) and without Gursky's knowledge. When Alma's mother receives a request from a mysterious man to translate *The History of Love*, Alma tries to track him down—an adventure that is also a story of coming of age and young love. The novel ends with an encounter between Alma and Gursky.

Krauss seems familiar with the concept of "late style" and certainly familiar with the sense of a different artistic bent in works by older artists. As I argued in the previous section, it was reasonable for her to expect that some of her readers would be familiar with the concept of artistic lateness and recognize it in Krauss's work. Alma Singer's art historian uncle, Julian, describes a self-portrait by Rembrandt where the painter looks old and weary; and yet, Julian explains, "There's a serenity in his face, a sense of something that's survived his own ruin" (179). Julian discovers in Rembrandt the confidence and authority that critics often identify with an artist's late production. Krauss wrote her MA in art history about the Dutch master and was especially fascinated with his *Self Portrait with Two Circles*. Krauss also references this painting in her third novel, *Great House*, as Elana Estrin noted in an interview. Responding to Estrin, Krauss describes the painting thus:

> In the early self-portraits, you have this painter who's putting on airs and costumes ... but he's really just a young, scrappy, ambitious guy. And then *late* in his life ... there come these amazing self-portraits that are quite brutal, frank, and unadorned. You feel a hurriedness in the brushstrokes. He's scratching into them with the back of the brush. You feel the sense of someone facing his death. Obviously, that's a position that I am drawn to in my work.[16]

By using the word "late," Krauss draws a connection between Rembrandt and her own production, claiming some of this lateness for herself.

Despite the invocation of late style in Alma's narrative, *The History of Love* mainly relates this kind of writing to Leo Gursky. As I have argued in Chapter 2 (see the section titled "Fiction and Public Identity"), fictional characters operate as a path to learning about the author herself; and, indeed, Krauss has linked herself with her octogenarian protagonist outside the bounds of the novel. The parts she shared during public readings while promoting the book were those narrated by Gursky, rather than by Alma, the more naturalistic casting choice. One reporter recounts his wonder at Krauss preforming Gursky: "The slim, 30-year-old woman behind the microphone at Vroman's Bookstore in Pasadena,

Calif., looks nothing like a wisecracking 80-year-old Polish locksmith living a threadbare retirement in New York City."[17] Krauss can be even more explicit: in an online book club interview carried out in 2011, one of the members asked if "Alma is based on Krauss." After a standard insistence on the fictionality of all of the characters, Krauss used the question to explain that, in the words of the interviewer, "it's Leo [Gursky] who is like her." Krauss elaborated: "He absolutely feels like me. He is the quickest, shortest cut I could make to exposing very vulnerable, very vivid parts of myself; things I just couldn't find a way to talk about in life."[18] She returns to these ideas in a 2017 interview while promoting *Forest Dark*.[19] Krauss affiliates herself with Gursky on several levels. In choosing him as one of the narrators of her novel, she shows that she can speak in his voice, and he in hers. She furthermore includes some pieces of Gursky's *The History of Love* and a series of fanciful obituaries, showing that she can write his fiction. Philippe Codde even goes as far as to argue that we should read Krauss's *History* as if Gursky had written it all and not just the segments he explicitly narrates.[20] In various degrees of explicitness, then, Krauss shows that readers should identify her with Gursky. She may even honestly feel herself to be, in some sense, an old man.

Gursky at first seems an unlikely candidate for the title of late stylists. He was never a well-known author and his two novels were published under other people's names. Nevertheless, he does come to possess a late style of sorts and the authority and prestige it grants the writer. Most crucial for this process is that Gursky writes a late text. After having a heart attack, Gursky writes the autobiographical *Words for Everything*. Previously, he has only written one book-length work, *The History of Love* (which gives its name to the novel and drives much of its plot). Thus, Gursky produces approximately half of his writing in old age. About *Words*, Gursky says, "At times I believed that the last page of my book and the last page of my life were one and the same, that when my book ended I'd end" (9). Gursky writes as a result of a near-death experience and, to him, it seems like the text with which his life will end.

Readers within the novel mistake this text for another author's last production. This mistake models how real readers may conflate Krauss and Gursky. After writing *Words for Everything*, Gursky sends it to Isaac Moritz, a well-known fiction writer and the son who never knew him. Soon after, Gursky learns from a newspaper obituary that Isaac died; but later we discover that the manuscript apparently reached him. Some weeks after his death, a magazine publishes an extract from *Words* under Isaac's name. Readers in the world of the novel receive

Words as an example of late style, especially because (having been written by someone else) it exhibits a new turn in Isaac's oeuvre—a feature often noted in discussions of late style. This book adds to Isaac's reputation, thus making him (inadvertently) a not-so-old author with a marked late work. Insofar as Isaac is dying, this is quite a suitable position for him to assume. Furthermore, Isaac belongs to the generation of Roth, Don DeLillo, and J. M. Coetzee, who were beginning to be associated with or to associate themselves with lateness at the turn of the century.[21]

The novel depicts how Gursky's personality might become attached to a young woman's identity. It does so through the connection between Gursky and the younger female protagonist of the novel, Alma. Through an ornate chain of events that involves Alma's brother thinking Gursky was her father, a meeting is set up between the two main narrators of the novel. In this meeting, and overall, Alma is presented as simultaneously a reincarnation of Gursky's love interest and his surrogate daughter or granddaughter. In the final scene of the novel— described from Gursky's and Alma's intercut perspectives—Gursky dies. A sense remains that Alma is now meant to become a writer like Gursky or to carry on his flame in other ways.

The idea that Alma inherits Gursky's inclination for writing is only suggested in *The History of Love* so I want to bring an example of another, very different, novel, where it is quite explicit. The 1992 *Hygiène de l'assassin* (*Hygiene and the Assassin* in the 2010 English translation), the first book by Belgian writer Amélie Nothomb (b. 1966), presents a similar case. In almost all respects, Nothomb's and Krauss's novels (and public images) are very different. However, both texts are by young women but about old dying authors. In *Hygiène*, a misanthropic, misogynistic, racist, gluttonous 82-year-old Nobel laureate for literature, Prétextat Tach, discovers that he has a rare cancer and will die within two months. *Hygiène*, structured as a series of five interviews, not only affiliates Nothomb with Tach but also dramatizes the flow of authority from the old novelist to a young woman. After four interviews conducted by men, Nina, a thirty-year-old journalist, appears. Readers can easily link Nina to Nothomb because they are close in age, are of the same gender, and write for a living. In order to see the transfer of authorship, my readers need to know that Tach equates writing with murder: "Les prix Nobel de la paix sont souvent des assassins, mais les prix Nobel de littérature sont toujours des assassins."[22] Indeed, Tach confesses that he murdered his young female cousin-lover. By the end of the novel, Nina becomes an "avatar" for Tach, fulfilling his legacy by murdering him and thus transforming into an author. Nothomb shows, grotesquely but memorably, authorship moving from an old man to a young woman. In *The History*, the process is more oblique but nonetheless affects the dynamics of identity building.

The History of Love flirts with the idea that Gursky already had a late period when he was a young man in Poland. Much of this sense of late style in youth comes from the series of obituaries. These also connect Gursky to the group of European Jewish writers who are as central to the formation of American Jewish literary identity. Obituaries are a recurring motif in the novel. I already mentioned that Gursky learns of his son's death by reading a newspaper. Yet the interest in obituaries begins in the opening lines of the novel: "When they write my obituary. Tomorrow. Or the next day. It will say, LEO GURSKY IS SURVIVED BY AN APARTMENT FULL OF SHIT" (3). The reader soon discovers that it is highly unlikely that anybody would write Gursky's obituary. The crude language of the headline, furthermore, suggests that it could never appear in a newspaper. It seems, then, that the only obituary he will ever have is the one he writes for himself. Gursky from the start is set up as a writer (and reader) of obituaries. It is tempting to say that, because of this introduction, the entire Gursky narrative is an obituary, something to be read after he dies in order to learn about his life. When we read it, we affirm that he was worth noticing. The novel ends with Gursky's death—or at least with Gursky believing he is about to die—but the final page is a text written by Gursky as a young man, as part of an obituary-like series of texts he composes about famous authors.

These poetic obituaries comprising Gursky's first late period are described in the sections about his early adulthood in Poland through the eyes of Litvinoff, the same man who will years later publish Gursky's *The History of Love* under his own name in a Spanish translation. Litvinoff writes an obituary for Isaac Babel for the newspaper, which he sees as one of his finest accomplishments as a journalist. Gursky also continues to connect with other European Jewish authors by writing obituaries, including one about Kafka and another about Osip Mandelstam, a Russian Jewish poet "who died at the bitter end of 1938 in a transit camp near Vladivostok" (117). Mandelstam thus is incorporated into the history of twentieth-century European totalitarian violence that affected Jews disproportionately, even under regimes that were not explicitly anti-Semitic. Even as he was living in Europe, Gursky aligns himself with the canon of Jewish writers (although Tolstoy is also treated) in a similar way to how Jewish American writers do.

Yet Gursky, in an attempt to join the ranks of the canonical Jewish writers, also writes about himself. Even as a young man, Gursky does not wait for his death in order to write his obituary: *"THE DEATH OF LEOPOLD GURSKY"* (117), presumably the same piece that closes the novel. In a way that makes the link with Krauss easier, she presents Gursky as approaching death and producing lateness even when he was young. McMullan argues that it is the nearness of death that is the defining feature of discourse around late style. Since even a young artist can have a late style, Gursky's deaths-of-authors series is seen as an example of late writing even though he was a young man when he composed it. The impending destruction of European Jewry already makes Gursky's life a confrontation with death. Furthermore, as Litvinoff reads the obituaries, Gursky is lying sick by his side and it is unclear to his reader (Litvinoff) whether he would live or die. Gursky dedicates the last obituary, which includes the line "he was a great writer," to himself. Though Gursky eventually survives into his eighties, his youthful production is colored by the nearness of death, just as our reading of a late Keats poem or listening to a late Mozart composition would be.

Litvinoff, who keeps Gursky's novel alive, also turns the "THE DEATH OF LEOPOLD GURSKY" into "a prayer for life" that keeps the author himself alive. Earlier, he had repeated this prayer over and over in order to save his sick friend, who is lying in a cold garret, fighting for his life. Later on, Litvinoff carries the page with him as a kind of talisman. Later still, this text is the only thing that links Gursky's name to the Spanish-language *The History of Love*, which displays Litvinoff's name as its author: after it is already accepted for publication, Litvinoff adds the unconnected text to the end of the novel (much as Krauss does in her own version of *The History of Love*). It is so important for him to keep this remnant of Gursky's authorship intact that he threatens to withdraw the manuscript if the editors insist on deleting it. Thus, though Gursky's name does not appear on the title page of the novel, it does appear on the final page as part of an obituary. The text about his own death, with Litvinoff's help, becomes an autograph, the closest thing to a signature Gursky is allowed to have. Thus, Gursky's announcement of his death becomes the announcement of his authorship.

Her investment in the intersection of age and European Jewishness is big enough to make Krauss bring back one of the most famous of these Jewish European writers as an old man. Gursky is a lonely person, but, when he is a retired old man, he unexpectedly finds a childhood friend who he believed was murdered during the Holocaust. His name is Bruno and, along with his interest in writing and Polish origins, it is not difficult to make the connection with Bruno Schulz, especially in the literary context that posits him as the writer-victim par excellence.[23] Bruno and Gursky become good friends again, even neighbors. Bruno often encourages Gursky to take actions that move the plot forward. Toward the end of the novel, we discover that the elderly Bruno was a figment of Gursky's imagination, but the sense of partnership with an old version of Schulz remains.

The Authority of Late Style

Krauss's novel, then, is an attempt to imaginatively inhabit the mind of an old Jewish man, but, in my context, it is also part of an effort to seem like one. Krauss's efforts to tinge her public image with a sense of age are visible beyond *The History of Love* and its immediate paratexts. She continues this association with older writers—this time women—in her third novel. *Great House* features five narrating voices telling only tangentially related stories, all of these revolve around an antique writing desk. One of the narratives concerns the life and death of Lotte Berg, a writer who escaped from Nazi Germany. Two of the other sections are narrated by Nadia, who, as an American writer, is the closest character to Krauss. In her fifties, she is not yet old but is older than Krauss. Her lethargic mood and writer's block make it seem as if she is at the end of her career. She is also connected to death in several instances. For example, her sections are narrated as a one-way conversation with an unconscious, possibly dying, patient in a hospital room.

Zeroing in on one passage, we can note that the only novel by Nadia that she discusses extensively (though not as extensively as she retells one of her short stories) is about her father and his death. Nadia presents herself as deeply connected to a damaged older man and narrates his final years. The description of this novel, which she "could not have written while [her father] was alive," connects her to the nearness of death and lateness. For some readers, this description will also connect Nadia to Roth, who wrote a memoir about his father's final years titled *Patrimony* (1991). In Krauss's novel, she writes about "the time he defecated in his pants and I had to clean him."[24] This passage recalls a memorable and detailed scene from *Patrimony* about Roth cleaning his father's excrement. No less importantly, it brings back Roth's discomfort with exposing his father so publicly, a theme Nadia also discusses.

Krauss also associates herself with older writers outside of fiction. On the occasion of her inclusion into the 2010 "20 under 40" *New Yorker* list Krauss was asked, "Who are your favorite writers over forty?" As I also said in Chapter 2 (see the section titled "Paratexts"), such questions are an opportunity for creating networks with other writers and thus affect authors' public images through those of other writers. Krauss named "Bruno Schulz, Samuel Beckett, Franz Kafka, Thomas Bernhard, W. G. Sebald, Rainer Maria Rilke, Zbigniew Herbert, Roberto Bolaño, Yehuda Amichai, David Grossman, Yoram Kaniuk, Jenny Erpenbeck, Saul Bellow, Philip Roth, Jorge Luis Borges, [and] J. M. Coetzee." In 2010, and apart from Jenny Erpenbeck and David Grossman, all the living novelists on the list were over sixty and have been associated to some degree with late style (Roth, Coetzee, Kaniuk), while some of the deceased authors have also been described as exhibiting it (Beckett, Borges). Compare Krauss's writers with the list presented by a fellow American Jewish author Gary Shteyngart to an identical question on the same occasion: "Jeffrey Eugenides, Jonathan Franzen, Chang-rae Lee, Mary Karr, Mary Gaitskill, Edwidge Danticat, Edmund White."[25] Again, as of 2010, with the exception of White, all the novelists on Shteyngart's list were in their forties. Shteyngart attaches his image to writers, who (barring misfortune) are in the position in which he will soon find himself, at mid-career.[26] Overall, then, Krauss charges her public image with associations of older writers. It is now time to offer conjectures about why she would do so.

I can continue this argument by examining one honor Krauss has garnered: the *New Yorker* list.[27] The list "20 under 40" has two contradictory implications vis-à-vis the role of youth in the literary world. One way of understanding the existence of such a list is that young writers attract readers; because youthfulness draws attention, it is profitable for the magazine to dedicate an issue to celebrating it. Conversely, one can argue that young authors are disadvantaged in the literary field. They, therefore, require a special league, in order to be noticed; "20 under 40" functions as the college basketball of literature. Matched against the NBA of writers over forty, the under-forties would have a lesser chance of scoring points with their readers. I think that both explanations are partly correct. However, the second one may help us understand why a writer would want to seem older than they really are: age has the potential of functioning as a source of prestige in the literary world. Of course, age is never sufficient for securing or maintaining a literary reputation.

A late phase, even a manufactured one, provides a sense of literariness. I believe that this sense of literariness or literary authority can be exchanged for what Pierre Bourdieu and his followers might call cultural capital.[28] In other studies, influenced by Bourdieu, the emphasis is on *canonization, consecration* in a global context, or *prestige* as circulated between artists and prizes.[29] The appearance of lateness increases literary authority because only great artists are said to have a late style. As McMullan puts it, "The late phase is something attributed by critics only to a very few creative artists, a limited handful of acknowledged geniuses. Death comes to all of us; old age to most; a late phase ... to very few indeed."[30] Krauss aligns her characters with the likes of Shakespeare, Henry James, Rembrandt, and Beethoven. Philip Roth, who is "quoted" praising Gursky's son in a newspaper obituary, can also be added to this list. The lingering belief in the wisdom of the elderly, the power of death as a moment of clarity, and the uniquely artistic idea of a late phase combine to give power to Gursky and other late stylists. By incorporating Gursky into her public persona, Krauss gains some of this prestige for herself, a kind of authority that is interconnected with her affiliation with European Jewish writers.

In order to show that my argument about transferring of identity has a basis in the social reality of reading literature and is not just a matter of my own interpretation or Krauss's desires, we can look at the reception of Krauss's novels. Indeed, some of the authority earned by Gursky as an old writer is transferred to his creator, Krauss. Janet Maslin, in a review for the *New York Times*, chooses to grant Krauss authority on the basis of *The History of Love*, writing that "[e]ven at their most oddball, these flourishes [of style] reflect the deep, surprising wisdom that gives this novel its ultimate heft." Krauss has a "deep ... wisdom"—a quality often associated, even in our deeply ageist society, with age and experience. Wisdom, then, would be associated with someone like Gursky. Maslin describes this "wisdom" as "surprising," because Krauss is young and relatively inexperienced. She insists that Krauss's work has "ultimate heft," a curious phrase for describing a 250-page book that weighs so little compared to contemporary maximalist tomes.[31] By heft, of course, she means literary and intellectual weight; she reacts to Krauss's newfound authority, which partly comes from Gursky.

Granted, *The History of Love* was not an uncontested critical success. Some hailed it as a major contribution to American fiction, but others derided it for stylistic faults and for playing too fast and loose with historical facts.[32] Sanford Pinsker—a long-time scholar and reviewer of Jewish American literature—wrote a favorable review but then, in a column for Yom Kippur, asked forgiveness for overpraising Krauss's book. He apologizes for not describing how "*manipulative*" the novel is, perhaps italicizing the word so his readers know that Krauss is more manipulative than most. I think Pinsker primarily intends to point to *The History*'s sentimentality; however, one sense of "manipulative" that registers here is how the novel causes the reader to give Krauss more authority—and therefore attention and praise—than she deserves (in Pinsker's view).[33] Certain reviewers were more willing than others to be manipulated, or they accepted that if the manipulation works, then the author deserves its fruits. The book succeeded in garnering a number of good reviews and many devoted readers—some of them can be spotted quoting from her novel on their blogs, some recommending it in bookstores, and some teaching it in university courses. In addition, the novel placed Krauss as a central author in the Jewish American literary field.

The novel continues to affect Krauss's public image. This sense of old age tinges even the reception of her next novel, *Great House*, where a connection with an old writer exists but is less extensive. Still, the authority of age can be sensed with the many critics who focus on loss and memory, two themes that are crucial to the novel but also invoke the losses that come with living a long life. In a different direction, *The Guardian* review begins by noting that profiles of Krauss inevitably mentioned her youth and a related attribute, beauty. Yet these are presented as a problem, something that prevents people from appreciating Krauss. While this problem accosts other writers, especially women, it is curious that this is the way at least one writer chooses to open a review of the novel. The decision to open a review of Krauss specifically in this manner suggests to me that the novel poses a solution to these problems.[34] An even more telling piece is Janet Byrne's review for the *Huffington Post*. It uses one setting of the novel, London's Hampstead Heath (near to where the Rembrandt portrait is housed), to frame the review with a recollection of "one summer [the reviewer] was taken under wing by Al Alvarez," a much older writer.[35] Through the textual prompts I have been discussing, Byrne senses that she should associate Krauss with this old man with whom Krauss has little in common.

Once a certain fact or association is set up, it shapes how we read other works of fiction. Thus, the novels Roth published after *Exit Ghost* were all received in the context of the old artist, even those focusing on young men, like *Nemesis* (2010), a novel about a polio epidemic in 1940s Newark whose protagonist is a physical education teacher in his twenties. For Krauss, the association with old age appears as a tinge rather than a full coat of paint. Still, in reading the novel that follows *The History of Love*, *Great House*, the sense of age does color the reading.

For example, the writer Nadia, one of the narrators of *Great House*, is middle-aged but is easier to decipher as the closest character to Krauss herself because of the previous sense of Krauss's identification with older writers. Any new novel also affects her public image further. Imagine if Krauss's latest novel, *Forest Dark* (2017), associated her with youth. Perhaps her link with Gursky would then be buried in the archives of her career. In fact, *Forest Dark* interweaves a plot about an early middle-aged novelist and an older man, so the mixing of age and youth seems likely to persist. This novel layers her image but does not erase the tinges I have traced here, just as Roth's association with Portnoy and Zuckerman as a young man is still part of his portrait.

The Jews as Old Men

I do not believe that Krauss, who is of course getting older herself all the time, will attempt to erase these ties with old age. Among other things, she is not likely to do so because they are deeply entangled with how she performs her Jewishness. There is a web of associations that connect Judaism, Jewishness, and the Jewish people with old age (especially gendered as old men, not women). Some of these associations date back to antiquity, some have to do with our current moment, some are part of Jewish culture, some are anti-Semitic in origin. Each alone would not be enough to make my argument, but the web that they create does present us with a deep association between age and Jewishness.

Even in antiquity, Judaism was considered an ancient tradition and afforded some leeway in Hellenistic and Roman law for this reason. This tolerance was in contrast to the way Christianity was treated in the first centuries CE. It was considered new and therefore not to be tolerated.[36] This idea of Judaism as old is, of course, crucial for Christianity. Traditionally, Christianity sees itself as inheriting and superseding an older, irrelevant form of monotheism and becoming the new people of God. This is a common way of understanding Paul's "In speaking of 'a new covenant' he has made the first one obsolete" (Hebrews 8:13). This sense deeply affects Western terminology. Think, for instance, of the term Old Testament for the Hebrew scripture. What Jews believe in is old; what Christians believe in is new.

This point of view takes on a more concrete form in post-Reformation Europe with the popularization of the Eternal or Wandering Jew. According to the Christian legend, the Wandering Jew was a man who mistreated Jesus Christ and was condemned to live in and travel the world till the end of days.[37] Cursed with near eternal life, but definitely not eternal youth, the Wandering Jew received many textual, folkloric, and visual representations, often depicted as old and weatherworn.[38] Some of the best-known images of the Wandering Jew come from a book designed and illustrated by Gustave Doré (1832–83) *La légende du Juif errant* (The Legend of the Wandering Jew [1856]). This book includes an introduction that states that the legend must have had its source in some "beautiful and impressive allegory" where the traits of the whole Jewish nation were attributed to the single Wandering Jew ("Cette légende fameuse a sans doute pris sa source dans une belle et imposante allégorie, imaginée par quelque prédicateur, ou plutôt par quelque poète qui a personnifié la nation juive sous les traits du Juif Errant").[39] Doré's images in this book depict the cursed Jew with tattered clothes, a deeply etched brow, and, most importantly, a white beard that reaches down below his knees. In the final image in the book, the Wandering Jew hears the trumpets of the end of days. He finally looks happy, but he also looks even older than the earlier images. Remember, this one infinitely old Jew is meant to stand for all Jews.

Figure 2 Detail from Gustave Doré's *The Wandering Jew* near a roadside crucifix, already looking old. Photographed by David Hadar.

Figure 3 Detail from Gustave Doré's *The Wandering Jew* at the end of days, looking even older. Photographed by David Hadar.

This idea of the Jewish man as old or at least part of an earlier generation has many representations in English literature, several of which Roth, Krauss, and many of their readers surely know. In English literature, the Jew is a father figure, often to a young Jewish woman who does not have a mother. The Jewish man, therefore, is old, while the Christian man who seeks and often seduces the daughter Jewess is young.[40] The most famous example must be Shylock from Shakespeare's *The Merchant of Venice* (c.1596-98). Shylock's daughter runs away from his house in order to live with a Christian man, whom he would never have allowed her to marry. He later loses all his possessions in a trial and seems to be close to the end of his life. Portia, the young woman responsible for his downfall, asks that her servant be led to Shylock's house so he might sign a deed: "show my youth old Shylock's house."[41] Portia puts "youth" and "old" together and thus highlights Shylock's agedness and perhaps obsolescence too, in an echo of the general Christian view of the Jew. Sir Walter Scott's Isaac of York from *Ivanhoe* (1820) and Charles Dickens's "bad" Jew Fagin and "good" Jew Riah from

Oliver Twist (1837–39) and *Our Mutual Friend* (1864–65) are other examples of the old Jewish father or father figure.[42] These gentile, sometimes blatantly anti-Semitic, images in classical texts and visual art shape how Jews are imagined, even how Jews imagine themselves.

Indeed, Jews too seem to find their representative image in older Jewish men. The crucial example is the figure of the elderly rabbi with his long white beard who leads his community and often is a symbol for it. The most widespread image of such a rabbi in the last thirty or so years must be Menachem Mendel Schneerson, better known as the Lubavitcher Rebbe. His photograph as a white-bearded old man waving to his followers is much reproduced by the Chabad organizations.[43] As one scholar explains, "The Rebbe is effectively Chabad's brand, and his smiling face, big white beard, and black fedora are a trademark as recognizable to some as McDonald's golden arches."[44] That is to say, the symbol for one of the most recognizable sects of Judaism worldwide and in the United States, and especially in New York where both of the novels discussed in this chapter are set, is an old Jewish man. This figure of the old rabbi has mythical correspondences with Moses and Elijah the Prophet (who according to the biblical narrative never died but rather were taken "into heaven by a whirlwind" [2 Kings 2:1]). In his Jewish folkloric incarnations (in contrast to his biblical one), Elijah is often mistaken to be simply a traveling old man, sometimes a beggar, visually reminiscent of the Eternal Jew. Only after a miracle happens do the benefactors realize it was Elijah all along. This tradition gives a sense that any strange old man might, in fact, be the mythical Elijah, a man who is also constructed as the protector of the Jewish people as a whole.[45] Perhaps Roth had some of these associations in mind when in his "Eli, the Fanatic," a story about a secular Jew first attacking and then dressing up as and identifying with an Orthodox Holocaust survivor, the transformed man was named Eli, short for Elijah. Like the old man revealed to be Elijah, the Americanized Eli is revealed to still be a Jew by donning old clothes.

The images of the bearded men from Eastern Europe from Roth's "Eli, the Fanatic" can lead us to the next point. The most visibly Jewish group, ultra-Orthodox men, wear beards as part of their devotions, making each individual look older than he is and the group as a whole seem older.[46] Older Jews are more likely to be closer to the Yiddish language and the experiences of immigration. This is reflected in the way that comedians, filmmakers, and novelists most associated with Jewishness, such as Jackie Mason (whom Gursky mentions), Mel Brooks, Woody Allen, Roth, and even Larry David, are in their seventies and eighties. This has not always been the case, but it has been since at least the 1990s. Larry David, the youngest of these, performed grumpy old manhood even in his fifties.

The connections between age and ties to Europe, Judaism, and the tragedies of Jewish history are often embodied in a custodian of a synagogue or a Jewish school. One such character appears in Roth's "The Conversion of the Jews," an early story with a young protagonist: "Yakov Blotnik, the seventy-one-year-old custodian." The story describes "old Blotnik": "To most of the students Yakov Blotnik's mumbling, along with his brown curly beard, scythe nose, and two heel-trailing black cats, made him an object of wonder, a foreigner, a relic … To Ozzie the mumbling had always seemed a monotonous, curious prayer." Blotnik belongs to the old world, and to the students he seems to be a strange survivor. In a story that is about leaving religion behind, the young Ozzie thinks of Blotnik as particularly representative of a dead religion: "Ozzie suspected he had memorized the prayers and forgotten all about God."[47] A more positive echo of this character-type appears in *The History of Love* in connection with Bird, Alma's younger brother. Bird, who is deeply attracted to Judaism as a religion, is in "the habit of following Mr. Goldstein, the janitor at Hebrew school who mumbled in three languages."[48] Mr. Goldstein, who is rumored to have survived Siberian labor camps and whose "heart was weak," is a source for much of Bird's Jewish knowledge (36).

The final point, and the one most relevant to Gursky in particular, is that the Holocaust survivor is one of the major images of the Jew of the contemporary era. Over the last three decades or so (over the entirety of Krauss's adult life), most Holocaust survivors have been elderly, creating an association between the survivor and old age. For Roth, this has not always been the case, but even he involves his aging character with an aging Holocaust survivor: in *The Ghost Writer*, Zuckerman imagined young Amy Bellette to be Anne Frank but, in *Exit Ghost*, readers discover that she has her own story of escape from the Nazis. The sense that survivors are now old can also be seen in Shalom Auslander's version of the idea that Anne Frank survived the Holocaust in *Hope: A Tragedy*. There, Anne Frank, who as a victim will always remain "a young girl" (as the title of her book usually indicates), is now imagined as an old woman. Aging in hiding somehow caused her to be more Jewish than she seems in either *The Diary* or *The Ghost Writer*. This sense is indicated, among other ways, by the fact she only eats "matzoh"—the unleavened bread of Passover. In fact, she "can't work [write in hiding] without matzoh."[49] Because of this entire field of associations, which deserves a book of its own, I am confident in saying that seeming old, especially by affiliating herself with an elderly Holocaust survivor who grew up in Poland, is also one of the ways Krauss has to appear and feel more Jewish.[50]

***

The History of Love is a novel about finding connections—about finding love. Finding and maintaining love is associated in the novel with writing and reading books. Gursky writes for Alma Mereminski in order to win her heart. His estranged son reads *The History of Love* so we know he knew his real father. Alma's father gave *The History of Love* to Alma's mother; she learned Spanish so she could read it. During the adventures that began in an attempt to figure out who commissioned a translation of *The History of Love*, Alma realizes that she is in love for the first time with her friend Misha (a Russian Jewish immigrant). Finally, the entanglements around the book bring Gursky and Alma together even if only for one final moment of compassion before his death (on a day when he was seen). The novel is about how books are agents of human connection and self-expression. I have not focused on this aspect of the book, but I highlight it now to forestall any idea that Krauss's path to Jewishness through Gursky is cynical in any way. Krauss seems to believe that fiction is a way to connect to others so they can see you and you are able to see them. Books are "the opposite of disappearing," the skill she thanks her grandparents for teaching her in the dedication page of the novel. This negation of invisibility is exactly what Krauss does with *The History of Love* by identifying with and through Gursky as an old man and a Jew.

5

New Networks with Israeli Writers

Jewish European writers have remained a fairly stable object for affiliation as a means of identity building over the past fifty years. Yiddish writers and more ancient Hebrew author-figures also continue to be available points of reference for authorial networking. Yet, since around the turn of the twenty-first century, Americans begin to use relating to Israeli writers as an important way for performing Jewish identity and for claiming the authority to write about Jews.

For a long time now, Zionism and the State of Israel have been on the Jewish American agenda. The Six-Day War (or 1967 War) is often marked as the moment when Israel and the question of support for Israel turned into a crucial aspect of identity for many Jewish Americans. Jewish American—and, to some extent, American—attentiveness to the State of Israel did leave its mark on fiction, both popular and highbrow, and many Jewish American writers of the second part of the twentieth century had some degree of interest in Israel.[1] Most discussions of these fiction writers' relation to Israel focus on the representation of Israel as a place or political entity, not so much on Israelis as individuals.[2] Generally speaking, the scholarship and often the fiction itself are far less concerned with the lives of Israelis than with the Jewish American experience of Israel. Even more so, critics rarely if at all write about how Americans think about the relation between Israeli writers and American ones, between modern Hebrew literature and literature written in English.[3] This is an oversight that causes us to miss an opportunity to understand literary identity making.

Indeed, until around the turn of the twenty-first century, highbrow American fiction about Israel was a literature of visits, not one about living in Israel or the lives of Israelis.[4] One can find a number of examples in Philip Roth's novels alone: the final chapter of *Portnoy's Complaint*, in which Portnoy tours Israel; one section of *The Counterlife*, in which Zuckerman travels to the West Bank in order to convince his brother to come back to the United States; and *Operation Shylock*, an autofictional novel in which Roth travels to Israel because a man there is pretending to be Philip Roth, preaching ideas about the abandonment of Israel for a new diaspora. At other moments in Jewish American fiction, Israel appears as a subtext and background.[5] In accordance with this trend, American writers did not connect significantly with Israeli writers as such.

The change that I will trace in this chapter may be related to larger changes in Jewish American attitudes toward Israel. The sociologist Theodore Sasson, going against those who diagnose a disengagement from Israel,[6] persuasively claims that American Jewish engagement has not disappeared. Rather, interest in Israel shifted from consensual support and commitment that do not involve much knowledge or experience of Israel to a more partisan and knowledgeable engagement with Israeli politics and culture. Sasson argues:

> Across multiple fields, including advocacy, philanthropy, and tourism, American Jews have stepped up their level of engagement with Israel. Attitudinally, they remain as emotionally attached to Israel as they have been at any point during the past quarter century. Nonetheless, the relationship of American Jews to Israel has changed in several important ways. Today, American Jews are more likely to advocate politically on behalf of their own personal views and target their Israel-bound donations to causes they care about personally. They are also more likely to connect to Israel directly, through travel and consumption of Israeli news and entertainment, often through the Internet.[7]

Sasson focuses on political, economic, and some cultural aspects of this relationship. However, there is a corresponding trend in literature. As part of this trend, Jewish readers may be interested in more authentic and nuanced fiction about living in and not just visiting Israel, even fiction about being an Israeli. Happy to answer the call, some twenty-first-century writers have intensified their engagement with Israel.

In contrast to more recent writers, the most important American Jewish writers who started their careers in the 1940s and 1950s do not often present themselves as deeply affected or connected to Israeli writers, even if the State of Israel is an important concern, and even in texts that are explicitly about Israel with their literary status having much less importance. When they align themselves with Israeli writers, they do so in ways that fall roughly into two categories. The first option is that Israeli authors are perceived as expert witnesses on Israel. As Bernard Malamud formulates it in an interview, "I'd … write about Israel if I knew the country. I don't, so I leave it to the Israeli writers."[8] Israeli writers, then, highlight Americans' lack of knowledge about Israel and perhaps even a lack of real concern. The second option is that Israeli authors are perceived as European Jewish authors, whose writing in Hebrew and life in Israel are not what makes them worth the connection, as we will see with Roth's treatment of Aharon Appelfeld. More recently, however, American writers show alignment with Israeli writers who are presented as both literary and Israeli. Several American writers—I will focus on Nathan Englander and Nicole Krauss—even present themselves as part of an Israeli literary community. This change, however, does not mean that writers abandon their other networks. In fact, the chapter will give special attention to Krauss's *Forest Dark* as a novel that entangles European and Israeli writers.

Expert Israelis and Displaced Jews

Saul Bellow engages with Hebrew and Israeli writers to some extent but still seems to keep them at a distance. In Bellow's travel book about Israel, *To Jerusalem and Back* (1976), he meets some Israeli colleagues. However, important writers like Haim Gouri (1923-2018) and David Shahar (1926-97) are for the most part presented as mere voices in a chorus of Israelis which also includes professors, politicians, kibbutzniks, and a barber. In Israel, Gouri is one of the central poets to give voice to the men and women who fought in the 1948 War. For example, his lyric *Shir haReuth* ("The Song of Comradery"), celebrating the fellowship of soldiers, is often sung at memorial services (it was famously Prime Minister Yitzhak Rabin's favorite song). Even if one does not agree with his ideology, there is much to be learned about Israel from discussing Gouri's literary writing. Yet, for Bellow, who describes him as "a poet and journalist," he is more like another political informant, useful for an anecdote about helping a Palestinian family regain its looted Peugeot after the Six-Day War. Shimon Peres (1923-2014) is the one Bellow calls a "fellow writer."[9] This is not Bellow reaching out, though. Instead, it is his way of satirizing Peres as a pretentious politician. Overall, *To Jerusalem and Back* exhibits how Bellow is an American and not at all an Israeli. In the same book, he fosters American identity through, among other things, alignment with Mark Twain and Herman Melville.[10] Yet Bellow not only reengages with the United States and its canonical authors but actively refuses to engage with Israeli writers as such. This lack of engagement is part of what gives the impression that what really interests Bellow is America and his own American identity. Not affiliating is also a way to form identity, and in *To Jerusalem and Back* Bellow performs an American identity almost like an anthropologist who performs and emphasizes his own status as a Westerner by writing about non-Western peoples.

Unlike Bellow, Roth does engage deeply with one Israeli writer. Aharon Appelfeld (1932–2018) was born (a year before Roth) in Romania. His life was irreversibly disrupted with the outbreak of the Second World War, much of which he spent alone in the forests of Eastern Europe. After the war, the fourteen-year-old Appelfeld immigrated to Palestine. He is considered a major voice in Hebrew literature and probably the most important prose writer in Hebrew on the Holocaust. Roth was instrumental in introducing Appelfeld to American readers. A deep and friendly interview between Roth and Appelfeld appeared in the *New York Times Book Review* in 1988, titled "Walking the Way of the Survivor; A Talk With Aharon Appelfeld"; it is now available in Roth's *Shop Talk*, a collection of interviews and essays (suggesting that Roth wanted or was at least willing to have this interview have a more lasting form from that of the newspaper piece). Furthermore, Appelfeld also appears as a character in not one but two of Roth's novels: *Deception* (1990) and *Operation Shylock* (1993). In the latter, some parts of the 1988 interview are reproduced. All of this might at first glance suggest that Appelfeld is a path through which Roth connects to Israel.

However, the way Roth relates to Appelfeld has relatively little to do with the latter being an Israeli. Rather, Roth connects with Appelfeld as a Jewish author and especially one with a unique perspective on the Holocaust. In *Shop Talk*, this emphasis is drawn in the order in which the chapters are presented. The Appelfeld interview is placed between an interview with Primo Levi (1919–87) and Ivan Klima (b. 1931), a Czech writer and survivor of Terezin. In the interview itself, Roth writes that he sees Appelfeld not as an Israeli writer, nor as a European writer, but rather as "a displaced writer of displaced fiction, who has made of displacement and disorientation a subject uniquely his own."[11] This definition takes Appelfeld back to a European history of displaced and diasporic Jewry, without connecting him to Israel, where the Jews are meant to have found their place.

There is a similar theme in *Deception*, a novel written in the form of dialogues, where one of the characters is an author named Philip. There, Philip describes an anti-Semitic incident he experienced while walking through the streets of London with Appelfeld and his sabra son:

> I was walking in Chelsea with my Israeli friend Aharon Appelfeld and his son Itzak. … We were on the left side of the street and coming along on the right side were two men in their thirties or early forties … As they were approaching

us, they began to cross over to our side of the street and I noticed that one of them ... was mumbling out loud ... and all the while glaring at me. ... then he gestured at his own clothes and he shouted, "You don't even dress right!"[12]

Philip has no doubt that this man was verbally attacking them because they are Jewish. Still, his point of view needs some interpretation:

> So—what he'd seen, you see, was a bearded, spectacled, darkish man dressed more or less like himself, talking animatedly to a smallish, bald middle-aged man wearing a sports jacket and a sport shirt and to a dark-haired boy of eighteen, both of whom had been listening and laughing as they all three walked along the quiet, civilized streets of Chelsea ... as though they owned the place ... And then I knew for sure what it was. I could have killed him ... in my best American accent, I said "Why don't you go fuck yourself?"[13]

Just after identifying himself as American, he recalls that he has an Israeli with him, not Aharon, but his son. Ironically, the son does not realize that what he is seeing anti-Semitism exactly because he is an Israeli:

> if there was going to be a brawl, I was counting very heavily on Itzak, Aharon's son, a big strong boy who does lots of push-ups every morning ... Itzak was just amused. He's an Israeli-born kid and he'd never actually witnessed an anti-Semitic incident before. To this boy from Jerusalem the man had just seemed ludicrous. But I come from Newark and I kept puzzling over the damn thing.[14]

The Newark Jew and the European Holocaust survivor are put on the same side of understanding that an anti-Semitic incident has taken place, while the Israeli son seems oblivious to anti-Semitism. The two writers comprehend that they were insulted as Jews, but the Israeli son—a brawny "New Jew" is mostly "amused."[15] The two diasporic writers seem similar, in a way that excludes the Israeli. Roth's diasporic sense of self is highlighted when he writes that, from the anti-Semite's vantage point, "with my beard and my looks and my gesticulations, I should have been wearing a caftan and a black felt hat" (that is what he meant by saying that they were not "dressed right"). Here, he is voicing the anti-Semite's point of view but also saying that he looks and sounds like a traditional Jew, only the costume is different, a sentiment that echoes Roth's own "Eli, the Fanatic." There, the story concludes with an assimilated American Jew donning the old markedly Jewish clothes of a religious Holocaust survivor. At least at this moment, Roth seems to buy into the idea that Israelis are a new kind of Jew and puts himself and Appelfeld on the side of diasporic old Jews.

Roth does not hide Appelfeld's explicit Zionism; and yet, when Roth explains Appelfeld to Americans, the main concern is not that he is an Israeli writer. Through Appelfeld, Roth connects himself to a displaced Jewish writer, not to a writer who describes himself as having found a home in Israel. It is crucial to note that the anti-Semitic scene occurs in a place that is not a home to either of them. Appelfeld is cherished by Roth as a displaced Jew and as a literary artist, not as an Israeli. Bellow uses Israeli writers for their Israeliness but downplays their role as writers. It is as if, from the point of view of two of the most important American writers of the time, one can be either a significant writer or significantly Israeli, not both.

Ignoring Israeli writers as such seems to be the rule between the inception of Israel and quite recently. Yet, of course, some exceptions are always to be found. Curt Leviant's *The Yemenite Girl* (1977) is a novel about an American who is enamored by an Israeli writer, turning him into "an old friend, an intimate, almost kin."[16] However, at a closer look one can see that the American is not exactly American, nor is the Israeli writer exactly a representative of Israeli literature. Instead, they are both part of a different network of international, mostly Europe-born, mostly Ashkenazi, Hebrew literature. Ezra Shultish, a scholar, writer, and translator, teaches Hebrew in New York but comes for a year's stay in Haifa in order to be closer to Yehiel Bar-Nun, a Nobel-winning Israeli writer and a clear stand-in for Shmuel Yosef Agnon (1888–1970), the only Israeli who has won the Nobel Prize in Literature. Agnon was born in a part of the Austro-Hungarian Empire that is now in Ukraine. In his twenties, he immigrated to Palestine but then moved again to Germany, where many of his most famous works were written. In his late thirties, he immigrated to Mandatory Palestine, settling permanently in Jerusalem. Despite living for many years in Palestine and then in the State of Israel, much (not all) of Agnon's production was dedicated to Jewish life in Eastern and Central Europe. Bar-Nun seems to have a similar career, though he lives for years in Vienna instead of Berlin and then settles in Haifa and not Jerusalem.

Shultish is a tourist in Israel, but not in Hebrew. He was part of the Hebrew literary scene before the war: he first met Bar-Nun when they were both living in Vienna. He continues to write Hebrew stories and produce scholarship about Hebrew literature. Unlike many Hebrew writers, he left Europe for the United States and not Palestine where Hebrew became an everyday language. So, this is not a narrative of an American connecting with Israel. The writer with whom Shultish entangles himself is also a Hebrew writer more than a typically

Israeli one. Bar-Nun (as Agnon) was not born in Palestine/Israel and many of his stories are about Europe and European Jews. Even as he lives in Israel, his literary fame has much to do with Europe. Unlike the many petty literary types who inhabit this novel and squabble over Israeli prizes and honors, Bar-Nun received the acknowledgment of Europe with his Nobel Prize (during Shultish's stay, Bar-Nun goes on a tour of Europe; his son is the Israeli ambassador to Switzerland). Shultish's connection with him is a reconnection with the European Jewish civilization that has mostly disappeared in the Holocaust, not with a representative of Israel. In Shultish's view, Israelis seem almost as distant from Bar-Nun's tradition-infused Hebrew as his own American students. He contemplates footnotes that need to be added to school editions of Bar-Nun's stories: "The sabras, teachers and students, had to work with a pony. Shultish remembered his shock when he first saw footnotes for words like mezuza, Siddur, and dozens of other terms that a European Jew or a Talmud Torah pupil in America took for granted" (170).[17] Sabras' knowledge of basic Jewish terms is contrasted with other groups of American Jews and European Jews, whether religious or not, like Shultish himself. Bar-Nun, who originated the text that now needs Sabra-oriented footnotes, clearly belongs to the European side of this equation. As far as Leviant uses this novel to connect himself to Agnon by way of Shultish and Bar-Nun, it is to Agnon as a writer in the European Hebrew tradition. He does not make himself more Israeli in the process, but perhaps he does turn himself into more of an Eastern European Jew.

Yet a major strand of the novel suggests an interest in Bar-Nun/Agnon as a writer who is, if not Israeli, still situated in Palestine-then-Israel and writes about this region. Shultish's favorite Bar-Nun story is "The Yemenite Girl." Many Yemenite Jews immigrated to the Holy Land around the time European Zionism started to make itself felt there. For many years, therefore, they were the main kind of Eastern Jews Ashkenazi Zionists were aware of. Shultish translated "The Yemenite Girl" into German many years earlier, records Bar-Nun reading it, and thinks of it many times during the course of the novel. Until the end of the novel, it is the one text that connects him most to Bar-Nun. In the story, a young man living in Rishon LeZion falls in love with an unnamed young woman from Yemen. Shultish never actualizes this love story. There, a connection between the European-born writer/narrator and a woman that seems more of a native of the Middle East never flowers because the Yemenite father refuses to let her be entangled with an Ashkenazi man. Shultish relives this story during his stay in Haifa by falling in love with a much younger Yemenite woman, Miriam, who works as a maid for one of his literary friends.[18] At first, it seems that this inappropriate infatuation is an attempt to connect with Israelis and the new Israel; but Miriam remains proof of the European American Jew's inability to connect to contemporary Israelis. Furthermore, she unwittingly assists in the creation of homosocial ties among Ashkenazi men. Because of these continued ties to Hebrew but not Israel, Leviant's *The Yemenite Girl* can be said to be part and parcel of how better-known writers have treated Israeli literature. Still, the deep love and understanding of Hebrew literature also prefigure interests that will emerge more fully about three decades after the book's publication.

The New Hebraists?

Around the turn of the millennium, a new generation of Jewish authors writing about Jewish characters and themes made its mark on American literature. This group includes both American-born and immigrant writers of Jewish descent who were born in the 1960s and 1970s. Josh Lambert marks the start of this change with Michael Chabon's work:

> When [he] won the Pulitzer Prize in spring 2001 for *The Amazing Adventures of Kavalier & Clay* (2000), his exuberant historical epic dramatizing links between Jews' experiences and the development of the popular American medium of the comic book, it was the first time that prize or the National Book Award, the two most prestigious national literary prizes, went to a work of fiction about Jews by a writer born after 1933.[19]

An enthusiastic piece in *Vanity Fair* dubbed the American-born group that includes Krauss, Englander, and others as "the New Yiddishists"[20] because of their interest in the Jewish Ashkenazi past. Notably, most of these authors do not speak much Yiddish and could just as easily have been named the New Hebraists (most of them not knowing much Hebrew either). My suggestion of "New Hebraists" is tongue-in-cheek but partly justified by the fact that some of them do speak or read Hebrew, engage with Hebrew texts from different time periods, and often deal with Israel, the country where Hebrew is the national language.

Lambert makes a convincing argument that this renewal in Jewish American literature should be explained by institutional changes. Considerable resources have been invested into encouraging young American Jewish people to learn about Jewish history and culture and into encouraging American Jews of all ages to read and discuss books by and about Jews. Jewish identity is currently an important resource in the literary marketplace. Writers are looking for Jewish themes and the authority to write about them. Israel takes a large role in Jewish identity and politics. To quote Krauss's description of how some Americans see Israel: "[it is] the strongbox of Jewishness, the place where the most vivid, authentic strain of its modern existence has been unfolding for the last sixty-five years."[21] One of Lambert's examples of institutional encouragement concerns a 1999 funded trip to Israel in which both Dara Horn and Jonathan Safran Foer participated. Meant to connect a group of promising young Jews to Israel and Jewishness, the "group met with politicians and major literary figures including Yehuda Amichai and A. B. Yehoshua."[22] Thus, we see that there indeed is an institutional drive to connect American and Israeli writers, creating the spaces to encourage and develop an interest in Israel. When adding to this the fact that Israel seems so important to the Jewish community and Jewishness is a major point of interest, it makes sense that some Jewish writers will want to connect their literary identity with it.

Indeed, almost all of the prominent names in this group of younger Jewish authors wrote about Israel in fiction or nonfiction.[23] They connect to the idea of Israel even if not to its everyday lived reality. Even if they imagine worlds where Israel never existed or is destroyed, they still show themselves to be preoccupied by it. Chabon's *The Yiddish Policemen's Union* (2007), for example, imagines a reality in which Israel never existed and another Jewish state is formed in Alaska. In addition, Chabon and his Israel-born wife, author Ayelet Waldman, edited *Kingdom of Olives and Ash: Writers Confront the Occupation* (2017), a collection of essays by international writers about the Israeli-Palestinian conflict. This collection includes a piece by one Israeli author, Assaf Gavron, who also translated both Roth and Englander. Foer's *Here I Am* (2016) features the destruction of Israel in an earthquake and a protagonist who is almost convinced by his Israeli cousin to join the efforts to save it but in the end stays in the United States. Less apocalyptic, Horn's protagonist in *A Guide for the Perplexed* (2013) is married to an intelligent, good-looking Israeli man. By the end of this Jewish-themed techno-thriller, mostly set in Egypt, the couple is living happily in Israel. Thus, the novel reenacts *Exodus* with both the United States and modern Egypt playing the role of the biblical Egypt. Furthermore, in an essay in an academic collection that cites both Agnon and Etgar Keret, Horn even states that she "write[s] in English as though it were Hebrew."[24] There are numerous other examples that exhibit a variety of political stripes.

We see several of these new voices depict Israel and Israelis in their fiction, building their Jewish identity by connecting to Israeli writers. Englander links up with Etgar Keret. Englander grew up on Long Island in an Orthodox Jewish community and lived in Jerusalem between 1996 and 2001. As he tells it, he immigrated to Israel out of a belief in the coming peace in the Middle East. Englander left Israel in despair over the slowing of the peace process to a virtual halt and the outbreak of the Second Intifada and yet still thinks that he might return to Israel.[25] His main identity as a writer is that of a former Orthodox Jew, but Israeliness, or at least having been a resident of Israel, is an important part of his persona as well. Etgar Keret (b. 1969) is an Israeli writer who emerged in the 1990s as a leading voice in the younger, leaner version of Hebrew literature. He is one of the most successful and well-known Israeli writers outside of Israel. Englander often promotes Keret's work on his Twitter feed, and, while he has translated some of Keret's stories, he has never translated whole books. Keret has done the same for Englander. This practice suggests that they translate as a labor of love and not as a professional task, making it a kind of bond between them. This also transpires in public statements.[26] Furthermore, several videos and photographs of them together circulate online. One photo on Englander's Twitter account shows them both on a subway in Tokyo, their bodies mirroring each

Figure 4 The caption reads: "Etgar Keret, Nathan Englander, twins reunited. #Tokyo."
Source: Nathan Englander's Twitter account, retweeted March 1, 2014.

other, their hair, smiles, and jackets looking similar. The caption for this photo is "Etgar Keret, Nathan Englander, twins reunited."[27] Obviously, there is some degree of irony in this proclamation of twinhood, but the message still comes through that one should look for similarities as well as differences, not only in appearance but also in identity and personality.

The importance of Englander's connection to Keret and Israeliness, in general, becomes clear when looking at his fiction. Of the eight stories in the collection *What We Talk about When We Talk about Anne Frank* (2012), one is set in Israeli-occupied West Bank ("Sister Hills") and one in Jerusalem ("Free Fruit for Young Widows"); the Anne Frank story deals with an American couple who live in Israel and are on a visit to Florida, and "How We Avenged the Blums" can easily be read as thinking about Israel. The latter story's theme is Jewish self-defense in the face of anti-Semitism, a major component of the Zionist ethos, and one that is troubled in Englander's story. Clearly, Israel is an important resource for Englander's imagination (as his 2017 novel *Dinner at the Center of the Earth* also suggests). Writing about Israel, but not residing in it, sets a certain problem for Englander: can he speak authoritatively about the intimate life of Israelis?[28] Malamud voiced such concerns and decided not to write about Israel. Englander does take up the challenge. Part of what Englander chooses to do is to remind readers that he has at least some degree of this intimate knowledge. This is especially the case with "Sister Hills" and "Free Fruit," which, unlike most American fiction about Israel (including the story about Anne Frank), present themselves not as American perspectives on Israel but as Israeli stories about Israelis.

One path Englander can take in showing that he is someone who has the ability to tell these stories is for him to associate himself with Israeliness. The references to the fact that he had immigrated to Israel do much of this work. For instance, "Free Fruit" is set in the Jerusalem neighborhood where Englander lived. For people who know this through Englander's interviews or public storytelling, the location helps build his status as a writer who is able or at least allowed to tell these stories. However, there is another way in which Englander fortifies his authentic Israeliness, and this additional connection is made within the book. In "Free Fruit," the main character is named Etgar. This is an uncommon name in Israel (its literal meaning is "challenge"); and, while its scarcity might not be known to all American readers, it should be to some, especially those likely to judge if a story is authentic or not. Hence, what Englander risks in seeming not to know about Israeli nomenclature, he gains in closeness to Etgar Keret.[29]

In the acknowledgments section, Keret is back, and he is the only writer mentioned. Englander gives thanks "to a truly generous soul, and my hairiest muse, Etgar Keret, who inspired not one story in this book, but two." Originally designating a Greek goddess of poetry, the word "muse" has come to be associated with a woman who inspires and cares for a male artist. By adding that Keret is a "hairy muse," Englander defamiliarizes the feminine word and invites us to think of its source. The hairiness works on other levels as well: it secures Keret's masculinity despite his role as a muse, but it also conjures up a certain stereotype about the hairy Middle Eastern/Israeli man. The hairy masculinity invokes images of the Zionist new Jew being much more in touch with his body and more masculine than his diasporic cousin. However, the term "muse" reengages Keret with the literary in a way that we cannot find in Bellow. Finally, the fact that Englander allows himself to joke about Keret's body hair suggests a degree of good-humored intimacy. Englander clearly wants people to know about his friendship with Keret and that this friendship influences him as a writer. He highlights his fraternal ties (his bro-mantic ties) with the Israeli writer and thus highlights the sense that he belongs to, or at least is welcome in, Israeli literature.

Paul Auster certainly does not belong to Israeli literature but, on occasion, can make himself welcome there. Auster is not part of the generation that I am describing nor usually thought of as a particularly Jewish writer. Nevertheless, under tragic circumstances, Auster found it appropriate to align himself with an Israeli writer, David Grossman (b. 1954). In an answer to a question about the relation of *Man in the Dark* (2008) to the 9/11 terrorist attacks, Auster said:

> There was another very important factor, too [in the construction of the novel]. I don't know if you noticed to whom the book is dedicated. David Grossman, he's an Israeli novelist and essayist. A great writer, in fact. And a very close friend of mine, someone I admire more than anybody I know ... His son Uri was 20 years old two years ago when he was killed in the war between Israel and Lebanon. I knew the boy, and it was just a shattering experience. Not just for David and his family, of course, who are still suffering horribly, but me too.

Auster ties the novel to a very Israeli story of a public intellectual and writer who lost his son in a war he protested against: "It was the very week when David and ... Amos Oz had gone to [Israeli Prime Minister Ehud] Olmert and were begging him to make a ceasefire. Two days later, Uri is killed, and two days after that, the ceasefire had gone into effect."[30] Auster makes it clear that the novel is not simply dedicated to Grossman as an act of friendship but that it was Grossman's experience that is at the heart of the novel. Indeed, if one reads the novel, it does seem to be thinking about Israel, or at least the question of what it would be like if the United States were more like Israel. That is to say, what if the United States, too, were entangled in a continuing domestic war? *Man in the Dark* features a retired literary critic named Brill who, suffering from insomnia, tells himself a story about an America that has become a war zone after the election of George W. Bush. Instead of fighting wars abroad, the war is internal and close to home, an experience highly foreign to contemporary Americans but all too familiar to Israelis like Grossman.

More tellingly yet, a young man who had dated Brill's granddaughter, and who Brill also mentored, is murdered by terrorists in Iraq. If one has any knowledge of Grossman's life (knowledge Auster provides in the above-cited interview and I assume on other occasions around the publication of the novel), they will know this is an echo of these fictional events. Since the entire novel is suffused with grief, and its ending offers a possible escape from it, one can say quite positively that the novel is a way of working through the loss of a friend's son. The direct association with Grossman allows Auster to put the novel and himself in this context. Overall, Auster's identity as an author is more associated with poststructuralism and postmodernism and not his ethnicity. However, during the first decade of the twenty-first century, he wanted to connect to an Israeli writer. In contrast to Englander's case, Auster's affiliation with Grossman is localized in this one novel, though he and Grossman continue to be friends and at times appear together in public events.

Nicole Krauss, too, makes a point of connecting herself repeatedly with Israeli writers. In interviews, she often mentions Hebrew and Israeli writers as influences, or just as people she reads (along with other international writers). Among them, Yoram Kaniuk (1930–2013) stands out, particularly because Krauss wrote a personal poetic obituary for Kaniuk, for the *New Yorker*. Part of the generation that fought in the 1948 War, Kaniuk is a prominent Israeli novelist, although for a long time he did not receive the full support of the literary establishment. Several of his books, including the postmodernist encyclopedic novel *The Last Jew* (1981; English translation, 2007), the closest thing in Hebrew literature to Thomas Pynchon's 1973 *Gravity's Rainbow*, were translated into English and other languages. His death prompted Krauss to present her personal and literary connection to him in the most extensive fashion to date. She opens the obituary by asserting their personal connection: "After receiving a hundred of his letters, meeting him fifteen times, either at his apartment on Bilu Street or at a Tel Aviv café, and receiving too many calls from his cell phone to ever hope to return, I gave up trying to count the number of times that Yoram Kaniuk had died."[31] This first sentence connects the two as correspondents and maybe intimate friends, putting Kaniuk in the position of the older family member who demands more attention than the younger generations can give them. It also initiates the main conceit of the piece: that Kaniuk has died many times. This idea connects Krauss and Kaniuk because, even though it comes from Kaniuk's narratives about himself, it is taken up by Krauss when she composes the piece that follows Kaniuk's final death. She is his ghostwriter, putting his stories to paper. She becomes a kind of medium for Kaniuk's story.

The obituary as a whole seems an integral part of Krauss's oeuvre, not only a way to honor her deceased friend. As discussed in Chapter 5, obituaries play a crucial part in *The History of Love*, Krauss's best-known novel. The novel opens with one of its protagonists, Leo Gursky, contemplating his own obituary. Later in the novel, it is from an obituary that he learns of his son's death. More importantly, as a young man, Gursky wrote a series of fanciful obituaries that, as we saw, connect him and Krauss to a series of mostly Jewish writers. The last obituary, which readers only find on the final page of the novel, after Gursky dies as an old man, is titled "The Death of Leopold Gursky" and is remarkably similar to the Kaniuk obituary that Krauss writes in her own voice. It begins: "Leopold Gursky started dying on August 18, 1920," presumably his date of birth. "He died learning to walk / He died standing at the blackboard" and it goes on in a similar manner for a few more lines. Like Kaniuk, Krauss's fictional character died many times. This parallel implies that Kaniuk (or a version of him) is in a way Krauss's creation. This close interconnectedness is miles away from Bellow's detached journalistic interest in Haim Gouri's anecdotes.

Later in Krauss's obituary of Kaniuk, Krauss quotes a letter from Kaniuk where he asserts some strange affiliations and filiations with her:

> I think that I have written your book. My English is so dull these days and I feel awkward writing to you in my pigs English, but apparently we are related, maybe I am your dead grandfather from the aunt of David's side who came from Gan Yavne where I was once in love with a girl who is by now dead and you were one year old when you had written your wonderful book and you had found it engraved in Phoenician on my grave.[32]

Kaniuk claims a family resemblance and a sense that he somehow wrote Krauss's book. This assertion echoes the plot of *The History of Love*, a novel that, as you will recall, features young love extensively and whose plot includes a man publishing a book that he did not write himself. Though Krauss does not accept that Kaniuk wrote her book, she does quote the letter, suggesting that there is something of value in the sentiment.[33]

Krauss's account of Kaniuk points to the connections between Israeli writing and current Jewish American writing. On the one hand, Krauss asserts that Kaniuk "was nothing if not Israeli" and speaks about his intimate connection to Tel Aviv and the history of Israel. On the other hand, she also depicts him as a deeply Jewish writer, partly because of his ongoing engagement with "failure," which puts him at odds with the Israeli ethos: "[He] worked against the grain of the favored Israeli narrative of strength, self-determination, and invincibility." Some of the Jewish diasporic qualities and themes in Kaniuk's work are said to be drawn from his time in New York. In the obituary, Krauss tells us that "[i]n the basement *batei midrash* [study houses] of East Broadway, he was introduced to the sort of Jewish learning deliberately excised from a Zionist education" and, later, that *The Last Jew*, which offers an alternate history of Jewish existence that encompasses both diaspora and the Land of Israel, could only have been written by "an Israeli born again [after one of his many deaths] on the Lower East Side."[34] The connection with the diaspora, and especially with the American diaspora, eases Krauss's literary affiliation with Kaniuk. With this thought about Kaniuk finding Jewishness on the Lower East Side, I suggest that affiliating with Israeli writers is not simply a fascination with the country as it exists today or with its literature. Rather, it is also a way to connect to Jewish identity. For Krauss and other writers of her generation, being Israeli and being connected to Israelis is one way to perform Jewishness.

Kafka in Israel

The generation I am describing continues to affiliate with other Jewish writers who are not Israeli, especially forming ties with other Jews writing in non-Jewish languages. This is a vein that seems not to have been exhausted by Roth and his generation (possibly it has been exhausted but contemporary writes mine it nonetheless). Indeed, Krauss's fourth novel *Forest Dark* combines an attempt at connecting with a European novelist but in a way that turns him into an Israeli. At the same time, *Forest Dark* also harkens back to the biblical author-figures, by presenting one of its characters as possibly a descendant of King David.

Krauss's novel follows two main characters. One is Epstein, a rich businessman who undergoes a process of giving away his worldly possessions. After being contacted by an eccentric rabbi, Epstein travels to Israel, where he disappears into the desert. The second is a writer named Nicole who shares many biographical facts with Krauss and whose story is narrated in the first person. Nicole suffers a writer's block as part of a quietly troubled marriage in Brooklyn and decides to spend some time in Tel Aviv. Contact made with a man who says he is a literature professor leads her into trouble with Israel's security forces and a hallucinatory fortnight in a lonely cabin in the Negev Desert that may have also housed Kafka. She returns to Brooklyn with renewed purpose as a writer and an understanding that her marriage is over.

As can be understood from the précis, both storylines are about Americans visiting Israel, but the characters see themselves as much more than mere tourists. Epstein was indeed born in Tel Aviv. Nicole, too, sees Israel as her personal provenance. Early in the novel, she contemplates the mystical idea that, for our entire lives, we are situated in the same location and only dream of other places. Continuing this notion, she writes "I knew unequivocally that if I was dreaming my life from anywhere, it was the Tel Aviv Hilton."[35] There she was conceived, she tells us, and there her family stayed many times when she was a child. This sense is part of what sends Nicole to Israel where she thinks that she might solve some of her personal as well as professional problems by returning to her place of origin. Israel as the place of inception corresponds to the Zionist ideology, expressed in Israel's Declaration of Independence: "The Land of Israel was the birthplace of the Jewish people. Here their spiritual, religious and political identity was shaped."[36] Even if at other moments she chafes at the role of the Jewish writer, in placing her origin in Israel, Nicole/Krauss reenacts the Jewish and Zionist myth of origin in her own prehistory.

Nicole tells Eliezer Friedman, who introduces himself as a professor of comparative literature and Kafka expert, that Tel Aviv "often felt to me more like my true home than anywhere else" ("Out in the Blue"). Later in that scene, she recalls her popularity in Israel, which is apparently due to the Jewish resonance of her books: "In Sweden or Japan they didn't care much about what I wrote, but in Israel, I was stopped in the street." Israelis are an important part of her readership, she imagines. Overall, Krauss and the novel's Nicole seem deeply connected to Israel, and Israel seems to be touched by her writing. In this, she repeats the gesture made in the Kaniuk obituary, in which Krauss shows that she is touched by Kaniuk just as he was touched by her. This sense of interconnectedness is echoed by the role of Hebrew in the novel. Hebrew at times remains untranslated as if meant just for Hebrew readers. For example, the dedication page reads "*To my father*" and then "ולג״ב״א" (and to Gimel, Beth, Aleph) in the Hebrew alphabet with no translation. To most American readers this would perhaps signify "Hebrew" or nothing at all. To readers of Hebrew, this signifies a dedication to a man or woman. One does not need an overly active imagination to think that perhaps this is the unnamed lover who is mentioned briefly toward the end of the novel. These are also the first three letters of the Hebrew alphabet in reverse order. That these mysteries are only open to Hebrew readers may be more important than any possible solution for them because they create an intimate bond, a dedication, with those who can decipher the letters.[37]

Nicole's connection to Israel and Jews is strong, but there is some disquiet that goes along with it as well. People stopping her in the street is not a pleasant experience. In one such incident, a woman catches Nicole on her way to an urgent restroom visit in order to show her a "red-faced infant" who is named, she says, after a character from Nicole's book: "because of you." Likely, the infant is named Alma, a popular name in Israel, which became even more popular after the publication of *The History of Love*, in which the young protagonist is also named Alma after a character in a book also titled *The History of Love*.[38] The next example Nicole proposes is even less pleasant. At Yad Vashem, Israel's "World Holocaust Remembrance Center,"[39] Nicole is "separated out from the other (non-Jewish) festival writers," a scene that echoes the systematic anti-Semitic actions that Yad Vashem records and memorializes ("Out in the Blue"). Nicole is presented with a blank notebook commemorating the liberation of Auschwitz. Essentially, she is told that, as a Jew, she is expected to be part of the Jewish national memorialization project that Yad Vashem represents. This is a grave intrusion on her identity as a writer. The novel hints at this infringement when Nicole cannot make herself write in this notebook: she tries to compose a mere shopping list but gives up halfway.

Krauss allows her alter ego Nicole to think about her desire to please and connect in terms of half voluntarily binding to the Jewish past. First invoking Isaac's binding by Abraham, she writes that its legacy was to "teach Jewish children to bind themselves." The self-inflicted, but never really chosen, bondage is what connects contemporary Jews with past Jews: "We bind and are bound because the binding binds us to those who were bound before us, and those bound before them, and those before them, in a chain of ropes and knots that goes back three thousand years, which is how long we've been dreaming of cutting ourselves loose" ("Out in the Blue"). The bond I am referring to is less arranged around a specific text (although Krauss is referring to the founding myth of the *Akida*) or ritual (which can be chosen or ignored). For Krauss, the binding is to other Jews, and suggests that a disposition or an identity for which *binding*, keeping in touch, telephoning your elders, reading your precursors, is of the utmost importance. Even as they dream of breaking free, Jews are joined together with the past, going all the way back to *Genesis*. Ironically, in complaining about this binding, Krauss affiliates herself even closer with the Jews, associating herself with Isaac and talking of the Jewish people in the first-person plural. The long ruminations about family, peoplehood, and authorship is triggered by the Israeli professor telling Nicole "I've read your novels. We all have … You're adding to the Jewish story. For this, we're very proud of you." The context in which another person tries to tighten the rope around the fictional Nicole and a "we" one can only assume is "the Jews" (or Israeli Jews, an important distinction intentionally left vague) suggests that, as one may expect, the issue of half-chosen binding to tradition is of urgent concern to Jewish writers as public figures, even more so than to most other, non-public Jews. As Krauss writes in the next paragraph, "The need to make one's parents proud is deforming enough; the pressure to make one's whole people proud is something else again" ("Out in the Blue").[40]

In this context of uneasiness about her role as a Jewish writer, especially one who was received so well in Israel, Kafka is first introduced into the novel (if we do not count the epigraph). Friedman says that he knows that she is interested in Kafka, "Once you even wrote an obituary for him." Friedman is likely referring to one of the Gursky obituaries from *The History of Love*. Here we see a character in a novel deducing an author's affiliation from her books (especially from the obituaries she writes). In addition, Friedman bases his decision to recruit Nicole for a special Kafka project on these affiliations. Curiously enough and despite or because of her ties to Israel, the Kafka with whom Nicole affiliates in *Forest Dark* is not only the European writer who died in 1924, but an imagined Kafka who survived his own death and becomes an Israeli. In Roth's "Looking at Kafka," Kafka becomes Americanized, even Jewish-Americanized, through the fantasy that he immigrated to New Jersey and became a Hebrew teacher. Through this metamorphosis, Roth can more easily connect himself to Kafka. Krauss's Kafka is Zionized, Israelized. Krauss can bind herself to him in a way that blends her drive to identify with European Jews and her drive to identify with Israelis.[41]

The details of Kafka's fictional secret immigration and his life in Israel are not very important to my argument, nor do they make much sense. It seems that for Krauss, some implausibility in her plots opens up room for emotional and artistic truths. What is important is that according to Friedman, Kafka continued writing in Palestine and later in the State of Israel, and that Max Brod (Kafka's friend, posthumous editor, and first biographer) inserted some of these writings into published material. These "facts" turn Kafka into a kind of Israeli writer, if not a Hebrew writer. We must remember that many Hebrew-Israeli writers were not born in Israel but immigrated to it, just as Kafka has in Friedman's narrative (see "Gilgul"). Furthermore, the idea that Kafka who wrote in German can be imagined as Israeli makes it more acceptable that Krauss could be an Israeli writer who writes in English. Of course, many writers continued writing in their native tongue despite living in Palestine and then Israel. Brod himself only one example.

Nicole is connected to Kafka is the writer who will finish his project, and will then be one who will present his true-life story to the world. She is charged with introducing his true post-1924 identity as a Zionist and then Israeli. She will be the one to write the Israeli Kafka. At first, Friedman tells her that among the manuscripts that were never published and are held by a private person, there is "a play that Kafka wrote near the end of his life" ("Out in the Blue")—only after hearing the tale of Kafka's immigration to Israel can we surmise that Friedman means that this play was written in Israel. Friedman plans to make a movie out of the play, but needs some changes to be made and an ending to be added, suggesting that Nicole is the writer to take up this task. Later on, after a drive to Jerusalem during which he lays out Kafka's life in Israel, Nicole gets

> [a] sense of what Friedman might be asking [her] ... not to write the end of a real play by Kafka, but to write the real end of his life. ... Did Friedman want ... to control how [the story] would be written? To shape, through fiction, the story of Kafka's afterlife in Israel, as Brod had shaped the canonical story of his life and death in Europe? ("Gilgul")

Nicole understands that she is being asked to rewrite Kafka's life according to an Israeli's narrative. By including the encounter with Friedman in the novel, Krauss indeed promotes this narrative (even if readers do not read the novel as alternate history). For a moment of fictional potentiality, Krauss is affiliated with Kafka as his editor, biographer, and collaborator.

Toward the end of the novel, Nicole finds herself in a deserted hut in the Israeli Negev desert, a place where Kafka may have lived. After spending a strange hallucinatory time in the hut, she returns to civilization leaving a suitcase of Kafka manuscripts behind. Nicole never becomes part of Israel nor of the plan to turn Kafka into an Israeli. Even when she does repeat Friedman's Kafka narrative, she tells it in a way that would make most readers doubt its veracity, even within the world of the novel. In other words, it makes sense to think Friedman might simply be a charlatan, lying about Kafka's Israeli fate. Instead of becoming one with the desert or the Israeli Kafka or some such, Nicole returns to Brooklyn, ends her marriage, and presumably finishes writing the book we are reading. At the end, then, she remains an American author with strong ties to Israel, not an Israeli writer.

Back to King David

It is quite possible that American writers will never find Israeli writers to be the most attractive partners for affiliation. The biggest factor working against this trend must be that Israeli writers do not have a prominent place in world literature that writers like Heinrich Heine, Isaac Babel, or even Isaac Bashevis Singer enjoy. Connecting to these European writers helps current Jewish writers connect to Jewishness but in a way that is legible to readers who are not especially familiar with Jewish literature. We saw how Auster needed to explain who David Grossman was;[42] within an American literary context, nobody is expected to explain who Kafka or Anne Frank are. Furthermore, affiliating with Israeli writers and with Israeliness can quickly be interpreted as political allegiance to the Israeli government. This allegiance is becoming more and more problematic every day because of the nationalistic policies of the Israeli government and the strengthening of pro-Palestinian movements. Unless some unexpected events arise, Israel, at least for the time being, will be more associated with its conflicts and politics than with its culture and literature.

This last point is thematized with a figure that takes us back to the beginning of the history of affiliation with Jewish writers, the biblical King David. David is often thought of as a poet-king. However, King David is also a conqueror and a builder of an empire, according to the Books of Samuel and Kings. Different American authors pick up different roles David has. Joshua Cohen is a younger and less well-known member of the recent wave of Jewish writing, though his

2010 novel *Witz* gained him a certain following. His well-received 2017 novel *Moving Kings* depicts several characters, one of whom is an Israeli ex-soldier working for a moving company that also carries out forced evictions. Cohen attempts to depict the Israeli character from the inside, partly by transferring him to New York. The owner of the moving company, an empire of sorts, is the Israeli's American cousin, whose name is David King. Despite the novel's obvious allusion to the biblical king, David King is a shallow moving-mogul who makes his money from the suffering of those who lose their houses (especially after the 2008 subprime mortgage crisis). There is almost nothing of the poet in him. Thus, even when Cohen invokes one of the Hebrew tradition's mythical poets, it is in his role as a conquering king. King's "brain wasn't wired for prayer, just panic";[43] he is no psalmist, then. Staunchly pro-Israel, this character is affiliated with Israel politically, but Cohen does not connect David King or himself to either current or historical Hebrew authors.

King David also plays a role in *Forest Dark*. Epstein, the second protagonist of the novel, is told by an eccentric rabbi that he is a descendant of the House of David (see "Ayeka"). King David here is utilized as a founder of dynasties and a mythical hero. Krauss does invoke his role as a poet but in a way that puts this role in a political context. In a passage that represents Epstein's thoughts after buying a used copy of the *Psalms* in Tel Aviv, we hear:

> Was there a more complicated hero in the Bible than David? ... A warrior, a murderer, hungry for power, willing to do whatever it took to become king. Betrayal was nothing to him. Killing was nothing. Nothing was left to stand in the way of his desires. He took what he wanted. And then, to let him rest from what he had been, the authors of David ascribed to him the most plaintive poetry ever written. ("Forests of Israel")

King David is seen as a figure to whom others have ascribed the gift of poetry in retrospect, only after he lived a brutal life. The novel is skeptical about any literal David, if there was such a man, actually writing the poems. Here, poetry or prayer cover up a life of ruthlessness and betrayal. Is this how most American authors are going to see writing originating from Israel? As a partially successful cover for its wars and empire building? If so, many American writers will find this affiliation rather unattractive. Time will tell what will remain from the contemporary trend of connecting to Israeli writers as a way to search for Jewish identity beyond the borders of the United States and the confines of the English language.

6

Negotiating Continuity: Writing about Philip Roth in Israel

How do Israeli writers create ties with Jewish American writers and to what ends? For the purposes of answering this question, an Israeli is anyone with an Israeli citizenship, whether born in Israel or not, living in Israel or not, and whether Jewish or not. In this chapter, I focus on responses in Hebrew, the most common language in Israel. I start with a narrative about the reception of Roth in Israel from 1959 to 2019. In Chapter 7, I zoom in on the response of one writer, Sayed Kashua, to Roth, showing how it parallels and differs from the general terms of the discussion taken up by other Israeli critics. Part of the difference is due to the fact that Kashua is Palestinian and is not Jewish. The two chapters tell different yet complementary stories of networking, both taking shape in the same landscape and vis-à-vis the same American writer.

Diaspora's Diaspora

There is a tendency to use Philip Roth and other Jewish American figures to perform Israeli and Jewish identity. In order to further explore the history of this reception, some additional theorizing and contextualizing is necessary. In *Letting Go So As to Touch*, Dan Miron rejects the idea of the unity of Jewish literature. Instead of a transhistorical, translingual unity, or as he calls it "continuity" (*hemshekhiyyut*), Miron suggests that there might be a sense of "contiguity" (his neologism in Hebrew, *magga'iyyut*). This contiguity seems to be a subterranean and rather mysterious intermittent connection between various strands of literature and thought produced by Jews.[1] It is a sense of connectedness that does not need to be supported by traceable, visible relays. It is perhaps like Gilles Deleuze and Félix Guattari's rhizome,[2] but it is not quite like the botanical source of the term (roughly speaking, the root system that connects seemingly autonomous plants). With plants, one can always find the spreading roots that connect seemingly individual organisms, at least if one digs deep enough. With Miron, contiguity is far more abstract. Inspired by Latour's demand in *Reassembling the Social* to trace the networks that build up our social constructs, I want to stay with the botanical rhizome and look for this visible connecting tissue. As I explained in the Introduction, I want to look for the links—textual ones for the most part—that forge connections between Jewish literary figures and communities. These ties build the contiguity that Miron senses, even if they cannot create the strict continuity that he is right to discard. It is important to emphasize that because much of this labor is carried out on the disposable pages of newspapers, periodicals, and somewhat more lasting but narrowly circulated academic books, it is largely forgotten. Often all that remains is a sense of contiguity in readers' minds or a consensus about contiguity in reading communities. That is why reading the archive is necessary to retrace these networks.

An important context for any discussion of an Israeli reading of Jewish American writers is the history of the response to diaspora. The official ideology that the State of Israel holds, and the one it was founded on, is Zionism. A central tenet of many strands of Zionism is "the negation of exile"—*shlilat ha-galut*. A leading critic of this concept, Amnon Raz-Krakotzkin, explains: "'Negation of exile' denotes a viewpoint that sees modern Jewish settlement in the Land of Israel, along with the establishment of Jewish territorial sovereignty, as the return of the Jewish people to a land defined as their own after two thousand years of exile." For him, it consists of the notion that the millennia of wandering among nations never took place. It is not a fantasy of return but one of never having left at all. Raz-Krakotzkin continues: "The negation of exile is understood by those who express and define Zionist consciousness as the 'normalization' of Jewish existence in terms of the full realization of Jewish history or, at least, its 'solution.'"[3] By downplaying and trying to forget two millennia between the destruction of the Second Temple and the inception of territorial Zionism, Jews might become a normal nation. This idea, when taken to an extreme that is no longer common in contemporary Israel, means that the history and culture of the Jews who lived and continue to live outside of the borders of the Land of Israel are of meager importance. Or as Raz-Krakotzkin puts it:

> [Zionists] perceive the period of exile as an intermediary period; even if in its context important cultural values were created, it was in and of itself meaningless, a condition of deficient existence, partial and abnormal—a time in which the "spirit of the nation" could not find expression due to the external bounds that prevented its realization.[4]

It is easy to understand, then, that historically mainstream Zionist Israelis were extremely suspicious, even disdainful, of Jewish literature produced outside of Israel, especially when not carried out in Hebrew or expressing a longing for Zion. Israelis, for example, marginalized Yiddish literature, the main rival for the literary attention of Eastern European Jews. Because of a mixture of the negation of exile and disdain for "the East," the literature of Jews who immigrated to the State of Israel from Muslim countries (Mizrahi Jews) was largely erased from mainstream narratives. The early years of Israel (established in 1948), when the Zionist ideology was at its most powerful, coincided with the rise of Jewish American fiction. Some of the novels by Saul Bellow, Bernard Malamud, and Roth were translated, just as novels by other Americans and Europeans were; but still, according to Amnon Hadary, who published a book in Hebrew about Jewish American literature in 1971, this literature met with a disdain based on the negation of exile.[5] The 1980s and 1990s saw the Americanization and globalization of great swaths of Israeli society and Israeli literature, along with the inception of identity politics, especially for Mizrahi Jews. These trends—along with a sense that Israel was more secure than in the past—meant that the idea of the negation of exile has weakened and even come under direct attack, opening up more room for Yiddish, Jewish Arab, and Jewish European writing as a resource for Israeli literature.

The trajectory of this study of Israeli reception gains contemporary relevance when twinned with debates about diaspora in the fields of Jewish studies and of Hebrew writing. The most prominent academic proponent of a revision of diaspora is the Talmud scholar Daniel Boyarin. In *A Traveling Homeland: The Babylonian Talmud as Diaspora*, Boyarin suggests a new definition: "diaspora [should] be understood as a synchronic cultural situation applicable to people who participate in a doubled cultural ... location, in which they share a culture with the place in which they dwell but also with another group of people who live elsewhere."[6] Boyarin bills both the Jewish Babylonian and the Jewish Palestinian cultures of late antiquity as diasporic to one another, rejecting any model of center and periphery, homeland and diaspora (*galut*). He explicitly frames other readings of the diaspora as Zionist, and thus implicitly suggests that we should think of today's Israel, or certain communities within it, as a diaspora rather than a homeland or center. Tal Hever-Chybowski expresses a similar point of view in reassessing the role that Israel plays for Hebrew literature. Since statehood, Israel has been considered the center of Hebrew language and culture. Israeli literature has taken a monopoly over Hebrew. Even when writers outside of Israel produce work in Hebrew these days, they often do so with reference to Israel.⁷ Hever-Chybowski reminds his readers that the centrality of Israel to Hebrew need not be the case, and that, over the millennia, there has been *Ivrit 'olamit*, global or world Hebrew, characterized by diasporic conditions.⁸ Accordingly, Hever-Chybowski edits *Mikan Ve'eylakh* ("From Here On Out"), a journal devoted to the promotion of Hebrew writing created without direct links to Israel. For him and Boyarin, texts written in Hebrew (and its close relative Aramaic) remain central to this rethinking of diaspora. With the added translingual dimension, my analysis is another step in thinking in this direction but without necessarily placing Jewish languages, especially Hebrew, at its center. In my analysis, Jewish communities can be in diasporic relations to one another through translation or through reading of a non-Jewish lingua franca, English.

A number of Israeli critics and writers take up Roth's writings and public image as a way to negotiate their identities as Israelis and Jews. For much of the time frame I examine here (1959–2019), Roth was the most frequently published and one of the best-known Jewish American writers in Israel. These literary or critical Israeli texts show how writers revise and reshape Roth's texts in their relation to the diaspora, and especially the American part of the diaspora. Some present Roth in a way that highlights how Israeli and diasporic identities powerfully diverge. Others put forward a view of a joint Jewish identity that belongs to both American and Israeli Jews. Still others, such as Kashua, find a place somewhere between these poles.⁹

Roth has periodically appeared in the Israeli press since the very beginning of his career, and, for almost as long, his name has been connected with the issue of continuity of Jewish identity—one of the main reasons I chose to focus on him. A brief note from 1959 reports on *Goodbye, Columbus* as a book that asks "the question that has been plaguing the Jews for many generations: 'to assimilate, or not to assimilate,'" suggesting that the book is indeed part of a Jewish tradition but a Jewish tradition of abandoning Jewish tradition ("to assimilate"). In accordance, this piece also emphasizes the character names, such as "Sheila, Kevin, Neil, and Brenda," that do not sound Jewish but rather sound very American. Readers are assured that the young author is, "of course, Jewish."¹⁰ Several years later, in 1963, Roth, not yet well known in Israel, appears explicitly in the Israel–diaspora context. He is invited to participate in a conference for "American-Israeli 'dialogue'" at the Hebrew University of Jerusalem; the subject of the second day is the issue of "[t]he Jewish international and Jewish identity in the United States and Israel."¹¹ Thus, even before he was famous, Roth's name (along with the names of other Jewish American writers) appears in the context of the crevice between Israeli and American Jews and the awareness that some cultural work ("dialogue," a conference) is needed to bridge this gap.

With the English publication of *Portnoy's Complaint* in 1969, an expected explosion of Israeli writing about both Roth and the novel occurred. The best-known example among Roth critics for the coverage that ensued comes from the great Kabbalah scholar Gershom Scholem, who wrote in *Haaretz* that the "revolting book" supplies anti-Semites proof that Jews lust after gentile women.[12] However, there were several other interesting responses, mostly ones that highlight Portnoy's weakness as a diaspora Jew. Before looking at some cases from 1969, I want to emphasize that most texts, just like Scholem's attack, are responding to the American publication of the novel. These are not routine reviews of new books in Israeli literary supplements, which usually review the Hebrew translations, but responses to the Portnoy phenomenon. They often incorporate reports that the book is a bestseller and has made its author a millionaire celebrity.

The penultimate chapter of *Portnoy's Complaint* (the final chapter is Spielvogel's "PUNCH LINE")[13] depicts the protagonist traveling in Israel and focuses on two encounters with young Israeli women and his suffering of impotence during his stay. It is a fairly short chapter, but it drew much attention from Israeli critics, as most of the 1969 Israeli commentary on *Portnoy* devotes large portions to this episode. It is often an opportunity to draw a line between Israelis and American Jews with clear echoes of the negation of exile. I will quote from the most explicit reading in this trend. R. Rabinowitz writes:

> Portnoy's alienation and loneliness are not resolved even when he reaches the Land of the Jews. One could imagine that precisely here [davka kan—Israel], in this new place in the extraordinary [bilti ragil] landscape, Portnoy will find his remedy. However, fate taunts him. He meets an Israeli girl, Naomi, a kibbutz member. She preaches to him, to him and to the capitalist society from which he comes. His attempt to conquer this girl turns out to be an impotent man's failure. At that moment the circle of solitude closes upon him. The contact [magga'] between the Israeli [Yisraelit—feminine] and the Jew ends with the Jew's failure. Without a doubt, in this, Philip Roth ... tried to exemplify the rupture between the two worlds. Between the world of the middle-class American Jew, who climbs the ladder of economic success in intellectual America on the one hand, and the "New Jew" type—the Israeli [Yisraeli—masculine] on the other.[14]

Rabinowitz moves from a psychological reading, Portnoy's complaints, to a national-allegorical reading, a fissure between the New Israeli Jew and the American diasporic Jew. The crucial sentence here is "The contact between the Israeli [woman] and the Jew ends with the Jew's failure." Portnoy is made to take on the role of the diasporic Jew by dropping the term American, while the Israeli is made to seem not a Jew at all but a new kind of entity, a *Yisraelit*. Later, we return to the language of New Jew and by implication old Jew, but at least for the moment, when contact is initiated, when there is a chance of (violent) sexual intercourse, the Israeli is made to seem a creature apart. For my argument, it does not matter if Rabinowitz's reading is correct. It is certainly not preposterous: Roth lets an Israeli character lecture Portnoy about "the negation of exile." He hears from her that he was "the epitome of what was most shameful in 'the culture of the Diaspora.'" In the end, she tells him, "you are nothing but a self-hating Jew."[15] What is interesting is how happily Israeli writers and journalists take up and condone such ideas, which the novel is at least highly ambivalent about. They seem enthusiastic about emphasizing a rift between Israel and the diaspora even as they engage with an American's narrative.

This pattern repeats in many of the pieces from 1969 but also persists when Roth's name comes up in other literary contexts years after the publication of *Portnoy's Complaint*. One can see this tendency in a column from 1977 by Shulamith Hareven (1930–2003), a well-known and highly regarded novelist and essayist. Her most widely read novel is *City of Many Days* (*Ir Yamim Rabim*, 1972), where she depicts a Jerusalemite Jewish family during the British Mandate. The 1977 essay, from the height of Hareven's powers as an essayist, begins with a friend asking whether the great events of our lives happen inside or outside of ourselves. Thus, a set of dichotomies is set up, with the introduction of an "exterior"/"interior" divide (Hareven uses those English words in Hebrew transliteration and quotation marks). In the typically Israeli manner of enmeshing the Jews within every problem, the dichotomy of Israel and the diaspora is inserted into this chain of associated oppositions. Diaspora writers are useful in explaining Hareven's concern with the interior/exterior dichotomy, though they are mixed with non-Jewish ones as well. Bemoaning the modern people's love for the interior, she writes: "we are all Proust, Robbe-Grillet, Saul Bellow." She goes on to say that some American writers like John Updike or Frank O'Hara use exterior settings, even knowing the names of trees and birds, but she suggests, invoking Mendele Mocher Sforim, that there is something typically goyish, inappropriate to diasporic Jews, in knowing such things. "A tree's a tree, a bird's a bird" is the (diasporic) Jewish thing to say. Hence, the interior is Jewish and the exterior is gentile. Yet the exterior is also Israeli. In Israel, she explains, "few can truly live only in the 'interior'" because of the army service (Hareven served as a combat medic in the 1948 War) and the culture of field trips. In accordance with Zionist ideology, the Israelis are like gentiles in their own lands. Israelis are more Updikes than Bellows.

Yet Hareven does sense that there is a longing in Israel for the Jewish interior, which she also associates with provincialism (*qartanut*). Roth suddenly appears in her essay as the paradigm for the oversophisticated, solipsistic writer who is nonetheless much more provincial than writers of the exterior, who are more likely to touch the sublime. Hareven admits that some Israelis long for the interior, especially those who live in Tel Aviv. Jerusalemites, like herself and most of her literary characters, are less likely to be such homebodies. Even in an essay that is mostly about social observation, she uses the rejection of Roth and Bellow to build her own affinity with the exterior and thus Israeliness.[16] Hareven, who was born in Warsaw but saw Israel as her only homeland and thought of herself as Levantine, a Mediterranean, uses Roth to perform this anti-*galut* identity.[17]

Even in the 2000s, some of this separatism remains, although it takes on a different tone and one with different political implications. Specifically, we find this with Yitzhak Laor (b. 1948), a well-known Israeli poet, novelist, and critic who is associated with the radical left.[18] In a review of a translation of Roth's *The Plot against America*, Laor writes that the idea of joint identity is based on an illusion:

> Perhaps this mutual misunderstanding [between American and Israeli Jews] contains within it a false delusion that understanding exists because "we are all Jews" and after all we all grew up watching *Exodus* [he uses the English title, and means the 1960 film version of Uris's novel] all of "us" [I am skipping an especially sexist clause] … worked in "moving" in New York, went into a Beverly Hills synagogue in order to marry a little [this last phrase is awkward in Hebrew as well]. But what we should really have known about each other is the kind of thing anthropologists research in foreign tribes … We must forget that we know everything in order to learn from the beginning. Read Roth as if he is writing about a distant people, very exotic, even if it has the potential of making Aliyah.[19]

Laor uses Roth as an opportunity to distance himself and his audience from the group of people Roth represents (in his novels and as a representative member of the group). Laor wants his readers to view American Jews as a strange tribe, despite shared misconceptions and despite the fact that according to the Israel

Law of Return these Americans could gain Israeli citizenship, solely based on their status as Jews, simply by deciding to immigrate to Israel. Laor thus challenges the assumption of Jewish continuity, while stressing Israeliness and not Jewishness. His predecessors do this with the belief that Israel may supersede the diaspora living according to the tenets of Zionism. Laor, I believe, has a different agenda in mind. In separating the Jew from the Israeli, Laor may be hoping for a non-Jewish Israeli identity. He points out a rift that is certainly there but of which size, importance, and permanence are up for debate. Laor is not a Zionist, but he too distances himself from Roth by pointing out this rift in order to create a new kind of Israeli identity for himself and perhaps his readers.

I now move to the opposite pole of the continuum between continuity and rift: the idea of full continuity between Israeli and American Jewish culture that is exemplified by Roth's relevance for the Israeli reader-writer. Though there are some hints of the potential for this move in earlier decades, the clearest examples can be found in texts from our own century. Writer and critic Matan Hermoni (b. 1969) was just about to publish his first novel, and was working on a dissertation about representations of America in Hebrew literature, when he wrote a review of a new translation of *Goodbye, Columbus*. There, Hermoni retells an anecdote about a woman meeting Isaac Bashevis Singer and saying to him "You are my writer." Hermoni then turned himself into that reader:

> Maybe one day I will meet mister Roth. And if I do, God is my witness, these are exactly the words I will say to him, *atta ha-sofer sheli, adoni, mar Roth*, "You are my writer, mister Roth" [English transliterated in Hebrew letters].

This review goes on to state: "I love Philip Roth. Philip Roth changed my life. Reading *Portnoy's Complaint* back then, towards the end of high school was a foundational moment. That was the moment a teenaged boy's hormones turned into a kernel that will later sprout something that looks like a mind. To a great extent, Philip Roth shaped my identity."[20] Hermoni writes that Roth shaped his identity, endowing him with the alchemical powers of turning hormones into intellect. He does not say explicitly that the attraction is connected to Jewishness, but the context of the Singer anecdote and the ideas of ownership ("you are *my* writer") suggest this context. I am especially willing to assert this Jewish connection in the context of Hermoni's debut novel *Hebrew Publishing Company* (again, transliterated English),[21] a Hebrew novel partly set in a Hebrew-speaking milieu in New York City during the early decades of the twentieth century.[22] This book and other projects that Hermoni undertook, like an edited volume of Yiddish and Hebrew stories about America,[23] situate him as a member of a movement to recall and perhaps revive the diasporic horizon of writing in Hebrew. In going against negation of exile, through showing how nourishing Roth is for him, Hermoni is building a Jewish identity that is at odds with standard Zionism.

It seems that, at least for a while, the association with Roth indeed stuck. The title of an interview with Hermoni in *Ynet*, "What's Bothering Mordechai Schuster" (a wordplay on the Hebrew title of *Portnoy*, "What's Bothering Portnoy") replaced Roth's protagonist's name with the very Ashkenazi Jewish-sounding name of Hermoni's protagonist. The subtitle of the article states that "It turns out that one can write Jewish American fiction here [in Israel] and even in Hebrew." The interviewer mixes references to Yiddish and Jewish American writing in English, as does the novel itself, and also compares Hermoni to the generation of younger American writers like Chabon and Krauss. In contrast with his Roth review, in the interview, Hermoni does push back on completely affiliating himself with Jewish American writers, but he lets the connection be part of the conversation about his book.[24]

In his most recent novel, Hermoni maintains his connection with Roth and does so in a way that emphasizes Roth's place in a Jewish literary network that includes Hebrew, Yiddish, and other languages. *Spielvogel, Spielvogel* (2019) is a sex comedy about the department of Hebrew literature at Tel Aviv University. The main character was a man up until the beginning of the novel, but one morning finds that he/she has turned into a woman named Yehudit Redler.[25] The connection to Woolf's *Orlando* and Kafka's *The Metamorphosis* is clear, but there is also a connection to Roth's *The Breast*, especially since the tone is comic. The strongest connection to Roth comes through the title, which refers to the psychologist that listens to Portnoy's complaint and also appears in *My Life As a Man*, two novels by Roth that are about men losing their sense of power and masculinity, a central theme in *Spielvogel, Spielvogel* as well. In the novel, Spielvogel is a relatively minor character but one who may be crucial to understanding the transformation because Spielvogel is Redler's rival and receives tenure just before the plot's beginning. The novel thus suggests that this loss to the rival underwrites the transformation. In several challenging and problematic ways, the novel equates powerlessness with femininity, at the same time that it depicts powerful women and the power of being a woman; but this is beyond the scope of this short discussion. Putting Spielvogel in the position of explaining the magical transformation but not doing much more,

Hermoni's novel reflects the minor yet crucial role Spielvogel plays in *Portnoy*. There he has no role in the plot but enables its telling by listening to Portnoy's complaint as his analyst.

Another Spielvogel appears in the role of a psychologist in a pastiche of erotic novels.[26] The novel also directly references one of the most iconic scenes of *Portnoy*: as satire of academia, the novel includes bibliographical and discursive footnotes and in one of them, before concerning the narrator's youthful encounter with Spielvogel, Roth is invoked directly as "the great poet of masturbation," admitting that "till this day I laugh a wild almost uncontrollable laughter when I go back and read the act Alex Portnoy performs with the raw piece of beef liver that would later be placed on the family's table" (64). In the same footnote, we are told that the narrator learned to masturbate from Spielvogel—the character with the name borrowed from Roth is the one who takes part in an important step in the narrator's sexual maturation. Roth is inserted into this early moment of formation, just as he is in the earlier review.

The novel helps us see that, for Hermoni, Roth is part of a Jewish literature that orbits around Eastern European writing in Jewish languages. Just as in the review, Roth is put in discourse with Singer, the novel entangles him with a world of Jewish literature that includes Europe, the Middle East, and America. I cannot offer a full reading of the novel here, but it is very clear that in terms of both style and content the novel recreates the atmosphere of late nineteenth- and early twentieth-century Jewish literature in both Hebrew and Yiddish—the literature of the Eastern European shtetl, only the shtetl here is a Hebrew literature department where this earlier literature is studied. For example, one plotline involves marrying off a pregnant PhD student, the daughter of one of the department's full professors, to another much less talented fellow PhD student who is not the baby's father, a kind of useful idiot. The narrator, a scholar himself, takes a paragraph to point out how this plotline is derivative:

> In Jewish literature, every time an idiot is described, he is described as marrying a slattern of a woman who was already with child begot by her fornication. The idiot is told that babies come in to the world after six months. And if the idiot says "but it is written nine are the moons of pregnancy," he is told that that line is from "Chad Gadya" [it is actually from a different song] and that that is from the [Passover] *Haggadah* and that the *Haggadah* is a fairytale [*agada*]. The best known story where this is told is Bashevis's "*Gimpel Tam*" ["Gimpel, the Fool"], but you can find stories like that ... elsewhere also. (55–6)

The paragraph ends with a reference to an article on this motif written by Hermoni himself, thus embedding him in the shtetl-style of the narrative. The passage puns irreverently on the name of the religious Jewish text of the *Haggadah*, turning it into a kind of fiction: a fairytale. The pun is used so as to fool a fool into believing something fundamentally incorrect about human biology. The final aim, though, is to serve the small community, perhaps at the price of humiliating one member of it. This plotline and its accompanying Jewish wordplay are somewhat out of place in modern Israel, where single mothers are not unheard of and sex outside of marriage is common. However, in Hermoni's shtetl of a literature department, it is necessary. With many moves like this one, Hermoni intertwines his text and persona in the galaxy of Jewish literature. Writing in and about the United States is part of this galaxy as well thanks to the fact that the United States is the subject of the narrator's PhD dissertation (10) and Redler's main research subject traveled in and wrote about the New World (35). In the web Hermoni spins, he also entangles Roth (as we saw above) and in the process making him seem to belong to a tradition that is far more Yiddishist and Hebraic, which it has sometimes been argued Roth has no part in (we saw Irving Howe actively disengaging Roth from this network and I also argued that Roth has little interest in it). Hermoni thus constructs Roth as an integral resource for a contemporary Hebrew writer. Hermoni's Roth is part of a continuity, not some contiguous cousin.

Suggestions of continuity are not restricted to liberal newspapers like *Haaretz*, where Hermoni published his review. In a reading of Roth's *The Plot against America*, the poet-novelist-critic-scholar Ortsion Bartana, writing for *HaTzofeh*, the organ of the Zionist National Religious Party (*Mafdal*), describes this novel about the United States being taken over by a pro-Nazi president as a warning to Jews outside of Israel. Bartana concludes in high literary style: "If I were sitting there [in the United States] upon reading this book, I would stand up and walk away."[27] Assuming the continuity of Jewish identity, Bartana can reimagine Roth writing a classical Zionist manifesto about the dangers of the *galut*. It is possible for different Israelis to imagine a different Roth for the purpose of revisiting the relations between the American Jewry and Israel—this time into a staunchly Zionistic Roth with a fantasy about mass exodus to Israel. Bartana uses Roth to reiterate one of Zionism's *raisons d'être*, saving Jews from anti-Semitism. He also makes the potential for *Aliyah*—which we saw Yitzhak Laor disregard and mock—as a central source for continuity between Roth's American Jews and Israelis. In this view, Jewishness is undivided and has its sole legitimate center in Israel.

In between these two poles (between rejection and embrace, rift and continuity), there is a significant middle ground that uses a certain version of Roth (or Jewish American literature) to draw attention to a difference between Israeli writers and Jewish American writers. Drawing this comparison, while highlighting difference, also assumes that some contiguity and even continuity exists or ought to exist. The approach that sees connections but also emphasizes the differences can be found in the initial reception of *Portnoy*, though it is less dominant than the strand that emphasizes the difference. Novelist and critic Ehud Ben-Ezer relates to Portnoy, saying early on in a review from 1969 that he did not "sense much difference between Petah Tikva and Newark,[28] New Jersey; between Eastern Europe in the Jewish colony [*moshavah*] where I grew up and Roth/Portnoy's Jewish American breeding grounds."[29] Ben-Ezer compares his hometown to Roth's and in so doing emphasizes his own Eastern European, diasporic roots and how they shaped his life. He tells us that he had the same suffocating Jewish mother and the same close-knit and overbearing family life as Portnoy's, one that stifles any ambitions for something more "spiritual." Still, when describing Portnoy's jaunt in Israel, Ben-Ezer emphasizes the distance between Roth and Israelis, and, unlike most commentators, he also takes Roth to task for portraying Israel and Israeli women in a superficial manner that is worse, he says, than Uris's shallow pro-Israel sentiment in *Exodus*.

Despite this critique, Ben-Ezer concludes that "Philip Roth's book is also our book." In a move that will be echoed in Kashua's response, Ben-Ezer explains that despite some reservations,

> I wish we [Israelis, or possibly only the Ashkenazi elite] could also write like that about ourselves. For if we are not able to see ourselves like that, to know how to hate ourselves, and to mock, and to write like that without being ostracized by public opinion—we will end up looking just like Mr. Portnoy sees us: a hollow nationalist poster. The Mayflower of Nahalal and Petah-Tikva.

Unexpectedly, Ben-Ezer argues that some Jewish self-hatred can do Israelis some good. Certainly, some satire and self-criticism should be part of Israeli writing, he argues. What happens if it is not? We become like the gentiles, like the American WASPs that the *Mayflower* represents (in *Portnoy*, the *Mayflower* is part of the logo used by the insurance company that does not promote Portnoy's father because of its institutional anti-Semitism). Petah Tikva and the northern agricultural settlement (*moshav*) Nahalal, associated, among others, with Moshe Dayan, are centers of power and symbols of the Zionist return to the land (the opposite of *galut*). These, according to Ben-Ezer, run the risk of becoming too goyish. Making *Portnoy's Complaint* into "our book" might prevent this threat.

In asking Israelis to learn from Roth, Ben-Ezer is a precursor to a trend that has expanded in more recent years. For example, literary critic and cultural studies scholar Omri Herzog uses a review of *Portnoy's Complaint* in the *Haaretz Sfarim* supplement to launch his own, hyperbolic, complaint against the lack of humor in Israeli literature:

> One tribe [of Jews] actually keeps away from irony and self-mockery like the plague. And when one reads *Portnoy's Complaint*—and laughs out loud at his and our expense—it is impossible not to wonder at the straight-faced seriousness, the righteousness, and the anxiety of this one tribe. How did it happen that the biggest tribe— "the Israeli Jews"—does not know how to laugh at its own expense?[30]

The assumption is, of course, that Israeli Jews can and should write more like the quintessential funny literary Jew Roth. Israelis here are not like American Jews; they are a different "tribe" but the same people. They have enough in common to make it surprising that their custom of fearing irony and self-mockery (in Herzog's view) is so different from the way American Jews are represented in their cultural artifacts. A review of *Portnoy* is a natural place for a critique of Jewish Israelis.

Humor and satire are not the only issues at stake. Another prominent literary critic, Arik Glasner of *Yedioth Ahronoth*, finds that certain Jewish American writers, including Roth, can serve as a model for the masculine literature that he sees Israel as lacking. Glasner proves their relevance by arguing that Jewish American literary masculinity was an American equivalent of the Zionist "New Jew," or Sabra:

> [Martin Amis reports that] Bellow stressed the extent to which the State of Israel was important for rehabilitating Jewish masculine identity. Accordingly, Bellow's generation and the immediately following Jewish American authors ... were very masculine[/manly] writers: Norman Mailer, Joseph Heller, and Philip Roth ... Roth's motto "let's put the id back in yid" became the motto for almost all of them. And their ideological project is not far from the project of the "sabra" in our tradition: bringing back the corporeal to the diasporic spiritual nerdy Jew.[31]

American Jews, thus, have a kind of debt to pay for making Jewish men great again. This debt might be cashed in on by "manly" Israeli writers, now that more masculinity is apparently needed. Glasner imagines a circle of exchange between these two groups of Jews, setting Israelis and Americans up in the same orbit; or, to reframe this issue in Boyarin's conceptualization, Israelis and American Jews are each other's diaspora. In making these comparisons, both critics (Herzog and Glasner) also implicitly build their own identities as closer to that of the American model: Herzog as a funny, witty, ironic Israeli writer and Glasner as a masculine writer, presumably.

Based on the examples I quoted and on some that I did not mention here (including some that relate to film and television), I can now generalize. For Jewish Israelis, writing about Roth is, among other things, an opportunity to set their relation to a different group of Jews. For some, this is the traditional Zionist relation of diaspora and homeland; for others, the idea of continuity is merely a Zionist myth that should be discredited. For many others, however, there is a movement to situate Israeli literature and Jewish American literature in a diasporic relation to each other. That is to say, there is a contiguity of the two cultures (they touch). There is much that is translocal and therefore unifying for Jews in both places. This makes sense because most of the Jews in the United States and around half of the Jews in Israel come from the same places: Central and Eastern Europe. Thinking of my own investment in Roth's writing (as an academic and reviewer—I have not mentioned the newspaper pieces I wrote about Roth in Hebrew and there were many; in fact, this chapter is an autoethnography of sorts), I will say that Roth and other Jewish American writers offer a way to be Jewish without pitting this identity against Palestinians, and of being a Jew of European origins without pitting this identity against Middle Eastern and North African Jews (Mizrahi Jews). Roth also offers an *Ashkenziyyut* that is neither nostalgic like some versions of *Yiddishkeit* nor traumatically vindictive like the version of Jewish identity that focuses on anti-Semitism and the Holocaust (one I associate with Benjamin Netanyahu but that is not unique to him). Identity without such conflicts is impossible for an Israeli Ashkenazi Jew because being an Ashkenazi in Israel means that you are part of the white hegemonic group. In many ways, this group has lost much of its Eastern European content and exchanged it for hegemonic Western European/American-influenced Israeliness. Attending an opera or a rock concert would seem more typically Ashkenazi in contemporary Israel than going to a play in Yiddish.[32] Negotiating identity through Roth and other American Jewish writers may lead to a less hegemonic, more diasporic version of *Ashkenziyyut*; I say this knowing that this approach is not a path most Israelis follow.

For Boyarin, diaspora entails "a doubled consciousness," a term that echoes the African American thinker W. E. B. Du Bois's "double consciousness."[33] The term "double consciousness" makes us see the self-contradiction that afflicts or empowers minority groups. What I want to cautiously suggest is that reading Jewish American literature, a literature of a minority group that is nonetheless now part of the white hegemony, gives access to some of this diasporic double-conscious thinking. And here lies much of the attraction to Roth and other Jewish writers for Israelis.

7

Kashua's Complaint: A Palestinian Writer Meets Roth

Sayed Kashua uses Roth to negotiate his identity as an Israeli, but his path is by necessity quite different from the Israeli Jews whom I discussed in Chapter 6. Indeed, Jews are the majority in Israel and are overrepresented in Hebrew-language media and literary circles. Ashkenazi men are especially represented in the media in greater numbers than their proportion in the population. Nonetheless, they are not the only voices heard and faces seen. In fact, one of the most intricate works of association with Roth comes from a Palestinian citizen of Israel. In a newspaper column titled "A New Translation of Philip Roth Made My Life a Living Hell," Kashua gripes in his usual ironic tone about how reading about Portnoy's father's chronic constipation has caused him to suffer from the same gastric affliction.[1] That people have physical reactions to literature is well known; but this complaint is, if I might say, too visceral. Why does Kashua align himself to such an extent with Roth's work?

Despite the fact that he now lives in the United States, Kashua (b. 1975) is one of the best-known writers in Israel. His fame comes from two partially autobiographical prime-time television shows, four books of fiction, and a now discontinued weekly column in *Haaretz*—currently the most liberal Hebrew daily. Some of Kashua's prominence is surely due to his position as a Palestinian Israeli writing in Hebrew, the language of the Jewish population, and not in Arabic, his mother tongue. Kashua is acutely aware of the drawbacks and benefits of this status and makes sure his readers are too. Again and again, he highlights his role as an Arab man living and working within a Jewish national society, writing to a Jewish audience in their native language, and not always depicting his people in a positive light.

Kashua is not remiss in acknowledging Roth as an influence.[2] In the newspaper column cited above, he willingly admits that he wants to be more like Roth and, in an earlier piece, he describes his giddiness at meeting the American author in New York. There are three main ways in which Kashua uses Roth's figure. The first, which I will discuss rather briefly, invokes Roth's status as an author who was maligned by his community. As such, Roth is presented as an inspiration for Kashua, who, like Roth, has been accused of self-hatred. The second application is related to the first—Kashua presents Roth as a merciless satirist, especially of Jewish life, thus positioning himself as a much milder, forgiving writer. The third function is more specific to the Israeli context. Kashua points out that Roth is Jewish but not Israeli, while Kashua is Israeli but not Jewish. Roth's position is only partially familiar and related to the Jewish Israeli public; Kashua stresses this position so as to foreground the way he, too, as an Israeli Arab, is only half-familiar to this same audience. These three issues can be placed under another agenda: fortifying Kashua's position as a literary author.

Kashua's background needs some explaining for readers unfamiliar with Israeli society. Kashua is an Israeli Arab, or an Israeli Palestinian—the term is contested; I use both. Approximately 20 percent of the citizens are part of the Palestinian minority. Most are descendants of Palestinians who remained in the parts of their homeland that became the State of Israel after the War of 1948. Unlike Palestinians in the West Bank and the Gaza Strip, these men and women have, by law, the full rights of Israeli citizens. Yet, while in theory they *are* equal citizens (as individuals), in reality they suffer from discrimination and inequality. Still, their everyday lives, identities, and histories are different from those of Palestinians living in the occupied territories or in the Palestinian diaspora. As Karen Grumberg shows, this spatial in-betweenness of Israeli Palestinians—neither fully in Israel nor fully in Palestine, geographical entities (as imagined as any other geographical unit) that in reality overlap—is vital for Kashua's self-perception.[3]

One reason to pay special attention to Kashua when studying authorial image management is that his archive of persona manipulation is large and diverse. Like other writers, he can manipulate his public image in his fiction, interviews, and other public appearances. Kashua, unlike most other novelists, also produced a weekly column. Even though these short essays are not opinion pieces, but nearly always autobiographical sketches, they often have political implications. The columns are dramatized and perhaps fictionalized to some extent, but their subject is their author, and often the theme is Kashua as a famous professional writer describing meet-the-author engagements and random encounters with people who recognize him. Such columns give a critic interested in image projection tens of short, often dense, texts that help learn how Kashua fashions and refashions his persona.

Kashua was born in Tira (*al-Ṭīra*), but much of his education took place at a prestigious Hebrew-language boarding school in Jerusalem and at the Hebrew University, where he majored in philosophy and sociology. He worked as a journalist, among other things, reporting on the West Bank. The columns here date from a time he was renting a house in a Palestinian neighborhood in East Jerusalem. Kashua now lives in the United States after deciding to leave Israel for good in 2014. Much of this information is well known to the readers of his weekly column in *Haaretz* and to an international audience through translations of his columns and some press, including a *New Yorker* profile.[4] This move west gives some additional relevance to my argument about Kashua's identification with an American author.[5]

His first novel, *Dancing Arabs*, is a fictionalized autobiography that includes references to his father's stint in an Israeli prison, his own studies, and his mixed emotions about his place as a Palestinian in Israel.[6] His second novel, *Let It Be Morning*, is a much more complex fiction about an Israeli Arab journalist returning to his hometown after years of living in a Jewish city.[7] After only a few weeks there, the town is put under siege without explanation and all communication with the outside world comes to a stop. The citizens must fend for themselves. This disaster scenario makes Kashua's narrator contemplate his Israeli Arab identity, examining under strain what is one of Kashua's most ubiquitous concerns. The way members of Kashua's community behave toward one another and toward Palestinians without Israeli citizenship is satirized, though with some sympathy. *Second Person Singular*, which also appeared in the UK as *Exposure*, is a novel of marital jealousy and ethnic passing, by and large, a more realistic and emotionally subtle affair.[8] His latest novel, *Track Changes* (2017), incorporates his experience with immigration to the United States. Kashua's tone, especially in his columns and television show, is comic and ironic.[9] He satirizes Jews, Palestinians, people in general, and himself in particular. Though political and ethnic issues are often at stake, he is just as likely to burlesque family dynamics or his role as a minor celebrity in a small country as he is to aim his darts at the way Jews treat Arabs.

In "Mister Roth and I," Kashua describes his first stay in New York City and closes with a nervously expected meeting with the prominent writer at an Upper West Side café. After some pleasantries, Roth asks, "'So, what do you want?' … and I didn't know where to start. What do I want? Get him to sign the books, get him to tell me about Portnoy, about Zuckerman, about *Operation Shylock*, about *Sabbath's Theater*, tell me how he got started, what it was like with Saul Bellow."[10]

Discarding the idea of asking him about the novels, or about another author, Kashua tells the readers what he really cares about, thus revealing as much about himself as about Roth:

> What do I really want? I know perfectly well what I want. I want to know what it is like to be the enemy of the people, how do you face attacks from the people you belong to … I wanted to ask him how he felt when all American Jewry's leaders attacked his works, what did he do, how does he feel about it today.

Kashua is referring to the periods in Roth's career after the publication of the stories of *Goodbye, Columbus* and the novel *Portnoy's Complaint*, when several Jews, some of them very prominent rabbis and scholars, accused Roth's writing of Jewish self-hatred and supplying fuel to anti-Semitic flames. These attacks are almost always mentioned in journalistic profiles of Roth and have been depicted and parodied in Roth's writing, most prominently in *The Ghost Writer*.[11] We never receive Roth's answer. In fact, we can't be sure Kashua ever asked these questions at all because the column ends with Kashua's realization that what Roth was asking him was what he wanted for *breakfast*.

This misprision notwithstanding, Kashua's message here is clear to readers who know, and many would because he discussed it in his columns and interviews, that he has attracted accusations of betrayal and self-hatred from members of the Palestinian Israeli community. Mahmoud Kayyal describes the reviews of Kashua's first novel thus:

> Almost all of them were severely critical of its derogatory view of Arab society, and its contribution to the perpetuation of a stereotypic view of the Arab in the eyes of Jewish society. Muhammad Hamza Ghanayim emphasizes that "Kashua jeers at us Arabs, in Hebrew"; he is, therefore, "a tragically schizophrenic cultural hero," who engages in "a spiritual examination of himself and of the 'other' in completely Israeli terms, which completely distort the fragrance of the Arab in this, his first literary production."[12]

Gil Hochberg also gives an account of Kashua's reception, showing how Palestinian Israelis critiquing Kashua's television show see it as "cater[ing] to an Israeli Jewish audience to whom Kashua chooses to speak in familiar terms by uncritically adopting their racist perspective."[13]

By invoking Roth's trials with the Jewish community, Kashua suggests that Roth could teach him how to cope with the problems he faces with his own ethnic group. Here, Kashua offers himself as Roth's pupil in the art of handling public contempt. Kashua is a less experienced Roth. Kashua points out that they occupy similar positions and are part of the same tradition of artists and thinkers scorned by their society, a tradition that includes James Joyce and Gustave Flaubert and goes at least as far back as Socrates—a lineage Roth invokes in *The Ghost Writer* but would be known to many readers even if they had not read that novel. Kashua thus presents his struggles in a heroic light, a light bestowed by the literary luminary Roth.

If the earlier column emphasizes similarity, the later one emphasizes difference. In "A New Translation of Philip Roth Made My Life a Living Hell," after complaining about his constipation caused by his reading of Portnoy's father's bowel consternation, Kashua stresses that he actually admires Roth a great deal:

> I wish I could write like Roth-Portnoy writes about his family specifically and the Jews in general. It's not that I want to write about the Jews, I want to write about Arabs, but it's hard, and to write about them like that in the enemy's language, well, that's impossible. I will only dare to produce such hate-filled descriptions that go hand in hand with the consciousness of a common destiny when I learn to write in Arabic. Roth wrote English, his mother tongue and the language of the American Jews he depicts in the book. He wrote about them for them, not about them for others.[14]

There is quite a lot going on in this portion of the first paragraph. Kashua writes that he wishes he could be more like Roth, suggesting that, though he should be measured on the same scale as Roth, he is not as extreme as the American author. Kashua compares the ways he and Roth depict family life and the ethnic or national community. It turns out that he is not as mean-spirited as Roth was; but, though their art is similar in some respects, Kashua is quick to remind the reader that he and Roth do not share an ethnic background: it is not about Jews that he needs to write but about Arabs; and, because of this difference, he will certainly not write like Roth—at least not yet.

The main reason he brings here for not being able to be as satirical as Roth is this: he will not write against Arabs in the "enemy's language," Hebrew. Since literary Arabic is difficult to master, and most of Kashua's formal education was in Hebrew—a background many of his readers are already aware of—he is stuck.[15] The term "enemy's language" is ironic because it is, despite the conflict, also Kashua's. It is meant to be taken as an echo of his Palestinian critics who might wish to ignore or suspect him simply for this choice. According to Kayyal, at least some Arab intellectuals find that

> Hebrew writing by Arab authors is ... strange and incomprehensible, and such an act is a denial of the rich Arabic cultural, literary and linguistic heritage,

which is an essential component of the national identity. Moreover, such acts constitute sycophancy and treachery in the face of Israeli aggression, and are useless, in view of the weakness and marginality of the Hebrew language.[16]

While "enemy's language" is used to ironize his critics, it is also expedient in making his position more vivid when contrasting himself with Roth, who is presumably writing in the unproblematic language of his own community.

Kashua is somewhat disingenuous about Roth's actual position in the United States, especially in the early years of his career. Though English is the language of most American Jews, it is also the language of American gentiles, some of whom are anti-Semitic—an issue Roth dramatizes in *The Ghost Writer* when Nathan Zuckerman's father worries that, if published, the story that the young writer has produced based on a family feud over money will corroborate some of the worst stereotypes non-Jews have about Jews, and implores his son not to publish the story. Kashua showed awareness of these issues when writing "Mister Roth and I," cited above, but, in the later piece, he stresses the differences rather than the similarities.

Kashua wants to show that he is not as provocative and provoking as Roth was in the novel he has been reading. To remind my readers, *Portnoy's Complaint* tells of the dysfunctions and absurdities of the Jewish family and his own masturbatory and amatory exploits in what was in the late 1960s an almost unheard-of directness or vulgarity. Kashua is glad to tell the world that he appreciates the novel, but, unlike Roth, he is holding back, not going all the way. He wants his readers to know that he could be meaner, he could be more hateful, more revealing, more of a traitor. He is saying: look at Portnoy and see how difficult to digest my writing might be; think of things you have heard of Roth and realize how timid I am. He is signaling to his Arab-speaking readers that he is not as bad as they make him out to be; and, at the same time, he tells other, mostly Jewish, readers that there is much about his world they do not have access to despite reading his columns and novels. If they want to know more, they must put in more work than reading a thousand words every week in the newspaper and a novel every three years.

A case in point for his gentleness can be found in the second section of the piece, in which he describes a phone conversation with his parents. His mother warns him about drinking alcohol (prohibited by Islam) and informs him that they are going on the Hajj, the sacred pilgrimage to Mecca. Kashua's father was a lifelong member of the communist party and therefore presumably an atheist, but, though flabbergasted, Kashua does not berate his father for hypocrisy or inconsistency. He only makes gentle fun of his mother's belief in holy water's healing power and her hope that Playmobil toys will be less expensive in Mecca than in Israeli branches of Toys "R" Us.

Kashua's conversation with his parents can be compared with—it was possibly modeled after—a conversation (or rather a yelling match) between Alex Portnoy and his father. It is Rosh Hashanah high holiday, the Jewish New Year. The elder Portnoy asks young Alex to come to synagogue with him or at least change from his street clothes to something more appropriate for the holiday. Alex refuses, stating that "I'm not going to act like these holidays mean anything when they don't! ... There is no such thing as God, and there never was and I'm sorry but in my vocabulary that's a lie."[17] This argument sends the entire family into tears. When Portnoy divulges that his mother was in the hospital at the time, recovering from surgery, it seems even more mean-spirited to deny his father's requests. While an older Portnoy may suggest that Alex was a "little prick" for being so unkind to his father on this occasion, his disdain for organized Judaism has not passed by the age of thirty.[18] This is obvious from the diatribe against Rabbi Warshaw who, as Portnoy tells his psychologist, is "a fat, pompous, impatient fraud, with an absolutely grotesque superiority complex."[19] I will save you the worst of it. Though these statements may be ascribed to a young Portnoy, it seems that even at thirty he is happy to repeat them. As for Roth, he decided to include them in a published work and accept the censure they may draw. Kashua's tolerance toward his parent's extemporized Hajj seems even more magnanimous when situated against Roth's viciousness toward organized religion and its representatives. Remember, he is speaking with them as he reads *Portnoy*.

The image Kashua projects through Roth, the satirist holding back, is complicated and undercut by its own presentation. By saying that he has much more he could criticize and mock, he is suggesting how despicable his ethnic or national group might be. This is especially striking as Kashua has been quite rough on his own people in his newspaper work and even more so in his fiction. His first novel, for instance, depicts violence against children in the home and at school. Looking back at such scenes makes one wonder how terrible the things he does not talk about could be.[20] The idea that Kashua's columns are depictions of reality and not fabrications is fostered by their appearance in the newspaper, which generally promises its readers true reportage rather than fiction. It might seem that by simply stating that there are more vicious things to write, he is leaving it up to the reader to imagine the worst. Is this move more dangerous than simply revealing everything? This question will lead to the next way Kashua deploys Roth: showing both of them as only partially legible to the Jewish Israeli audience.

Jewish Israeli readers might be satisfied that, even if they do not hear everything, they know a lot about what is going on in Kashua's life and know that there might be more to tell. They might even imagine that it is possible to guess what Kashua would report if he dared. This potential is registered by the many Jewish Israeli critics, myself not excluded, who are happy to interpret or explain Kashua's writing to other Jewish Israeli and international readers. It is especially noticeable with those critics who, while not wrong in doing so, interpret Kashua as writing in a Jewish tradition or, figuratively, as a Jewish writer. Hanna Herzig, writing in Hebrew for an online magazine, shows how Kashua presents himself as a "comic anti-hero, pretty cowardly, passive." Thus, he is reminiscent of the "diaspora Jew" who "does not know quite how to deal with gentile society," which, for Kashua, is, as Herzig points out while invoking Woody Allen, Jewish Israeli society (Israelis as gentiles is a recurrent feature of Israeli discourse about diaspora, as you see). Yet, as Herzig underlines, Kashua is not totally estranged from this society; he always finds himself integrating into it, again very much like the widespread representations of the American Jew (Herzig writes before Kashua's move to the United States). In fact, Kashua's "Jewishness" is a recurring theme in academic engagement with his works. Thus, Adia Mendelson-Maoz and Liat Steir-Livny, focusing on his fiction and script writing, have found that Kashua often endows his protagonists with qualities that correspond with Jewish stereotypes, while Batya Shimony makes the case that Kashua integrates Jewishness into his Palestinian Israeli identity.[21] Clearly, part of Kashua's project is to make himself seem familiar to his audience, often through using a Jewish cultural vocabulary, a vocabulary that one must remember has also become familiar to American and international audiences through literature, film, and television. Indeed, the alignment with Roth can be read in those terms. We might say that reading *Portnoy* so viscerally is a way to simply emphasize a family resemblance between the Palestinian and the American. However, this framework needs some refinement.

Kashua will not let the readers stay satisfied thinking that they know what is going on in Kashua's life, nor will he let them think that they can fully understand him. Nor does he let us simply peg him as the Arab Philip Roth. Still in pain from constipation, Kashua appears in a panel discussion on the future of Jerusalem. He inevitably speaks about the clogged sewage system faced by Palestinian East Jerusalemites. This indeed may be a real problem but has a special (and humorous) significance for Kashua because of his gastric complaint. After the show is over, a deeply moved middle-aged woman comes up to him and says: "Your talk made me ashamed to be an Israeli … your pain was simply … so, so sincere." The butt of the joke is Kashua's Israeli audience. The woman sees the pain, which is indeed sincere, visceral in fact, but she mistakes its origin and therefore its significance. Instead of national Palestinian pain, it is personal physical pain and has nothing or little to do with her being an Israeli (though it does have everything to do with reading Roth).

The column that began with Kashua reading Roth ends with an example of an Israeli misreading Kashua, a case where a crucial piece of information was hidden from the Israeli auditors. The way Roth is partially readable to Israelis is important in seeing why Kashua is only half visible to the same public. Just before the scene I described, Kashua foregrounds Roth's distance from Israeli life: "I went on stage with tears in my eyes. The pain was unbearable, I cursed Roth and his father and Portnoy's mama [*im-imma shel Portnoy*]. Why should I suffer in twenty-first century Jerusalem because of some perverted Jewish man from the sixties?" Almost half a century and an ocean separate Kashua and Portnoy. (The column includes an illustration by Amos Biderman of Roth and Kashua with a toilet separating their images.) It is therefore unjust that their suffering should be shared, and indeed their complaints are not really the same. Kashua is fixated on a minor aspect of that novel; *Portnoy's Complaint* is more about sexual dissatisfaction and impotence (what Kashua suggests by calling Portnoy, or maybe Roth, perverted) than about constipation. The scenes depicting the father's battle with his bowels may be memorable but they are not the obvious center of the novel in any way. Nor is it insignificant that he does not mention that Portnoy visits Israel in the final section of that novel. The same chasm that exists between Kashua and Roth also appears between Roth and most of his Israeli readers. Jews but not American Jews, they only share part of Roth's cultural background.

In Kashua's *Second Person Singular*, this point is hinted at by invoking *The Human Stain* (translated into Hebrew in 2000), Roth's novel about Coleman Silk, an African American passing as a Jew. Amir, one of the two protagonists of Kashua's novel, finds himself assuming the identity of a young Jewish man who tried to commit suicide—passing as Jewish, just like Roth's Silk. Though not all of Kashua's readers would think of Roth's novel, I believe some do.

Racial or ethnic passing occurs in Israel. One example of passing has reached the headlines when it led to a rape conviction. Saber Kashour had sex with a

Jewish woman after presenting himself as an Israeli Jew named Dudu. He was first prosecuted for violent rape but agreed to a "rape by deception" plea bargain. Critics of the court's decision to accept this plea have said that in so doing the courts are justifying racism and subverting the rape laws.[22] Despite its occurrence, the phenomenon of Palestinians passing as Jews did not register in fiction, as far as I could ascertain, until *Second Person*. There are no other novels of ethnic passing about Arabs in either the Hebrew or the Palestinian tradition, though there are several novels about ambivalent and mixed identities: Yoram Kaniuk's *Confessions of a Good Arab* (1984, English 1988), for instance, is a story about a man with a Jewish mother and a Palestinian father.[23] To the best of my knowledge, *The Human Stain* is the only American novel about racial passing that was translated into Hebrew before the publication of the texts discussed here.[24] Kashua writes that, while fluent in English, he only reads translations from English.[25] This is the case with many educated Israelis. Kashua is probably not thinking or expecting anyone else to think of other American novels of passing, such as James Weldon Johnson's *The Autobiography of an Ex-Colored Man* or Nella Larsen's *Passing*. However, a reader who knows Roth's novel—or even its widely available if not especially successful screen adaptation—may recall *The Human Stain* when reading Kashua's novel. They would note that *The Human Stain*'s subject matter was quite distant from their experiences, even more alien than the Palestinian lives Kashua is describing. Racial and ethnic relations in Israel, though arguably as complex, are worlds apart from those in the United States.[26]

There is an additional aspect of Roth's identity that Kashua does not share. Roth is a Jew; Kashua is not. This gap also exists between Kashua and many of his readers. At the same time, Kashua's readers are also distant from Roth. Kashua and the public he seems to have in mind are Israeli citizens, lacking certain knowledge and assumptions that American authors and readers share. By calling attention to how Roth—an American Jew—is not wholly in sync with their understanding as Israeli Jews, Kashua stresses that he too is not absolutely legible to his readers as an Israeli Arab. They might easily understand Kashua as an Israeli but they run into difficulties when trying to understand him as a Palestinian. At the same time that Kashua makes efforts to make himself available to his Jewish readers by using their language, familiar cultural stereotypes, and aligning himself with Jewish authors, he is also keeping the readers at a distance, showing them that they can easily misread his motives and meanings. They should not jump to conclusions about what he does not tell them.

By playing with identification and identity, Kashua takes one step in a long-term project of marking himself as a half-decipherable figure and thus one deserving the attentive reading that goes along with the literary authority he seeks. Aligning and misaligning himself with Roth is one of the ways Kashua shapes his own role as a central Israeli author, at the same time as he adjusts his position vis-à-vis Israeli and Palestinian milieus. By playing with his location in the literary network, Kashua shapes the perceptions concerning his cultural-political significance and the value of his work.

Just as some other Israelis use Roth in order to be both (diasporic) Jewish and Israeli at the same time, Kashua uses Roth to be Jewish and not Jewish at the same time. These paradoxical constructions, much like others I described in this book, are enabled by the logic of affiliation that goes beyond but also corresponds with family resemblances. It is now possible for a writer to be entangled with Jewish identity and sometimes even be called Jewish by others without needing to ever claim any religious, racial, or ethnic filiation. This possibility is not an altogether new phenomenon. Since the late 1960s, John Updike, who is also known as a quintessentially white Protestant—goyish—writer, also managed to sport some Jewishness through his association with the likes of Bellow and Roth, as well as a series of stories and novels about a Jewish American writer alter ago named Henry Bech. As I have shown throughout this book, such complex contradictory identities based on networking are possible within the realm of literature. In the Coda that follows, I ask to what extent this identification by way of chosen networks functions for people who are not literary writers.

Coda

An August 23, 2018 headline in *Tablet*, a Jewish online magazine, asked, "Who Is Julia Salazar?" By posing this question, the reporter, Armin Rosen, suggests that there might be something less than straightforward about her identity. Salazar was then a candidate for the New York State Senate and receiving much more attention than most other state senate candidates. This was partly because of her membership in the Democratic Socialists of America—a leftist organization with commitments to the Democratic Party. As such, and as another young Latina woman (she was born in 1990), she was perceived as a close ally of Alexandria Ocasio-Cortez, who was beginning to gain the extensive attention that exploded after the November 2018 midterm election (Ocasio-Cortez's name comes up six times in Rosen's report—more than any other name apart from Salazar's). Another reason—important for my argument—that Salazar gained attention is her Jewishness. However, Rosen's piece undermines Salazar's Jewish identity with evidence that comes directly from the world of filiation, of family ties. Later commentators and Salazar herself will use a mix of discourses about affiliation and filiation to insist on Salazar's Jewish identity. The play of filiation and affiliation is the reason I want to begin this final section of the book with an examination of Salazar's story, all the time remembering the point made in the Introduction that there is no agreement over the question of what defines Jewish identity: nationality, genetics, ethnicity, religion, a combination of all of these, or something else altogether.

My interest lies not with Salazar's genealogy or psychology but with her self-presentation and how others reacted to it. This story will ask how people today identify Jews (outside of literary milieus) and what kind of evidence for Jewishness might be deemed legitimate in the diverse landscape of American Jewish media. I focus on responses that come from the explicitly Jewish publication *Tablet* and, by and large, the more liberal *The Forward*. My argument is about a certain strand in current Jewish thought; it does not imply that all American Jews would accept it. In fact, many would not.

To be fair, Rosen never actually writes that Salazar is not Jewish or is lying about being a Jew. What he does write is that her Jewishness is "largely self-created,"[1] that is to say, not inherited, not handed down from her family. He is accusing her of lying about her status as an ethnic Jew, even if he does not use the word "lie." True, some evidence comes from her former activity: "in her early 20s Salazar was a right-wing pro-Israel Christian," Rosen reports. This Christian past, he writes, is part of a longer history of inconsistency, inaccurate reports, lies, and extreme changes of direction, not all of which are connected to Jewishness. Nevertheless, his main issue with her Jewishness seems to be ancestry, not her old religious affiliations. According to Rosen, Salazar suggested that she grew up Jewish and that she is of Jewish descent. In order to show that she is misleading her audience, Rosen checks up on Salazar's family. Salazar's brother is quoted: "There was nobody in our immediate family who was Jewish ... my father was not Jewish, we were not raised Jewish."[2] From the brother he goes to the mother. In Orthodox Judaism, the mother—not the father—is the one who determines if the child is Jewish at birth. Therefore, if your mother is Jewish and you never converted to another religion, you are considered halachically Jewish, even if you have no religious knowledge or cultural affiliations. However, Salazar's mother is not Jewish (nor, to the best of my understanding, has Salazar ever claimed she was).[3]

Unlike Orthodox Halacha law, in our story the father is of greater importance than the mother. Ben Fractenberg at *The Forward* writes (before the Rosen exposé): Salazar "came from a unique Jewish background. She was born in Colombia, and her father was Jewish, descended from the community expelled from medieval Spain."[4] These reports are likely based on Salazar's own information. Here, genetic or ethnic Jewishness is invoked, not one that is based on Orthodox religious law (Reform Judaism accepts either matrilineal or patrilineal descent but demands an exclusive and public commitment to Judaism).[5] Rosen brings some proof to disrupt the idea that her father was indeed Jewish, questioning Salazar's filiation with Jews, even in a Reform context. The evidence is the brother's quote cited above and the father's funeral notice, which indicates "Prince of Peace Catholic Church."[6] Neither pieces of evidence disprove the story Salazar tells about her own life—perhaps the father was not involved in his funeral arrangements; it seems he died quite young and may not have expected a funeral; a partner or someone else could have chosen a Catholic service. The brother—who seems to have little contact with Salazar—could have his own reasons not to affiliate his family with Jewishness. After all, many people dislike complications—and being a Sephardi Jew of color is rather complicated. However, Rosen certainly shows that Salazar's story is less straightforward than it seems at first. At any rate, Rosen questions her ties to a Jewish family or to a Jewish past. He does not try to question the many Jewish affiliations with individuals and organizations she currently has. To return to the central terms of my project, he implies—never saying so explicitly—that affiliation cannot substitute for genetic filiations.

In the exposé's ending, the piece, which was focused on Salazar's individual shortcomings, turns into a case study in contemporary identity making, targeting a whole worldview rather than one politician. He writes: "The Jewish left ... has staked out a Jewishness that is proudly at odds with many of the longstanding markers of communal belonging—Julia Salazar is right at home in a milieu where religion, nation, denomination, and ethnic peoplehood don't matter as much." But as much as what? As they once did? As much as political like-mindedness? It seems like Rosen does not complete the thought. He does point to a milieu where old definitions of Jewishness do not matter but does not quite stipulate what defining attributes do matter. Rosen seems to be returning to the idea that in the current left everything and anything goes. Thus, he fears a kind of postmodern Jewishness where there is no anchoring for identity and anyone can take up the position of Jew if it so pleases them. Accordingly, he also suggests that, in the current "dislocation" of American politics, "identity is both obsessed over and self-fashioned."[7] Salazar's supporters are depicted as obsessives. They latch on to the fact that they have a woman with an intriguing minority background, a Sephardi Jewish woman of color with a history of immigration from Latin America, who shares their political views. Rosen disparages these supporters by showing that they seem not to care that much if this identity is based on lies or is, as he puts it more politely, "self-fashioned."

Some who would go to Salazar's defense—beyond her own statements, I will quote two other texts published in *The Forward*—argue that her identity is neither predicated on the question of her father's beliefs or descent nor was it plucked out of thin air. Rather, her Jewish identity is real because of the connection she created with Jewish individuals and institutions. After the appearance of the article, Salazar insisted that her Jewish identity is not made up. Rather, it has a basis in familial ties. At the same time, she gives up the idea that she has direct parental ties to Judaism, saying to a reporter: "Some of my extended family are Jewish; many are Catholic. Others converted from Judaism to Catholicism. My dad didn't identify as Jewish ... I converted, but my engagement with Judaism came from learning about my family background."[8] So, she did go through a reform conversion, in a way admitting that her family ties are not enough. Nonetheless, the way she sees it, this technical and educational process is not really what made her a Jew. She says, "I felt Jewish," which may sound like exactly the kind of self-fashioning Rosen derides. It is not! This Jewish feeling is due to a network of connections with a selective group of "extended family." However, I would argue that this filiation is so cherry-picked that it really constitutes more of a voluntary affiliation in the sense that I have been tracing in regard to writers. Salazar chose to affiliate with the members of her extended family in a way that runs parallel to how writers from Emma Lazarus to Nicole Krauss chose to affiliate with other Jewish writers.

Some commentators on Salazar's story explain how one can be Jewish by choosing to connect with Jews. Arielle Levites, an academic in the field of Jewish education, makes this point in an opinion piece for *The Forward*. In order to frame her commentary on Salazar, Levites describes how members of her own family believe, but are not able to prove, that they are descendants of illustrious rabbis. She accepts her family's unsubstantiated story because it gives her a sense of her own potential and a sense of belonging. She generalizes in a way that would have fit into the Introduction of this book: "personal narrative is not only about individual self-making. It's also about interpersonal relationship-making and in-group community-making as well."[9] Hanging on to imaginary (or real) ancestors helps her know who she is or can be. Her sense that her identity is built on potentially fictional filiation makes her accept Salazar's own identification as a Jew. For Levites, Salazar does not self-fashion her Jewishness; rather her "story about her Jewish identity tells us about who she *believes* her people are." The point is not who Salazar thinks she is but with whom she thinks she belongs. Levites makes the cogent point that, in contrast with some other identity groups, there is an accepted process for joining the Jewish people, conversion. One can decide to be Jewish in a way that is not possible if you wish you were or even feel you are an African American.[10] Yet the most crucial point for Levites is the connection to Jewish groups: "Most importantly, Salazar is known to be an active member of Jewish groups. She has been busy working to realize a version of a vibrant, moral Jewish worldview. You or I may not agree with that worldview, but she has been credibly affiliated with the Jewish community."

A letter, also published in *The Forward*, written by a group of Jewish men and women who associated with Salazar during their college years allows for an even more intimate example. The letter was written "to affirm who we know Julia to be as a Jew and as someone with moral character that we believe more than qualifies her to represent North Brooklyn in the New York State Senate."[11] This group acknowledges that Salazar's path to Jewishness was not straightforward: "her college years [were] a key period where her ... Jewish identity [was] shaped and formed." In other words, they knew her as she was becoming a Jew or reconnecting to Jewishness. Note that the verbs "shaped" and "formed" are in the passive. The letter's writers are going against, consciously or unconsciously, the notion that Salazar was actively self-fashioning her identity (a path Rosen's piece equated with lying). Instead, they hint that external factors came together to shape Salazar's identity. More explicit evidence for her Jewishness comes next: "During Julia's time on campus, we shared Shabbat dinners with her. We prayed with her. And we knew her in the many informal ways that living in a Jewish community draws its members close to one another." They show her practicing Judaism, yes; but, more importantly, they show that she practiced Judaism together with them. She is part of the group, not only performing that identity. The authors of the letter explain that they connected to Salazar in specifically Jewish ways—Shabbat dinners, prayer—and some less religious yet still Jewish activities that remained unspecified but marked with the word "community."

Mijal Bitton—a Jewish academic and community leader of Sephardi and Latino background—is unhappy with how these and other commentators in *The Forward* and elsewhere have defended Salazar's identity. Much like Rosen, she sees Salazar and her defenders as indicative of certain problems in liberal discourse and "identity politics." Bitton sees a contradiction in the discourse around Salazar. According to her analysis, the defenders argue that, on the one hand, people who do not understand Salazar's unique position as Latina, Sephardi, and a Jew of color cannot be allowed to comment on her identity (it is "protected property") and that, on the other hand, they argue that Jewishness is a malleable identity that may be appropriated by anyone who wishes to do so.[12] Fluid, anti-essentialist, so-called postmodern concepts of identity are applied only to Jewishness, Bitton fears. As she describes it, this position is inconsistent and, worse, suggests that "Jewish identity has less value than other minority identities and Jews as a collective do not have the right as a group to own their own self-representation." It seems to me, however, that Bitton is ignoring something crucial about the way in which many of these defenders understand Jewishness. It is not open for appropriation as she describes; the label Jew is not part of a so-called postmodern market of identities. It is not a T-shirt you can buy online. It is, however, an identity you gain if you put in the effort of connecting to it, its institutions, and with people who already hold it. Jewishness is a club you can join. Not everyone can be a Jew or speak for the Jews, but anyone could presumably connect themselves to enough Jews and Jewish institutions to achieve this right. Perhaps from Bitton's point of view or Rosen's this amounts to the same thing. However, the difference is the gap between a so-called postmodern or individualistic conception of Jewish identity and a conception that is based on networks and affiliation, between a concept of identity that is afloat in a sea of discourse and one that is anchored in social (or literary) networks, in community. It seems to me that the networked conception is more prevalent than some critics understand, while the more free-floating "postmodern" view of Jewishness is not as common as these commentators fear.

The reactions to Salazar's public persona show that there is a strand of thought in the contemporary Jewish community that predicates Jewish identity on networks of affiliations with other Jews and Jewish organizations. Birth or rulings by religious authorities are not the sole criteria and are perhaps less important than questions such as, Who do you spend your time with? How do you spend that time? And in which institutional contexts? So, in line with the argument I have been making about literary writers, Salazar is Jewish because she put in the work of connecting with Jews. Her Jewishness is not invented; it is affiliated. Furthermore, it seems that many American Jews would accept this kind of basis for Jewishness.

Julia Salazar was elected as a New York State senator in November 2018. Her victory cannot tell us how prevalent the belief in affiliated Jewish identity is. Nor can I answer this question by way of qualitative discourse analysis. I have no doubt that this strand of thought is not universal among American Jews, not even among secular ones. However, some evidence gathered by social scientists does suggest that versions of this approach have a hold in the American Jewish community. Ari Kelman and his colleagues point out that, at least for a portion American Jews, Jewishness is primarily thought about in terms of connection to others. Kelman and his colleagues interviewed Jewish men and women born after the Baby Boom generation and found that these Jews do not identify their Jewishness in terms of religion or genetically determined ethnicity. Instead, the interviewees used the word "tradition," which they—and this is the crucial point—associate with social ties. They practiced some Jewish rituals and felt culturally Jewish, but they did so in order to feel connected to the past and present Jewish community and as a justification for congregating with their friends and family (not necessarily Jewish friends and family).

For these interviewees, however, untying Jewishness from genetics or religious authority does not mean an embrace of an "everything goes" approach to Jewishness or identity in general. They are not "postmodern" Jews. Kelman and his colleagues report that "the implicit freedom to opt out of Jewishness never presented itself fully." They add: "tradition suggests a sense of a binding connection to other people in their immediate families—past and future—which our interviewees willingly subjected themselves to."[13] Tradition is a willing submission to binding (to return to the word Krauss chose when discussing Jewish ties), to filiation and affiliation, but it also suggests to what extent maintaining and creating this tradition is an identity-building labor that needs to be undertaken. A Jew must network Jewishly in order to maintain some of this sense of belonging. A Jew must attend a Passover dinner once in a while to maintain this kind of sense of tradition. Identifying as a Jew in the United States might not be a lot of work but it is more work than simply saying that you are a Jew. It is more similar to joining and keeping up appearances at a club than to buying a T-shirt. The world being what it is, some club members will always want to restrict membership or at least define "keeping up appearances" differently for people of different backgrounds. More would be expected when proving Jewishness from a Latina woman with Catholic relatives than from a man with an Ashkenazi-sounding name who looks like his entire family tree must be Jewish.

Armed with the idea that the concept of affiliated identities is also relevant to segments of the nonliterary Jewish population, we can return to literature. So, what is the relation between the affiliated identity for contemporary American Jews and affiliated identity in American Jewish literature? One could argue that fiction writers reflect this tendency. Jewish writers are part of the community and, to varying degrees, write for the Jewish American community. It would make sense for them to take up the idea of affiliated identities in their work. Inviting Kafka, Anne Frank, I. B. Singer, or Maimonides into their novels is the literary equivalent to inviting a distant aunt for Passover dinner; and, as we saw, two prominent writers, Englander and Foer, collaborated on a new *Haggadah*, incorporating the holiday into their body of work and their network of affiliations. It is what they do to be part of how American Jewry thinks of itself: people who celebrate Passover together.

However, I can offer a different, more ambitious view and one that will bring this book near its close. As I have shown, the tendency to acquire and shape literary Jewishness has been with American Jewish literature from early on. Emma Lazarus—a founder of Jewish American literature—connected both with biblical writers and with Heine at the end of the nineteenth century. Thus, writers have been concerned with affiliating identities even at a time when the prevalent idea of Jewishness was much more oriented toward religious authority than it is today. I suggest that writers and other public figures affiliated their public image with other Jews in order to form their identities and this is one of the forces that turned American Jewish identity into one that is self-consciously predicated on networks. Writers like Philip Roth negotiated their own identity but, in the process, also modeled for their public a certain way of forming and preforming identity. They showed how people could anchor their own Jewishness by way of affiliation. One path in this network is through the role of a reader of Jewish American writers. Becoming a reader of Jewish writers (American and otherwise) is a method for enmeshing within the Jewish network. It is a path many chose and one encouraged by a number of organizations, led by the Jewish Book Council.[14]

It is also the path I have chosen. Let me end with some thoughts about my own Jewishness and my own bonds, and to do so in relation to the image of the tied straps I chose for the cover of *Affiliated Identities in Jewish American Literature* (the choice was made in conversation with Lilac Hadar, my partner, who also drew the image).[15] Religious Jews (in contemporary Orthodox Judaism, only men) perform their morning prayers wearing *tefillin* (phylacteries). These are two boxes containing parchment with lines of scripture, one box is for the forehead and the other is for the arm. The Jew binds these boxes to his arm and head with leather straps. In a sense, they are the daily echo of the binding of Isaac, which we saw Krauss associate with the willing binding to Jewishness. In fact, one of the texts recited as part of the morning prayers is from the biblical verses about the binding of Isaac. The straps almost literally tie you to a textual tradition and, less literally, to other Jews performing the ritual, to those who performed it over the centuries and, if you are a believer, to your God. For observant Jews, every morning includes a ritual of binding, of tying, of affiliating. It is a voluntary self-binding, even if it is commanded by a higher law and might not feel voluntary to all practitioners.

On Israeli streets, it is common to meet religious men and adolescents—often associated with Chabad—asking other Jewish men to put on the *tefillin* (they keep several sets on hand) and pray. When I was younger, I would stop every once in a while and put on the *tefillin* with the help of the Orthodox man and read the short prayer from their little cards. I did so not out of faith but as a way to connect to my past or a different version of myself. After all, my grandfather

Fishel and grandmother Leah, who were considerably more *frum* than I am, had purchased a set of *tefillin* for me when I reached the age of thirteen and was supposed to commence the routine of daily prayers as a Jewish man. I used this set only once or twice; its leather straps were hard and stinging, not soft like the well-worn ones offered by the Chabad men on the street. This set of *tefillin* is stored somewhere deep in some closet of my parent's apartment along with my father's set, thirty years older, their straps probably still hard, having never been worn since my Bar Mitzva. I write "probably" because when my mother recently looked for them (I asked her to find them so Lilac could use them as a reference for her drawing), they could not be found. Still, they must be there. One does not throw away such gifts, nor pass them on. Perhaps they will be found by the time of my son's Bar Mitzva (if he chooses to have one)—perhaps he will find some interest in them, perhaps my daughter might. But, I am falling back on the convenient discourse of filiation: grandparents, parents, and children.

These days, I politely decline the public *tefillin*. I have grown intolerant of the Israeli versions of Orthodox Judaism, more resentful of the role its most powerful representatives play in some of the ills of my society. I am also less patient with practices that exclude women. My identity as a secular person is more secure, less negotiable. And anyway, I have less time—did I mention I have two children?—to stand around and playact tradition. But also, more importantly here, I found other ways to voluntarily bind myself with other Jews, ways I learned in part from Jewish American literature, from Philip Roth. I will not say that *Affiliated Identities in Jewish American Literature* is a kind of *tefillin*. That would be untrue, intolerably boastful, and more of a sacrilege then I am willing to commit in print. However, I can afford to say that my book can operate as the *tefillin*'s straps, the part of the *tefillin* depicted on the cover, connecting me, binding me, to the texts and authors that help me feel and show what kind of Jew I am.

Notes

Introduction

1. Philip Roth, *The Ghost Writer* (New York: Vintage, 1995), 47.
2. See Michael P. Kramer, "Race, Literary History, and the 'Jewish' Question," *Prooftexts* 21, no. 3 (2001): 287–321, https://doi.org/10.2979/PFT.2001.21.3.287. This paper will be discussed in further detail later on in this Introduction.
3. I elaborate my reading of *The Ghost Writer* in Chapter 1.
4. Erving Goffman, *Stigma: Notes on the Management of Spoiled Identity* (New York: Simon & Schuster, 1986), 2.
5. Goffman, 56–7, 62.
6. Goffman, 57.
7. Goffman, 71.
8. Thresholds is the literal translation of his French title: *Seuils*.
9. Gérard Genette, *Paratexts: Thresholds of Interpretation*, trans. Jane E. Lewin (Cambridge, MA: Cambridge University Press, 1997), 7–8.
10. See Chapter 2 for the development of this idea.
11. Saul Bellow, *Great Jewish Short Stories* (London: Vallentine, Mitchell, 1971).
12. See Ruth R. Wisse, *The Modern Jewish Canon: A Journey through Language and Culture* (New York: Free Press, 2000), 15–16.
13. Kramer, "Race, Literary History, and the 'Jewish' Question," 290.
14. Benjamin Schreier, *The Impossible Jew: Identity and the Reconstruction of Jewish American Literary History* (New York: New York University Press, 2015), 23.
15. I recommend also reading Schreier's working out of this argument in relation to film: Benjamin Schreier, "Filming Identity in the Jewish American Postwar; Or, on the Uses and Abuses of Periodization for Jewish Studies," *Shofar* 34, no. 3 (April 1, 2016): 76–101, https://doi.org/10.5703/shofar.34.3.0076.
16. See Schreier, *The Impossible Jew*, 211, n. 4.
17. Dan Miron, *Letting Go So As to Touch* (Tel Aviv: Am Oved, 2005), 158–9 [Hebrew]. Available in English: Dan Miron, *From Continuity to Contiguity: Toward a New Jewish Literary Thinking* (Stanford: Stanford University Press, 2010). I am referring to the Hebrew version here. I return to Miron in Chapter 6.
18. Miron, 165. For Deleuze and Guattari's own introduction of the term rhizome as a way of thinking through ever-changing, ever-developing networks, where any point could be an entryway and any sense of closed-off unity is illusory, see Gilles

Deleuze and Félix Guattari, *A Thousand Plateaus: Capitalism and Schizophrenia*, trans. Brian Massumi (Minneapolis: University of Minnesota Press, 1987), 3–24.

19 Bruno Latour, *Reassembling the Social: An Introduction to Actor-Network-Theory* (Oxford: Oxford University Press, 2005), 182–3.
20 Latour, 187.
21 Latour, 177. The example there is a linguist's office.
22 Latour, 252.
23 Latour, 203–4.
24 For a review of the importation of Latour into literary studies, see Rita Felski, "Latour and Literary Studies," *PMLA* 130, no. 3 (2015): 737–42. For some interesting adaptations, see Rita Felski, *The Limits of Critique* (Chicago: University of Chicago Press, 2015); Heather Love, "Close but Not Deep: Literary Ethics and the Descriptive Turn," *New Literary History*, 41, no. 2 (2010): 371–92; Elizabeth Outka, "Dead Men, Walking: Actors, Networks, and Actualized Metaphors in *Mrs. Dalloway* and *Raymond*," *Novel* 46, no. 2 (June 20, 2013): 253–74, https://doi.org/10.1215/00295132-2088130; David J. Alworth, "Melville in the Asylum: Literature, Sociology, Reading," *American Literary History* 26, no. 2 (2014): 234–61.
25 Felski, "Latour and Literary Studies."
26 Josh Lambert's work stands out in this respect. See Josh Lambert, *Unclean Lips: Obscenity, Jews, and American Culture* (New York: New York University Press, 2013); and, for more recent work: Josh Lambert, "The Gordon Lish Lineage of Jewish American Writing," *Literary Hub*, September 25, 2018, https://lithub.com/the-gordon-lish-lineage-of-jewish-american-writing/. Josh Lambert, "Publishing Jews at Knopf," *Book History* 21, no. 1 (December 4, 2018): 343–69, https://doi.org/10.1353/bh.2018.0011.
27 Amy Hungerford, *Making Literature Now* (Stanford: Stanford University Press, 2016).
28 James F. English, *The Economy of Prestige: Prizes, Awards, and the Circulation of Cultural Value* (Cambridge, MA: Harvard University Press, 2008).
29 Charles Horton Cooley, *Social Organization: A Study of the Larger Mind* (New York: Schocken Books, 1963), 168–210.
30 Goffman, *Stigma*, 47.
31 Eric Hayot, *The Elements of Academic Style: Writing for the Humanities*, Kindle (New York: Columbia University Press, 2014), chap. 5.
32 There is no need to be sad for the cut material because a good deal of it can be found in the book you are now reading. See David Hadar, "Medium and Author: Margaret Atwood on the Writer's Place in the Network of Literature," *Studies in Canadian Literature/Études en Littérature Canadienne* 42, no. 2 (2017): 109–31.
33 Albert Goldman, "'Portnoy's Complaint' by Philip Roth Looms as a Wild Blue Shocker and the American Novel of the Sixties," *Life* (1969) 58d.

34 J. Hoberman, "Wallace Markfield, Contender," *Tablet Magazine*, August 13, 2012, http://www.tabletmag.com/jewish-arts-and-culture/109053/wallace-markfield-contender.

35 Alfred Kazin, "The Writer as Sexual Show-Off: Or, Making Press Agents Unnecessary," *New York Magazine*, June 9, 1975, 36, https://books.google.co.il/books?id=g-kCAAAAMBAJ&lpg=PA3&dq=New%20york%20magazine%201975%20alfred%20kazin&hl=iw&pg=PA36#v=onepage&q&f=false.

36 Daniel L. Medin, *Three Sons: Franz Kafka and the Fiction of J.M. Coetzee, Philip Roth, and W.G. Sebald* (Evanston, IL: Northwestern University Press, 2010).

37 Zohar Weiman-Kelman, *Queer Expectations: A Genealogy of Jewish Women's Poetry* (Albany, NY: SUNY Press, 2018), xxv.

38 Charles Kadushin, "Social Networks and Jews," *Contemporary Jewry* 31, no. 1 (April 1, 2011): 65, https://doi.org/10.1007/s12397-010-9030-y.

39 A footnote for my readers who know something about Hebrew literature: that Brenner and Uri Nissan Gnessin were friends and perhaps even lovers is not of interest in this project. That Brenner wrote a moving canonical eulogy for Gnessin is; that many writers and critics have been obsessed with this relationship is also relevant.

40 Richard Jean So and Hoyt Long, "Network Analysis and the Sociology of Modernism," *Boundary 2* 40, no. 2 (2013): 148, https://doi.org/10.1215/01903659-2151839.

41 Mark McGurl, *The Program Era: Postwar Fiction and the Rise of Creative Writing* (Cambridge, MA: Harvard University Press, 2009), 55.

42 Patrick Cheney, "Influence," in *The Princeton Encyclopedia of Poetry and Poetics*, ed. Roland Greene et al. (Princeton: Princeton University Press, 2012), 705, https://www.degruyter.com/viewbooktoc/product/452252.

43 Harold Bloom, *The Anxiety of Influence: A Theory of Poetry* (New York: Oxford University Press, 1997), 11.

44 Bloom, 96.

45 Julia Kristeva, "The Bounded Text," in *Desire in Language: A Semiotic Approach to Literature and Art*, ed. Leon Roudiez, trans. Thomas Gora and Alice Jardine, rev. edition (New York: Columbia University Press, 1980), 36.

46 For a succinct history of intertextuality in its two versions, see Heinrich F. Plett, "Intertextualities," in *Intertextuality*, ed. Heinrich F. Plett (Berlin: Walter de Gruyter, 1991), 3–30; for a longer discussion that also includes influence, see Graham Allen, *Intertextuality* (New York: Routledge, 2000).

47 Richard Dyer, *Stars*, new edition (London: BFI Publishing, 1998). Several scholars have engaged with the idea of writers as celebrities and stars. Some good monographs on this subject include Timothy W. Galow, *Writing Celebrity: Stein, Fitzgerald, and the Modern(ist) Art of Self-Fashioning* (New York: Palgrave Macmillan, 2011); Loren

Glass, *Authors Inc.: Literary Celebrity in the Modern United States, 1880–1980* (New York: New York University Press, 2004); Graham Huggan, *The Postcolonial Exotic: Marketing the Margins* (London: Routledge, 2001); Aaron Jaffe, *Modernism and the Culture of Celebrity* (Cambridge: Cambridge University Press, 2005); Joe Moran, *Star Authors: Literary Celebrity in America* (London: Pluto, 2000); Lorraine York, *Literary Celebrity in Canada* (Toronto: University of Toronto Press, 2007); Lorraine York, *Margaret Atwood and the Labour of Literary Celebrity* (Toronto: University of Toronto Press, 2013). I will only have occasion to refer to a few of these books in the course of my argument, but they have all been part of opening up the possibility of discussing the issues of celebrity and public image in the context of literature.

Chapter 1

1   McGurl, *The Program Era*, 53.
2   McGurl, 51.
3   Ross Posnock, *Philip Roth's Rude Truth: The Art of Immaturity* (Princeton: Princeton University Press, 2006), 20.
4   Additional proof of the importance of Roth to the study of public image is that Joe Moran's *Star Authors*, the first book to extensively broach contemporary literary celebrity, dedicates a chapter to Roth (100–15). Another important scholar of literary celebrity dedicates a paper to him (Loren Glass, "Zuckerman/Roth: Literary Celebrity between Two Deaths," *PMLA* 129, no. 2 (2014): 223–36). Public image has often been acknowledged as an important tool for understanding Roth by Roth scholars as well; see especially the edited volume on the subject Aimee Pozorski, ed., *Roth and Celebrity* (Lanham, MD: Lexington Books, 2012).
5   The comparison to Joyce is not mine but Roth's. In *The Ghost Writer*, one of the chapters is named "Nathan Dedalus" (75), clearly invoking not only the mythological inventor but also Stephen Dedalus, the protagonist in Joyce's *Portrait of the Artist As a Young Man* and *Ulysses*. Joyce is invoked again as part of a group of writers, also including Flaubert and Thomas Wolfe, who were in conflict with their societies: a "literary history … of novelists infuriating fellow countrymen, family, and friends" (110). After aligning himself with Joyce there is a moment of disaffiliation on account of filiation: "But what about sons? It wasn't … Joyce's father who had impugned me for my recklessness—it was my own. Nor was it the Irish he claimed I had maligned and misrepresented, but the Jews. Of which I was one. Of which, only some five thousand days past, there had been millions more" (110–11). In acknowledging the connection to his father and the Jews, he shows that the Joycean exemplum is one that he will not be able to follow fully. For a much more

detailed examination of Joyce's role in *The Ghost Writer*, see Jeffrey Rubin-Dorsky, "Philip Roth's *The Ghost Writer*: Literary Heritage and Jewish Irreverence," *Studies in American Jewish Literature* 8, no. 2 (1989): 168–85.

6   Hermione Lee, *Philip Roth* (London: Methuen, 1982), 33.
7   Philip Roth, *Reading Myself and Others* (London: Vintage Books, 2007), 204.
8   Philip Roth, *The Counterlife* (New York: Farrar, Straus, and Giroux, 1986), 50–140.
9   Roth, *The Counterlife*, 278.
10 Edward Said, *The World, the Text, and the Critic* (Cambridge, MA: Harvard University Press, 1984).
11 Said, 17.
12 Said, 19.
13 Posnock quotes the same passage to introduce his chapter about the non-Jewish literary heritage. See Posnock, *Philip Roth's Rude Truth*, 88.
14 Ludwig Wittgenstein, *Philosophical Investigations*, trans. G. E. M. Anscombe, 2nd edition (Oxford: Blackwell, 1986), section 66, 32e.
15 Kramer, "Race, Literary History, and the 'Jewish' Question."
16 Philip Roth, *I Married a Communist* (London: Vintage, 1999), 106.
17 Bloom, *The Anxiety of Influence*, 11.
18 Virginia Woolf, *A Room of One's Own* (Adelaide: eBooks@Adelaide, 2015), chap. 3, https://ebooks.adelaide.edu.au/w/woolf/virginia/w91r/index.html.
19 Alice Walker, "In Search of Our Mothers' Gardens," in *Within the Circle: An Anthology of African American Literary Criticism from the Harlem Renaissance to the Present*, ed. Angelyn Mitchell (Durham, NC: Duke University Press, 1994), 407.
20 I am bypassing biographical and autobiographical works that take a parent as their direct subject. The most important example in Jewish American literature would probably be Art Spiegelman's *Maus*.
21 Grace Paley, *The Collected Stories* (New York: Farrar, Straus, Giroux, 1994), 3, 14.
22 Grace Paley, *Just as I Thought* (New York: Farrar, Straus, Giroux, 1998), 191.
23 This is not the case in *My Life as a Man* (1974), where two stories by the protagonist appear as the first section and are later commented on by the characters of the main narrative. Incidentally, these stories are the first appearance of Nathan Zuckerman in Roth's oeuvre. This Zuckerman has a somewhat different personal history than the one in *The Ghost Writer*.
24 See Philip Roth, *Portnoy's Complaint* (London: Jonathan Cape, 1969) 82, 85, 142–8. For the role of the shiksa in *Portnoy's Complaint*, see Sam B. Girgus, "Portnoy's Prayer: Philip Roth and the American Unconscious," in *Philip Roth's Portnoy's Complaint*, ed. Harold Bloom (Philadelphia: Chelsea House, 2004), 43–60. For the crucial place language has in Portnoy's sexuality, see Robert Forrey, "Oedipal Politics in *Portnoy's Complaint*," in *Philip Roth's Portnoy's Complaint*, ed. Harold Bloom (Philadelphia: Chelsea House, 2004), 119–28.

25 Eve Kosofsky Sedgwick, *Between Men: English Literature and Male Homosocial Desire*, 30th anniversary edition (New York: Columbia University Press, 2016).
26 "In his fantasy [Zuckerman] uses Anne Frank, who has become the symbol of innocence engulfed by evil, and more specifically of the tenders shoot of Jewish life exterminated by the Nazis, in order to regain the acceptance of the Jewish community offended by his art." Hana Wirth-Nesher, "The Artist Tales of Philip Roth," *Prooftexts* 3, no. 3 (September 1, 1983): 268.
27 The ties with Anne Frank are crucial for *The Ghost Writer*'s reception and for understanding Roth more generally. See, for instance, Debra Shostak, *Philip Roth: Countertexts, Counterlives* (Columbia: University of South Carolina Press, 2004), 123–8, 201–4; Aimee Pozorski, "How to Tell a True Ghost Story: The Ghost Writer and the Case of Anne Frank," in *Philip Roth: New Perspectives on an American Author* (2005), 89–102; R. Clifton Spargo, "To Invent as Presumptuously as Real Life: Parody and the Cultural Memory of Anne Frank in Roth's 'The Ghost Writer,'" *Representations*, no. 76 (Autumn 2001): 88–119; Emily Miller Budick, "The Haunted House of Fiction: Ghost Writing the Holocaust," *Common Knowledge* 5, no. 2 (1996): 121–35.
28 Philip Roth, "Acceptance Speech by Philip Roth for the Saul Bellow Award," *PEN America* (blog), May 31, 2007, https://pen.org/acceptance-speech-by-philip-roth-for-the-saul-bellow-award/. Augie March is the narrator of one of Bellow's major novels, *The Adventures of Augie March*. Like many of his novels, it is set in Chicago.
29 Michael Chabon, *Maps and Legends: Reading and Writing along the Borderlands* (London: Fourth Estate, 2010), 179.
30 Roth's characters often have few qualms about romantic relationships with students. In *The Dying Animal*, the protagonist, David Kepesh, finds a way to bypass sexual harassment laws by initiating romantic ties only after courses are over (but doing so every year). This is one of the areas in which Roth's preoccupation with sexual freedom prevents him from seeing ethical problems.
31 Nathan Englander, "In Conversation: Nathan Englander and Jonathan Safran Foer," *The Guardian*, February 10, 2012, sec. Books, https://www.theguardian.com/books/2012/feb/10/nathan-englander-conversation-jonathan-safran-foer.
32 Ari Y. Kelman et al., "Traditional Judaism: The Conceptualization of Jewishness in the Lives of American Jewish Post-Boomers," *Jewish Social Studies* 23, no. 1 (2017): 153–5, https://doi.org/10.2979/jewisocistud.23.1.05.
33 Saul Bellow, "Foreword," in *Preserving the Hunger: An Isaac Rosenfeld Reader*, by Isaac Rosenfeld, ed. Mark Schechner (Detroit: Wayne State University Press, 1988), 13–17.
34 Roth, *Reading*, [v].
35 Spargo, "To Invent as Presumptuously as Real Life," 97.

36 Set in Early Modern Spain, Donna Clara falls in love with a mysterious knight, pledging her feelings by way of anti-Semitic comments such as "Yes, I love thee, O my darling, / And I swear it by our Saviour, / Whom the accursèd Jews did murder, / Long ago with wicked malice." At the end of the poem, the knight presents his identity as "the son of the respected / Worthy, erudite Grand Rabbi, / Israel of Saragossa" (Emma Lazarus, *Selected Poems*, ed. John Hollander (New York: The Library of America, 2005), 129, 131).

37 Julian Levinson, *Exiles on Main Street: Jewish American Writers and American Literary Culture* (Bloomington: Indiana University Press, 2008), 28.

38 See Emily Miller Budick, *The Subject of Holocaust Fiction* (Bloomington: Indiana University Press, 2015), 23-5. For a different version, see Budick, "The Haunted House of Fiction." See also Patrick Hayes, *Philip Roth: Fiction and Power* (Oxford: Oxford University Press, 2014), 173-4.

Chapter 2

1 Galow, *Writing Celebrity*, 25. Italics mine.
2 Pozorski, *Roth and Celebrity*. See especially Miriam Jaffe-Foger, "Philip Roth: Death and Celebrity," 67-85; Mark Shechner, "Fanfare for Agoraphobia," 175-82.
3 Glass, "Zuckerman," 224.
4 Stefan Kjerkegaard, "Getting People Right. Getting Fiction Right: Self-Fashioning, Fictionality, and Ethics in the Roth Books," *JNT: Journal of Narrative Theory*, 46, no. 1 (Winter 2016): 121-48.
5 Liesbeth Korthals Altes, *Ethos and Narrative Interpretation: The Negotiation of Values in Fiction* (Lincoln: University of Nebraska Press, 2014), vii.
6 Korthals Altes, viii.
7 I should mention that the book includes a more nuanced analysis of one Roth novel, *The Human Stain* (Korthals Altes, 124-7, 138-9).
8 Korthals Altes, 55.
9 Boris Tomaševkij, "Literature and Biography," in *Readings in Russian Poetics: Formalist and Structuralist Views*, ed. Ladislav Matejka and Krystyna Pomorska, trans. Herbert Eagle (Cambridge, MA: MIT Press, 1971), 55.
10 Pia Masiero, *Philip Roth and the Zuckerman Books: The Making of a Story World* (Amherst, NY: Cambria, 2011), 8.
11 Rita Felski, *Uses of Literature* (Malden, MA: Blackwell, 2008), 14.
12 I am not the first critic to point this out: Barbara Hochman, coming from a tradition of reception studies, shows that what she calls "reading for the author," or seeing the author as a friend, was the prevalent view of reading throughout

much of the nineteenth century in the United States. She also writes that, even though the idea is "no longer readily apparent, at least to academics ... the desire for an author has never entirely disappeared" (Barbara Hochman, *Getting at the Author: Reimagining Books and Reading in the Age of American Realism* [Amherst: University of Massachusetts Press, 2001], 7). Carla Benedetti goes even further when she writes that "The act of enjoyment consists in the processes of attribution to an author," including what we know of his personal life, "necessary for the valorization of a text as work of art" (Carla Benedetti, *The Empty Cage: Inquiry into the Mysterious Disappearance of the Author*, trans. William J. Hartley [Ithaca, NY: Cornell University Press, 2005], 60).

13 Moran, *Star Authors*, 62–3.
14 Erving Goffman, *The Presentation of Self in Everyday Life* (Garden City, NY: Doubleday Anchor Books, 1959), 1.
15 James Phelan, *Reading People, Reading Plots: Character, Progression, and the Interpretation of Narrative* (Chicago: University of Chicago Press, 1989), 2.
16 Phelan, 2.
17 Phelan, 3.
18 Another option for naming this component is *genetic*. The term would make sense because this component concerns the creation of the character by the author in the same way genetic criticism is concerned with the process of creating a text.
19 Choice of narration is of great importance for this issue of public image negotiation, but, in order to stay focused on the issue of character, I must only reference Susan Lanser's contribution to the question of when the narrating "I" is likely to be identified with the author and Korthals Altes's development of it. See Susan S. Lanser, "The 'I' of the Beholder: Equivocal Attachments and the Limits of Structuralist Narratology," in *A Companion to Narrative Theory*, ed. James Phelan and Peter J. Rabinowitz (Malden, MA: Blackwell, 2005), 206–19; Korthals Altes, *Ethos and Narrative Interpretation*, 160ff. Some empirical testing on the question of author image creation has been carried out in Eefje Claassen, *Author Representations in Literary Reading* (Amsterdam: Benjamins, 2012).
20 Roth, *Reading*, 252–3.
21 Amy Fine Collins, "Once Was Never Enough," *Vanity Fair*, August 26, 2013, http://www.vanityfair.com/culture/2000/01/jacqueline-susann-valley-of-the-dolls-books.
22 Robert Towers, "The Lesson of the Master," *New York Times*, September 2, 1979, sec. Book Review, BR1.
23 John Leonard, "Fathers and Ghosts," *New York Review of Books*, October 25, 1979, 85, http://www.nybooks.com/articles/archives/1979/oct/25/fathers-and-ghosts/.
24 The issue of the close relation between the biographical Roth and his characters is a recurring theme in Roth criticisms. See, for example, Shostak, *Counter*, 159ff.

25 This example will be greatly expanded in Chapter 4.
26 Shalom Auslander, *Hope: A Tragedy*, Kindle (New York: Riverhead, 2012), chap. 13.
27 See Jennifer Glaser, *Borrowed Voices: Writing and Racial Ventriloquism in the Jewish American Imagination* (New Brunswick, NJ: Rutgers University Press, 2016), 22.
28 Bernard Malamud, *The Tenants* (New York: Farrar, Straus and Giroux, 1971), 60.
29 For a deeper reading of Malamud's problematic text, see Emily Miller Budick, *Blacks and Jews in Literary Conversation*, (Cambridge: Cambridge University Press, 1998), 11–19, http://search.ebscohost.com/login.aspx?direct=true&db=nlebk&AN =55548&site=ehost-live. Glaser, *Borrowed Voices*, 15–40.
30 James D. Hart and Phillip W. Leininger, "Humboldt's Gift" in *The Oxford Companion to American Literature*, 6th ed. (Oxford: Oxford University Press, 1995), http://www.oxfordreference.com/view/10.1093/acref/9780195065480.001.0001/ acref-9780195065480-e-2309. Italics mine.
31 Keith Cushman, "Discriminating Gusto," *Chicago Review* 27, no. 3 (1975): 147; see also Jack Richardson, "A Burnt-Out Case," *Commentary* 60, no. 5 (1975): 76.
32 Edmund Fuller, "Cowing Before the 'Gorgeous Project,'" *Wall Street Journal (1923 - Current File)*, 1975; Daniel Golden, "Money and Madness: Saul Bellow's 'Humboldt's Gift,'" *Studies in American Jewish Literature (1975–1979)* 2, no. 1 (1976): 23–30.
33 Roger Shattuck, "A Higher Selfishness?," *New York Review of Books*, September 18, 1975, 22.
34 Jane Barnes Casey, "Bellow's Gift," *Virginia Quarterly Review* 52, no. 1 (1976): 151.
35 Philip Roth, *The Breast* (New York: Vintage, 1994), 78.
36 Adam Kirsch, "Since When Is Philip Roth an Idol?," *The New Republic*, January 9, 2014, https://newrepublic.com/article/115970/philip-roth-claudia-roth-pierponts-biography-fan-fiction.
37 Michael Kimmage, "Philip Roth, Feminist," *Los Angeles Review of Books*, January 27, 2014, https://lareviewofbooks.org/article/philip-roth-feminist/.
38 Claudia Roth Pierpont, *Roth Unbound: A Writer and His Books*, Kindle (New York: Farrar, Straus and Giroux, 2013), chap. "Kafka's Children."
39 Roland Barthes, *Camera Lucida: Reflections on Photography*, trans. Richard Howard (New York: Hill and Wang, 1981), 67.
40 The first tweet is from July 15, 2013, while the photo must be earlier as David Foster Wallace died in 2008. At the time of writing, the tweet could not be found online; the photo can be found here: https://www.wikiwand.com/en/Antonio_Monda. The second tweet is from February 2, 2014, but the photo must also be somewhat older as it is labeled "#ThrowbackMonday": https://twitter.com/NathanEnglander/ status/430403809542950912.

41 Bob Peterson, *Author Philip Roth Posing Next to a Photo of Author Franz Kafka Whom He Resembles in Appearance & Whom He Owes Much in the Way of Inspiration as a Writer, 1968*, January 1, 1968, Photograph, https://www.gettyimages.com/detail/news-photo/author-philip-roth-posing-next-to-a-photo-of-author-franz-news-photo/50561635.

42 Goldman, "Wild Blue," 58c.

43 York, *Margaret Atwood and the Labour of Literary Celebrity*.

44 Rita Felski, *The Limits of Critique* (Chicago: University of Chicago Press, 2015), 170.

45 It is not by accident that some editions of Harold Bloom's *The Western Canon* use Raphael's masterpiece as their cover image.

46 Raphael, *The School of Athens*, fresco, 1509–1511 (Stanza della Segnatura, Papal Palace, Vatican); Raphael, *The Parnassus*, fresco, 1509–1511 (Stanza della Segnatura, Papal Palace, Vatican).

47 David Sax, "Rise of the New Yiddishists," *Vanity Fair*, March 31, 2009, https://www.vanityfair.com/culture/2009/04/yiddishists200904.

48 For some systematic discussion of the role interviews play in the literary system and the research done on this issue, see Anneleen Masschelein, Christophe Meurée, David Martens, and Stéphanie Vanasten, "The Literary Interview: Toward a Poetics of a Hybrid Genre," *Poetics Today* 35, no. 1–2 (March 1, 2014): 1–49, https://doi.org/10.1215/03335372-2648368. For a more detailed analysis of the genre as a path to authorial self-fashioning and as literary texts than I can provide here, see John Rodden, "The Literary Interview as Public Performance," *Society* 50, no. 4 (2013): 402–6, https://doi.org/10.1007/s12115-013-9684-7; and Galia Yanoshevsky, "On the Literariness of the Author Interview," *Poetics Today* 37, no. 1 (March 1, 2016): 181–213, https://doi.org/10.1215/03335372-3452668.

49 Roth, *Reading*, 18.

50 Roth, *Reading*, 281.

51 Roth, *Reading*, 282.

52 Bharati Mukherjee, *Darkness: Stories*, Fawcett Crest (New York: Fawcett Crest, 1992), xv.

53 Mukherjee, xvi.

54 Jonathan Freedman, *Klezmer America: Jewishness, Ethnicity, Modernity* (New York: Columbia University Press, 2008), 288. Affiliation is not the main issue in Freedman's book but only one tool among many.

55 Freedman, 287–91.

56 A very similar argument can be found in Bellow's review of Roth's first book. See Saul Bellow, "Goodbye, Columbus, by Philip Roth," *Commentary Magazine*, July 1, 1959, https://www.commentarymagazine.com/articles/goodbye-columbus-by-philip-roth/.

57 I shall have more to say about this hairy muse in Chapter 5.
58 Genette, *Paratexts*, 134.
59 For a discussion of blurbs that includes an extensive map of who wrote a blurb for whom, see Michael Maguire, "The Literary Blurb Economy," *Post45*, November 30, 2018, http://post45.research.yale.edu/2018/11/the-literary-blurb-economy/.

Chapter 3

1 Levinson, *Exiles*.
2 Glaser, *Borrowed Voices*.
3 Posnock, *Philip Roth's Rude Truth*, 91ff.
4 Hana Wirth-Nesher, *Call It English: The Languages of Jewish American Literature* (Princeton: Princeton University Press, 2009).
5 Jacobson was born a decade after Roth but only began publishing fiction in the early 1980s after Roth was already a celebrated even a canonical writer. He is sometimes called the "English Philip Roth," suggesting mainly his Jewishness but also, I believe, his interest in masculinity and the use of a comic tone in many of his novels. Jacobson reflects on this comparison, telling one interviewer that he was once asked: "How do you feel about being described as the English Philip Roth?" Politely but swiftly he answers "Flattered," suggesting that it is mostly a matter of the quality of their work that is in question. He adds: "'but I am more accurately the Jewish Jane Austen.' A spontaneous, reactive quip, designed to release me back into English Literature—for I am more English than anything else—though I guess the 'Jewish' didn't exactly help drive that home." Jacobson is explicit here about affiliation as a manner of performing identity—he is English because he is a version of Austen. Though the introduction of Jewish emphasizes how such formulations can also show up difference, it stresses that he is not exactly Austen because of his Jewishness (he could have said a modern-day or a male Austen). At any rate, both being a Jewish Austen and an English Roth stuck. Such titles are extremely useful for journalists, critics, and Wikipedia article writers. They use them to quickly place Jacobson as Jewish, English, and a serious literary writer who is at the same time also funny. See Gregory McNamee, "British Novelist Howard Jacobson on Being the Jewish Jane Austen," *Kirkus Reviews*, October 16, 2012 accessed April 5, 2018, https://www.kirkusreviews.com/features/british-novelist-howard-jacobson-being-jewish-jane/.
6 Adam Gopnik, "Mordecai Richler," *New Yorker*, July 9, 2001, https://www.newyorker.com/magazine/2001/07/16/mordecai-richler.
7 Because her Statue of Liberty poem "The New Colossus" (1883) is her best-known and most influential poem, some scholarly attention has been given to its biblical

resonances. Daniel Marom argues that the Statue of Liberty is the biblical matriarch Rachel, while Shira Wolosky identifies the Statue of Liberty with Deborah of the Book of Judges. The association is especially significant for me because Deborah was a prophet and a poet, producing the victory hymn known as "The Song of Deborah" (Judges 5:2–31). See Daniel Marom, "Who Is the 'Mother of Exiles'? An Inquiry into Jewish Aspects of Emma Lazarus's 'The New Colossus,'" *Prooftexts* 20, no. 3 (September 1, 2000): 250–2, https://doi.org/10.1353/ptx.2000.0020; Shira Wolosky, "An American-Jewish Typology: Emma Lazarus and the Figure of Christ," *Prooftexts* 16, no. 2 (1996): 114.

8   Lazarus, *Selected Poems*, 85.
9   H. L. Mencken, "The New Poetry Movement," in *Prejudices, First Series* (New York: Knopf, 1919), 83–96.
10 For an approach to the mixing of images of Jews and Asians in the United States in that period, see Freedman's chapter "Asians and Jews in Theory and Practice" in Freedman, *Klezmer America*, 251–81.
11 Mencken, "The New Poetry Movement," 87.
12 James Oppenheim, *Songs for the New Age* (New York: Century, 1914), 23, 79, http://archive.org/details/songsfornewage01oppegoog.
13 Oppenheim, 23.
14 "When the morning stars sang together, and all the sons of God shouted for joy?" (King James Version).
15 Daniel Boyarin, *A Traveling Homeland: The Babylonian Talmud as Diaspora* (Philadelphia: University of Pennsylvania Press, 2015). Boyarin's point of view is not uncontroversial.
16 Let me give you a taste of some of this introduction to the Talmud that is part of *The Rise of David Levinsky*: "The Talmud is a voluminous work of about twenty ponderous tomes. To read these books, to drink deep of their sacred wisdom, is accounted one of the greatest 'good deeds' in the life of a Jew." A little later he, like many a lecturer, asks a rhetorical question, "What is the Talmud?" and quickly answers:

> The bulk of it is taken up with debates of ancient rabbis. It is primarily concerned with questions of conscience, religious duty, and human sympathy—in short, with the relations "between man and God" and those "between man and man." But it practically contains a consideration of almost every topic under the sun, mostly with some verse of the Pentateuch for a pretext. All of which is analyzed and explained in the minutest and keenest fashion, discussions on abstruse subjects being sometimes relieved by an anecdote or two, a bit of folklore, worldly wisdom, or small talk. Scattered through its numerous volumes are priceless gems of poetry, epigram, and story-telling.

This goes on a little longer. Abraham Cahan, *The Rise of David Levinsky*, bk 2, chap. 1, accessed August 19, 2019, http://www.gutenberg.org/cache/epub/2803/pg2803-images.html.

17 Ezra Cappell, *American Talmud: The Cultural Work of Jewish American Fiction* (Albany: State University of New York Press, 2007), 17.

18 Irving Howe, *World of Our Fathers* (New York: Schocken Books, 1989), 589, http://archive.org/details/worldofourfather00howe.

19 Levinson, *Exiles*, 172.

20 Levinson, 188.

21 Levinson, 189.

22 Levinson, 190.

23 Cynthia Ozick, *The Pagan Rabbi and Other Stories* (New York: Schocken Books, 1976), 52. Further citations in the text will refer to this edition.

24 "It is not hard to concur with the many readers who have come to believe that Ozick based 'Envy; Or, Yiddish in America' on the acrimonious relationship between Isaac Bashevis Singer and other Yiddish writers during the time of Singer's ascendancy into the American literary mainstream through his translation into English," Kathryn Hellerstein writes before mentioning that Ozick never admits this connection. Kathryn Hellerstein, "The Envy of Yiddish: Cynthia Ozick as Translator," *Studies in American Jewish Literature* 31, no. 1 (2012): 25, https://doi.org/10.5325/studamerjewilite.31.1.0024.

25 Opening a short 1987 book about Ozick with a paragraph describing I. B. Singer's reputation, Pinsker writes in the second paragraph that "it would be hard to think of a contemporary Jewish-American writer *more* aware of tradition, of history, of the grip of the past." Sanford Pinsker, *The Uncompromising Fictions of Cynthia Ozick* (Columbia: University of Missouri Press, 1987), 1.

26 Philip Roth, *Shop Talk: A Writer and His Colleagues and Their Work* (Boston: Houghton Mifflin, 2001), 78.

27 Chabon, *Maps*, 166–7.

28 Chabon, 169–75, 179.

29 Levinson, *Exiles*, 28–9.

30 He publicly cut his ties with Ezra Pound.

31 Delmore Schwartz, *Once and for All: The Best of Delmore Schwartz*, ed. Craig Morgan Teicher (New York: New Directions, 2016), 212–13.

32 Schwartz, 213.

33 If we include Jewish intellectuals, the picture looks somewhat different with German-speaking expatriates Martin Buber and Hannah Arendt referred to in *Herzog* and *Mr. Sammler's Planet,* respectively (but not respectfully).

34 See Birte Christ, "The Aesthetics of Accessibility: John Irving and the Middlebrow Novel after 1975," *Post45*, July 1, 2016, http://post45.research.yale.edu/2016/07/the-aesthetics-of-accessibility-john-irving-and-the-middlebrow-novel-after-1975/.

35 Irving Howe, "Philip Roth Reconsidered," *Commentary*, December 1972, 74. Further citations in the text will refer to this publication.
36 Roth, *The Breast*, 77–8.
37 Roth, *Portnoy's Complaint*, 191.
38 Paley, *Just As I Thought*, 229–30.
39 Nicole Krauss, *The History of Love* (London: Penguin, 2006), 110–18.
40 Paley, *Just As I Thought*, 221.
41 Budick, *The Subject of Holocaust Fiction*, 127.
42 Foer's version:

> Felix Landau, a Gestapo officer in charge of the Jewish labor force in Drohobycz, became aware of Schulz's talents as a draughtsman, and directed Schulz to paint murals on the walls of his child's playroom. This relationship brought Schulz certain privileges, most importantly protection. Like a modern Scheherazade, he was kept alive for as long as his creation continued to please his captor. But, on November 19, 1942, Landau killed a Jew favored by another Gestapo officer, Karl Günther. Soon after, Günther came upon Schulz, on the corner of Czacki and Mickiewicz Streets, and shot him in the head. "You killed my Jew," he is said to have later told Landau, "I killed yours."

Jonathan Safran Foer, *Tree of Codes* (London: Visual Editions, 2010), 138.
43 Sanford Pinsker, "Jewish-American Literature's Lost-and-Found Department: How Philip Roth and Cynthia Ozick Reimagine Their Significant Dead," *MFS: Modern Fiction Studies* 35, no. 2 (1989): 234.
44 Budick, *The Subject of Holocaust Fiction*, 127–45.
45 Budick, 129.
46 Margaret Atwood, *Negotiating with the Dead : A Writer on Writing* (Toronto: Anchor Canada, 2003), 156.
47 Maurice Blanchot, *The Space of Literature*, trans. Ann Smock (Lincoln: University of Nebraska Press, 1982).
48 For my perspective on this theme in Atwood, see Hadar, "Medium and Author."
49 Philip Roth, *The Prague Orgy* (Harmondsworth: Penguin, 1987), 8. Further citations will refer to this edition.
50 Sisovsky may be referring to some Kafka critics' tendency to overemphasize biography as a tool for interpretation. Milan Kundera, who may be a source for Sisovsky, complains: "When people speak of [Kafka], they leave him only one context: Felice, the father, Milena, Dora; he is flung back into the mini-mini-mini-context of his biography." Milan Kundera, *Testaments Betrayed: An Essay in Nine Parts*, trans. Linda Asher (New York: HarperCollins, 1995), 270–1.
51 Mark Shechner, *Up Society's Ass, Copper: Rereading Philip Roth* (Madison: University of Wisconsin Press, 2003), 97–8.

52 Donald Kartiganer, for example, interprets the *Zuckerman Bound* volume that includes *The Ghost Writer* and for which this novella is the epilogue, thus: "[Zuckerman] links himself to the victimized, the muted, the dead as a vehicle for his voice." Kartiganer asserts that the Holocaust is "the powerful yet ghostly force" in *Zuckerman Bound*. Donald M. Kartiganer, "*Zuckerman Bound*: The Celebrant of Silence," in *The Cambridge Companion to Philip Roth*, ed. Timothy Parrish (Cambridge: Cambridge University Press, 2007), 150–1. David Brauner connects the issue of cultural continuity to fatherhood: "Like Lonoff in *The Ghost Writer*, Sisovsky's father represents a Jewish cultural patrimony for Zuckerman (a literary legacy that he can claim as his own)." David Brauner, *Philip Roth* (Manchester: Manchester University Press, 2007), 42.
53 Budick, *The Subject of Holocaust Fiction*, 147.
54 On Roth's visits to Prague, see Pierpont, *Roth Unbound*, chap. "Kafka's Children."
55 For example, Norman Ravvin, *A House of Words: Jewish Writing, Identity, and Memory* (Montreal: McGill-Queen's University Press, 1997), 53.

Chapter 4

1 James Wood, "Parade's End: The Many Lives of Nathan Zuckerman," *New Yorker*, October 15, 2007, http://www.newyorker.com/arts/critics/books/2007/10/15/071015crbo_books_wood?currentPage=all. Italics mine.
2 Theodor Adorno, "Late Style in Beethoven," in *Essays on Music*, ed. Richard Leppert, trans. Susan H. Gillespie (Berkeley: University of California Press, 2002), 564–8; Edward Said, *On Late Style: Music and Literature Against the Grain* (New York: Vintage, 2007).
3 One scholar writing on Adorno goes so far as to say that "the idea of a radical breakthrough in Beethoven's late work [drawn from Adorno] has become almost a literary trope or even cliché": Sven-Olov Wallenstein, "Adorno and the Problem of Late Style," *Site*, no. 31–2 (2012): 98.
4 John Updike, "Late Works," *New Yorker*, August 7, 2006, http://www.newyorker.com/magazine/2006/08/07/late-works.
5 Peter Boxall, "Late: Fictional Time in the Twenty-First Century," *Contemporary Literature* 53, no. 4 (2012): 681–712, https://doi.org/10.1353/cli.2012.0038; Matthew Shipe, "*Exit Ghost* and the Politics of 'Late Style,'" *Philip Roth Studies* 5, no. 2 (2009): 189–204, https://doi.org/www. See also Ira Nadel, "The Fate of Sex: Late Style and 'The Chaos of Eros,'" *Philip Roth Studies* 9, no. 1 (2013): 75–88, https://doi.org/www; Adam Zachary Newton, "'I Was the Prosthesis': Roth and Late Style," in *Roth after Eighty: Philip Roth and the American Literary Imagination*, ed. Aimee Pozorski and David Gooblar (Lanham, MD: Lexington Books, 2016), 127–49.

6 It is "as if Roth is summoning or channeling an orchestra of ghostly late styles to harmonize with his own" (Boxall "Late," 703). Adam Zachary Newton, who opens his paper on late style by insisting that the *Nemeses* quartet is not comparable to Strauss's *Songs*, points out that in one of these later novels, *Indignation*, Beethoven's last significant piece of music, Opus 135, also plays a noteworthy role. There, the protagonist smashes a record of Opus 135, opening the possibility, for Newton, that Roth may be trying to discourage his identification with late style. See "'I Was the Prosthesis': Roth and Late Style."
7 Philip Roth, *Exit Ghost* (London: Vintage, 2008).
8 See, for example, Robert J. Hughes, "Roth Says: Goodbye, Nathan," *Wall Street Journal*, September 28, 2007, https://www.wsj.com/articles/SB119093825978441978.
9 "On the one hand, [readers] are pressured to link beginning with end and—implicitly—to consider the Zuckerman books as a unified whole. On the other hand, they are invited to organize their interpretation around the concept of ending" (Masiero, *Philip Roth and The Zuckerman Books*, 216).
10 Nelly Kaprièlian "Philip Roth: 'Némésis Sera Mon Dernier Livre,'" *Les Inrockuptibles*, July 10, 2012, http://www.lesinrocks.com/2012/10/07/livres/philip-roth-nemesis-sera-mon-dernier-livre-11310126/.
11 David Daley, "Philip Roth: 'I'm done,'" *Salon*, November 9, 2012, http://www.salon.com/2012/11/09/philip_roth_im_done/.
12 Panio Gianopoulos, "Philip Roth: A Eulogy for a Living Man," *Salon*, November 10, 2012, http://www.salon.com/2012/11/10/philip_roth_a_eulogy_for_a_living_man/.
13 Glass makes a similar argument. See Glass, "Zuckerman," 234–5.
14 Adam Gopnik, "Happy Birthday," *New Yorker*, March 11, 2013, http://www.newyorker.com/talk/comment/2013/03/18/130318taco_talk_gopnik; David Remnick, "Philip Roth's Eightieth-Birthday Celebration," *New Yorker Blogs* (blog), March 20, 2013, http://www.newyorker.com/online/blogs/books/2013/03/philip-roth-eightieth-birthday-celebration.html.
15 Charles McGrath, "Struggle Over, Philip Roth Reflects on Putting Down His Pen," *New York Times*, November 17, 2012.
16 Elana Estrin, "Q&A With Nicole Krauss, Author of Great House and The History of Love," *Huffington Post: Books* (blog), September 15, 2011, http://www.huffingtonpost.com/elana-estrin/qa-with-nicole-krauss-aut_b_965230.html; emphasis added.
17 Ann Marsh, "The Emergence of Nicole Krauss," *Stanford Alumni*, September/October 2005, https://stanfordmag.org/contents/the-emergence-of-nicole-krauss.
18 Genevieve Fox, "Nicole Krauss on The History of Love," *Telegraph Book Club* (blog), February 6, 2011, http://www.telegraph.co.uk/culture/books/bookclub/8300960/Nicole-Krauss-on-The-History-of-Love.html.

19 Alice O'Keeffe, "Nicole Krauss," *The Bookseller*, May 19, 2017, 23.
20 Philippe Codde, "Keeping History at Bay: Absent Presences in Three Recent Jewish American Novels," *MFS Modern Fiction Studies* 57, no. 4 (2011): 689, https://doi.org/10.1353/mfs.2011.0097.
21 Boxall, "Late."
22 Amélie Nothomb, *Hygiène de l'assassin* (Paris: Albin Michel, 1992). It was translated thus: "Nobel Peace Prize winners are often assassins, but the literature winners are always assassins." Amélie Nothomb, *Hygiene and the Assassin*, trans. Alison Anderson (New York: Europa, 2010).
23 Budick, *The Subject of Holocaust Fiction*, 133.
24 Nicole Krauss, *Great House* (Camberwell: Penguin, 2010), 27.
25 Jennifer L. Knox, "20 Under 40: Q. & A.," *New Yorker*, June 7, 2010, www.newyorker.com/magazine/20-under-40-q-a.
26 One can also point out how Jewish, masculine, and non-American Krauss's list is comparted with others. For Krauss's further affiliation with Kaniuk, see the obituary she wrote for him, which echoes her Gursky texts: Nicole Krauss, "Born Again," *New Yorker Blogs*, June 12, 2013, http://www.newyorker.com/online/blogs/books/2013/06/yoram-kaniuk-postscript.html. In Chapter 4, I argue that Krauss, along with others of her generation, chooses to affiliate herself with Israeli writers. Going back to Shteyngart's relative disinterest in affiliation with Jewish and Israeli writers, I can argue that, as an immigrant from Russia, he has other ways to perform his Jewishness and other priorities when he creates his literary network.
27 I turn to such an honor partly because prizes and accolades are crucial features of the contemporary cultural scene and its economy of prestige: see English, *The Economy of Prestige*.
28 Pierre Bourdieu, *The Rules of Art: Genesis and Structure of the Literary Field*, trans. Susan Emanuel (Stanford: Stanford University Press, 1996); Pierre Bourdieu, "Social Space and Symbolic Power," trans. Loïc J. D. Wacquant, *Sociological Theory* 7, no. 1 (April 1, 1989): 14–25, https://doi.org/10.2307/202060.
29 John Guillory, *Cultural Capital the Problem of Literary Canon Formation* (Chicago: University of Chicago Press, 1993); Pascale Casanova, *The World Republic of Letters*, trans. M. B. DeBevoise (Cambridge, MA: Harvard University Press, 2004); English, *The Economy of Prestige*.
30 Gordon McMullan, *Shakespeare and the Idea of Late Writing: Authorship in the Proximity of Death* (Cambridge: Cambridge University Press, 2007), 10.
31 Janet Maslin, "The Story of a Book within a Book," *New York Times*, April 25, 2005, https://www.nytimes.com/2005/04/25/books/the-story-of-a-book-within-a-book.html.

32 See Louis Begley, "The Custom of the Country," *New York Review of Books*, June 23, 2005, http://www.nybooks.com/articles/archives/2005/jun/23/the-custom-of-the-country/.
33 Sanford Pinsker, "My History with *The History of Love*," JBooks.com: The Online Jewish Books Community, NA, http://www.jbooks.com/interviews/index/IP_Pinsker_Krauss.htm.
34 Patrick Ness, "Great House by Nicole Krauss," *The Guardian*, February 19, 2011, sec. Books, http://www.theguardian.com/books/2011/feb/19/great-house-nicole-krauss-review.
35 Janet Byrne, "Nicole Krauss's 'Great House' Reviewed," *Huffington Post* (blog), October 4, 2010, http://www.huffingtonpost.com/janet-byrne/nicole-krausss-great-house_b_747489.html.
36 See Paula Fredriksen, "Christians in the Roman Empire in the First Three Centuries CE," in *A Companion to the Roman Empire*, ed. David S. Potter (Malden, MA: Wiley-Blackwell, 2006), 595, https://doi.org/10.1002/9780470996942.ch30.
37 See R. Edelmann, "Ahasuerus, The Wandering Jew: Origin and Background," in *The Wandering Jew : Essays in the Interpretation of a Christian Legend*, ed. Galit Hasan-Rokem and Alan Dundes (Bloomington: Indiana University Press, 1986), 1–10, http://archive.org/details/wanderingjewessa00hasa.
38 See Galit Hasan-Rokem and Alan Dundes, *The Wandering Jew: Essays in the Interpretation of a Christian Legend* (Bloomington: Indiana University Press, 1986), http://archive.org/details/wanderingjewessa00hasa.
39 Paul Lacroix, "Notice bibliographique sur la legende du Juif errant" in Gustave Doré, *La légende du Juif errant* (Paris: M. Lévy, 1856), 7, http://gallica.bnf.fr/ark:/12148/bpt6k1045490m.
40 See Efraim Sicher, *The Jew's Daughter: A Cultural History of a Conversion Narrative* (Lanham, MD: Lexington, 2017).
41 William Shakespeare, *The Merchant of Venice*, ed. M. M. Mahood, New Cambridge Shakespeare (Cambridge: Cambridge University Press, 2003), l. 4.2.11.
42 Fagin is first introduced as "a very old shriveled Jew." Charles Dickens, *Oliver Twist* (New York: J. G. Gregory, 1861), 98, http://archive.org/details/olivertwist01dick. One character describes Riah in anti-Semitic terms that emphasize his age and role as a father: "Quite a Shylock, and quite a Patriarch. A picturesque gray-headed and gray-bearded old Jew, in a shovel-hat and gaberdine." Charles Dickens, *Our Mutual Friend* (New York, Continental Press, [n.d.]), 573, http://archive.org/details/ourmutualfriend00dickuoft. For a very extensive discussion of Dickens's depiction of Jews, especially the contrast between Fagin and Riah, see Harry Stone, "Dickens and the Jews," *Victorian Studies* 2, no. 3 (March 1, 1959): 223–53.
43 "Today one can find Schneerson's smiling visage gazing down from billboards in Brooklyn, staring up from the covers of books, and peering out from the walls

of Chabad members' homes, not to mention printed on countless other surfaces and objects. Although rabbi portraits are not new to contemporary Judaism, the sheer volume and intensity of Schneerson's photographic representations are unique in modern Jewish visual culture … The Rebbe's portrait was, and still is, deployed by various outreach campaigns led by Chabad emissaries, and also serves as a devotional icon for members of the Chabad movement itself." Ranana L. Dine, "The Age of Messianic Reproduction: The Image of the Last Lubavitcher Rebbe in Chabad Theology," *Journal of the American Academy of Religion* 85, no. 3 (September 1, 2017): 776, https://doi.org/10.1093/jaarel/lfx002.

44 Dine, 777.
45 For a study of the parallels between these characters, see Harold Fisch, "Elijah and the Wandering Jew," in *Rabbi Joseph H. Lookstein Memorial Volume*, ed. Leo Landman (New York: Ktav, 1980), 125–35. For some of these tales and their analysis in a wider context of Jewish lore about Elijah, see Kristen Lindbeck, *Elijah and the Rabbis, Story and Theology* (Berlin: Columbia University Press, 2010), 136–70, https://doi.org/10.7312/lind13080. For Elijah's role as protector, see Chana Shacham-Rosby, "Elijah the Prophet: The Guard Dog of Israel," *Jewish History* 30, no. 3-4 (December 1, 2016): 165–82, https://doi.org/10.1007/s10835-017-9262-4.
46 For a study of how beards make men look older, see Barnaby J. Dixson and Paul L. Vasey, "Beards Augment Perceptions of Men's Age, Social Status, and Aggressiveness, but Not Attractiveness," *Behavioral Ecology* 23, no. 3 (May 1, 2012): 481–90, https://doi.org/10.1093/beheco/arr214.
47 Philip Roth, *Goodbye, Columbus* (New York: Vintage, 1993), 144.
48 Krauss, *The History of Love*, 36. Further quotes will be from this addition.
49 Auslander, *Hope*, chap. 7.
50 I turned to Facebook to solidify this network of associations and I should thank Saul Noam Zaritt, Anna Bareretz Mowszowski, Tali Artman, Elana Gomel, Adriana Jacobs, Galit Hasan-Rokem, and others for their useful comments and feedback.

Chapter 5

1 Naomi Sokoloff points out that, compared to the central role Israel plays in other Jewish American fields of discourse, it is "a relatively minor topic in … imaginative writing." Naomi Sokoloff, "Israel in the Jewish American Imagination," in *The Cambridge History of Jewish American Literature*, ed. Hana Wirth-Nesher (Cambridge: Cambridge University Press, 2016), 362.
2 For example, Ranen Omer-Sherman explicitly focuses on more abstract notions of homeland and diaspora in his book on Zionism, Israel, and American Jewish

literature; even so, he does deal with texts depicting modern-day Israel as well. See Ranen Omer-Sherman, *Diaspora and Zionism in Jewish American Literature: Lazarus, Syrkin, Reznikoff, and Roth* (Hanover: Brandeis University Press, 2002). The most extended treatment of this subject, Andrew Furman's *Israel through the Jewish-American Imagination*, does deal with Israeli issues but almost always in a political context and almost always in ways that relate it back to Jewish American concerns. Andrew Furman, *Israel Through the Jewish-American Imagination: A Survey of Jewish-American Literature on Israel, 1928–1995* (Albany: SUNY Press, 1997). I must say that my aim is not to critique these scholars. I think it makes perfect sense for Jewish American critics reading Jewish American writers to focus on the American aspects of the texts.

3 There are some comparative studies, especially around issues relating to the Holocaust. These critics perform the work of affiliation but rarely discuss the authors' active networking. For example, Efraim Sicher, "In the Shadow of History: Second Generation Writers and Artists and the Shaping of Holocaust Memory in Israel and America," *Judaism* 47, no. 2 (Spring 1998): 169–85; Naomi Sokoloff, "Reinventing Bruno Schulz: Cynthia Ozick's *The Messiah of Stockholm* and David Grossman's *See Under: Love*," *AJS Review* 13, no. 1–2 (1988): 171–99, https://doi.org/10.1017/S0364009400002348.

4 The situation in popular and middlebrow fiction is significantly different, with Uris's *Exodus* providing a primary example.

5 Andrew Furman, "The Jewish-American Writer, Emergent Israel, and Allegra Goodman's 'The Family Markowitz,'" *Shofar* 16, no. 2 (1998): 8–24.

6 In the public sphere, this diagnosis is associated with the journalist Peter Beinart: Beinart, "The Failure of the American Jewish Establishment," *New York Review of Books*, June 10, 2010, https://www.nybooks.com/articles/2010/06/10/failure-american-jewish-establishment/. Beinart bases his argument on social research; see, for example, Steven M. Cohen and Ari Y. Kelman, "Thinking About Distancing from Israel," *Contemporary Jewry* 30, no. 2/3 (2010): 287–96. In a more recent book, Dov Waxman discusses the fracturing of American Jewry over Israel: Waxman, *Trouble in the Tribe: The American Jewish Conflict over Israel* (Princeton: Princeton University Press, 2016). The truth is that recent developments in Israel and the United States have been swift and often surprising, so academic and even journalistic accounts of American Jewish public sentiment and opinion have a hard time keeping pace.

7 Theodore Sasson, *The New American Zionism* (New York: New York University Press, 2015), 2–3.

8 Bernard Malamud, *Conversations with Bernard Malamud*, ed. Lawrence M. Lasher, Literary Conversations Series (Jackson: University Press of Mississippi, 1991), 42.

9 Saul Bellow, *To Jerusalem and Back* (New York: Penguin, 2012).

10 Emily Miller Budick, "The Place of Israel in American Writing: Reflections on Saul Bellow's *To Jerusalem and Back*," *South Central Review* 8, no. 1 (1991): 59–70, https://doi.org/10.2307/3189299.
11 Roth, *Shop Talk*, 20.
12 Philip Roth, *Deception* (London: Vintage, 1990), 101–2.
13 Roth, 102–3.
14 Roth, 103–4.
15 For a detailed description of the Sabra—the Zionist ideal of the Israel-born tough Jew—see Oz Almog, *The Sabra: The Creation of a New Jew*, trans. Haim Watzman (Berkeley: University of California Press, 2000). A more introductory description of the Zionist version of "New Jew" can be found in Cynthia M. Baker, *Jew* (New Brunswick, NJ: Rutgers University Press, 2017), 99–110.
16 Curt Leviant, *The Yemenite Girl* (New York: Avon, 1978), 182. Further references are to this edition. Despite the fact that on the novel's release it received a blurb from Saul Bellow, a number of reviews in major papers, a paperback edition, and even a Hebrew translation, *The Yemenite Girl* has received little to no scholarly attention. I suspect this situation will not change any time soon.
17 Saying that Israelis do not know what a *mezuza* or a *Siddur* are is quite an overstatement, I believe.
18 Mimi Haskin and Dina Haruvi explore the recurring and often degrading role Yemenite maids have in Hebrew literature from the 1930s on. In this at least Leviant is spot on regarding the conventions of Israeli culture. See Mimi Haskin and Dina Haruvi, "Yemenite Women Maids and Cleaners in Israeli Literature," in *Light Glistening with Tears: The Mizrahi Question in Educational and Cultural Contexts*, ed. Mimi Haskin and Nissim Avissar (Tel Aviv: Resling, 2019), 325–55.
19 Josh Lambert, "Since 2000," in *The Cambridge History of Jewish American Literature*, ed. Hana Wirth-Nesher (Cambridge: Cambridge University Press, 2016), 622 [Hebrew].
20 Sax, "Rise of the New Yiddishists."
21 Krauss, "Born Again."
22 Lambert, "Since 2000," 623. Lambert's source is an interview with Horn.
23 This is at least true of Jewish writers whose parents are Americans. This generation also includes Jews born in the former USSR—the most successful of these is Gary Shteyngart, who was mentioned a couple of times in this book. These immigrant or second-generation writers often have different ways to perform their Jewish affiliation. Lambert discusses this group, but see Deborah Wallrabenstein, *Sounds of a New Generation: On Contemporary Jewish-American Literature* (Bielefeld: Transcript, 2017), 147–86.
24 Dara Horn, "Living in Hebrew: On Jealousy and Creativity," in *What We Talk About When We Talk About Hebrew: (And What It Means to Americans)*, ed. Naomi B. Sokoloff and Nancy E. Berg (Seattle: University of Washington Press,

2018), 32. But note that her allegiance is to Hebrew (and its connection of Judaism) more than to Israeliness or Israeli Hebrew. This prioritization is visible with her favoring Agnon over Keret (though, to be fair, most readers of the Hebrew literature would agree that Agnon is the better writer and certainly the more canonical of the two).

25 The information about his stay in Israel and his attitude about it is taken from The Moth, a storytelling event series, *The Moth and the World Science Festival Present Nathan Englander: Man on the Moon*, 2012, https://www.youtube.com/watch?v=PXUExgJxSvI.

26 See, for example, Chicago Humanities Festival, *Etgar Keret and Nathan Englander in Conversation (1 of 4)*, accessed July 31, 2018, https://www.youtube.com/watch?v=Zlyl-2WgwtY.

27 @NathanEnglander, "Etgar Keret, Nathan Englander, twins reunited," *Twitter*, March 1, 2014, https://twitter.com/NathanEnglander/status/439936137591681024. This is a retweet (posting someone's else's Twitter message) from the original poster called @AragiAuthorNews. Since the post, this account seems to have been taken over by spammers. However, the name Aragi suggest that it once belonged to the literary agency Aragi Inc. I emailed the agency regarding the photograph, but they did not reply. I also tried to contact Englander directly without success.

28 Furman explains why there is less American Jewish fiction about Israel than one would expect by noting that "most Jewish-American writers ... lack the palpable and intimate knowledge of Israel that could stimulate good literature." Furman, *Israel through the Jewish-American Imagination*, 2. That's true, but lack of intimate knowledge has not stopped Malamud from writing about Russia in *The Fixer* or Italy in several short stories, nor has it stopped Ozick from writing about Poland in *The Shawl* or Sweden in *The Messiah of Stockholm*. Lack of experience and knowledge cannot be the sole explanation.

29 Its reasonable to assume that Englander does know that Etgar is an uncommon name.

30 Gregg LaGambina, "Interview: Paul Auster," *The A.V. Club*, September 6, 2008, https://www.avclub.com/paul-auster-1798214720. Square brackets are LaGambina's.

31 Krauss, "Born Again."

32 Krauss, "Born Again."

33 I want to acknowledge that the interactions between the two could easily be read as an example of the too common occurrence of an older man taking credit for a young woman's work and overtaxing her time. I am, however, focusing on what Krauss does with these interactions, not the broader gender dynamics they fit into.

34 Krauss, "Born Again."

35 Nicole Krauss, *Forest Dark*, Kindle (Bloomsbury, 2017), chap. "Out in the Blue." Further chapter titles refer to this edition.

36 Provisional Government of Israel, "The Declaration of the Establishment of the State of Israel," May 14, 1948, www.knesset.gov.il/docs/eng/megilat_eng.htm
37 Incidentally, an *Elle* profile reports that Krauss was in a relationship with Gon Ben-Ari, an Israeli writer. The initials match. See Keziah Weir, "Nicole Krauss Talks Divorce, Freedom, and New Beginnings," *Elle*, September 12, 2017, https://www.elle.com/culture/books/a12119575/nicole-krauss-profile-october-2017/.
38 Was *The History of Love* instrumental in making Alma a popular name? I would say yes, but cannot prove it. Krauss, at any rate, seems to think it was or at least has her character thinks so.
39 As it is described in the English version of the Yad VaShem website: [https://www.yadvashem.org/[18/2/2019]
40 I return to the image of binding in the book's Coda.
41 Krauss's move is an echo of the National Library of Israel's claim to some of Kafka's unpublished manuscripts, but I cannot elaborate on this context here.
42 Possibly now, after Grossman received the Man Booker International Prize, a little less explaining is necessary.
43 Joshua Cohen, *Moving Kings*, Kindle (London: Fitzcarraldo Editions, 2017), chap. "David."

Chapter 6

1 Dan Miron, *Letting Go So as to Touch* (Tel Aviv: Am Oved, 2005), 158–9 [Hebrew]. Here, I am expanding a point first presented in the Introduction to the present book.
2 See Deleuze and Guattari, *A Thousand Plateaus: Capitalism and Schizophrenia*, 3–24.
3 Amnon Raz-Krakotzkin, "Exile Within Sovereignty: Critique of 'The Negation of Exile' in Israeli," trans. Aviv Ben-Or, in *The Scaffolding of Sovereignty*, ed. Zvi Benite, Stefanos Geroulanos, and Nicole Jerr (New York: Columbia University Press, 2017), https://doi.org/10.7312/beni17186-021.
4 Raz-Krakotzkin, 394.
5 Amnon Hadary, *To Royal Estate: The Jewish Novel in America* (Tel Aviv: Am Oved, 1972), 15 [Hebrew].
6 Boyarin, *A Traveling Homeland: The Babylonian Talmud As Diaspora*, 19.
7 Yaron Peleg, "A New Hebrew Literary Diaspora? Israeli Literature Abroad," *Studia Judaica* 18, no. 2 (2016): 323, https://doi.org/10.4467/24500100STJ.15.014.4605.
8 Tal Hever-Chybowski, "Neither Alive, nor Dead: Hebrew as a Global Language," *Moznaim*, December 2015, 13–18 [Hebrew].
9 A note on my sources: I focused on Israeli periodicals in Hebrew. Almost all of the pieces I quote appeared in dailies. Israeli newspapers are overall not as well

cataloged as one would wish, despite laudable efforts. For the first half of Roth's career, I leaned heavily on the Historical Jewish Press Database, based in the National Library of Israel, where I could find a great variety of mentions of Roth, even in articles where he is not the main subject. For pieces published after 1990, I used the Beit Ariela Computerized Key to Daily Press, which is incomplete, to find pieces that have Roth as their main subject. I used Google searches, friends' recommendations, and my own alertness and recollection for the latter period to augment the findings in the Beit Ariela Key. I have not found or read everything written about Roth and other Jewish American writers in Israel, but I did cover a large amount of material. Obviously, not all of it can be included here. Several of the reviews (often by women) are not concerned with relating their identities to Roth but deal with the themes or problems raised by the individual novel. For example, most reviews of *The Humbling* and *Everyman* dealt with old age or depression, the themes of those late novels. Study of the Hebrew translations of Roth's texts is beyond the purview of this chapter; for a paper on this subject, see Inbar Kaminsky, "Jewish Mischief in the Land of Pranks: The Mistranslation of Philip Roth's *Operation Shylock* into Hebrew," *Philip Roth Studies* 8, no. 2 (2012): 197-208, https://doi.org/10.5703/philrothstud.8.2.197.

10 K. Yosef, "International Writers and Artists," *Herut*, May 22, 1959, p. 5. *JPress* [Hebrew].
11 "American-Israeli Dialogue Conference Commences," *HaTzofeh* June 17, 1962, p. 4. *JPress* [Hebrew].
12 Gershom Scholem, "Things As They Are," *Haaretz*, June 6, 1969, p. 22 [Hebrew]; or "Portnoy's Complaint," trans. E. E. Siskin, *CCARJ (Central Conference of American Rabbis)* (June 1970): 56-8. Alan Cooper discusses this piece not as an Israeli text but as one that represents European Jewish sensitivities: Cooper, *Philip Roth and the Jews* (Albany, NY: SUNY Press, 1996), 110-12. I believe he is right to do so, and I therefore do not dedicate further space to this piece. For a fascinating reading of Scholem's reaction to Portnoy that contextualizes it within his scholarly work on Jewish mystics—some of these mystics also lusted after gentile women—see Eli Shai, "Gershom Scholem's Attitude toward Sexual Subjects in the Works of Philip Roth and Agnon," *Jerusalem Studies in Jewish Thought* 21 (2007): 543-60 [Hebrew].
13 Roth, *Portnoy's Complaint*, 274.
14 R. Rabinowitz, "The American Jew on the *Psychiatrist*'s Couch," *Maariv*, June 27, 1969, p. 27. *JPress* [Hebrew].
15 Roth, *Portnoy's Complaint*, 265.
16 Shulamith Hareven, "The Great Crested Grebe and the Scandinavian Sofa; or, Springtime Impatience," *Maariv*, March 4, 1977, p. 37. *JPress* [Hebrew].
17 For an explicit statement on her adopted Levantine, Mediterranean identity, see Shulamith Hareven, "On Being a Levantine," in *The Vocabulary of Peace: Life, Culture,*

and Politics in the Middle East, trans. Malka Jagendorf (San Francisco: Mercury House, 1995), 81–7, http://archive.org/details/vocabularyofpeac00hare. There she is more anti-European, anti-Christian even, than anti-*Galut*. In the Israeli context, however, being against European cultures also has implications in the diaspora/homeland dichotomy. The idea that a woman born in Europe to European parents can take on the Levantine identity and say that the Levant has always been her true home echoes the negation of exile, even if it takes it in a direction that is not Zionist in a straightforward way.

18 I use this quote halfheartedly because Yitzhak Laor has been accused of rape and sexual harassment many times, and one can see some sexual violence in the review. See Lidar Gravé-Lazi, "Following Public Outcry, National Lottery Reconsiders Landau Prize to Poet Yitzhak Laor," *Jerusalem Post*, December 17, 2014, http://jpost.com/Israel-News/Following-public-outcry-National-Lottery-reconsiders-Landau-Prize-to-poet-Yitzhak-Laor-384930.

19 Yitzhak Laor, "The Bathroom was Small," *Haaretz, Tarbut ve-Sifrut* sec. 2, May 25, 2007 [Hebrew].

20 Matan Hermoni, "Beef Liver Instead of the Nobel Prize," *Haareztz, Sfarim* sec. 12, September 1, 2010, https://www.haaretz.co.il/literature/1.1219441 [Hebrew].

21 Giving Hebrew novels names in transliterated English is not an uncommon practice, though it obviously gives some indication that the novel has an international horizon. Some examples include *Dolly City* (1992) by Orly Castel-Bloom, *My First Sony* (1994) by Benny Barabash, and *Moving* (2003) by Assaf Gavron (who translated *Portnoy's Complaint* and stories by Englander).

22 Matan Hermoni, *Hebrew Publishing Company* (Modi'in: Kinneret, Zomora, Bittan, 2011) [Hebrew].

23 Matan Hermoni, ed., *America: The New World in Yiddish and Hebrew* (Tel Aviv: Am Oved, 2012) [Hebrew].

24 Shiri Lev-Ari, "What's Bothering Mordechai Shuster," *ynet*, March 24, 2011, https://www.ynet.co.il/articles/0,7340,L-4036704,00.html [Hebrew].

25 The Hebrew could be transcribed as Radler as well, but Hermoni, via email, suggested Redler. If the novel is translated into English, another decision might be made. (Personal communication, July 10, 2019.)

26 Matan Hermoni, *Spielvogel, Spielvogel* (Moshav Bet Shemen: Keter, 2019), 142 [Hebrew]. Further references will be to this edition.

27 Ortsion Bartana, "Black Wind Blowing," *HaTzofeh*, August 17, 2007, p. 14 [Hebrew].

28 The Hebrew actually says "New York," which I want to believe is a typesetter's or editor's mistake and not Ben-Ezer's.

29 Ehud Ben-Ezer, "On 'Portnoy's Complaint,'" *Al HaMishmar*, September 19, 1969, p. 6 [Hebrew].

30 Omri Herzog, "It's Not Easy Being a Jew: On *Portnoy's Complaint* Author Philip Roth's Wild Humor," *Haaretz Sfarim sec.*, March 2, 2010, p. 4 [Hebrew].

31 Arik Glasner, "A Short Note on Masculinity in Israeli Literature," *Free Critic*, June 13, 2014, https://arikglasner.wordpress.com/2014/06/13 [Hebrew]. A shorter version of this piece was published in *Yedioth Ahronoth*.
32 I am writing from my own perception of things as a member of Israeli society. Other researchers, however, have also described *Ashkenziyyut* as "the product of a local, dynamic, social-historical construction that is identified with Western culture and habitus," but because it is hegemonic, one of the "characteristics of the category of Ashkenaziness is that its members often avoid ethnic self-definition." Orna Sasson-Levy, "A Different Kind of Whiteness: Marking and Unmarking of Social Boundaries in the Construction of Hegemonic Ethnicity," *Sociological Forum* 28, no. 1 (2013): 29–30, https://doi.org/10.1111/socf.12001. See also her article (with Avi Shoshana) about passing as Ashkenazi, where this process "means Westernization," not identifying with Eastern European culture: "'Passing' as (Non) Ethnic: The Israeli Version of Acting White," *Sociological Inquiry* 83, no. 3 (August 2013): 561, https://doi.org/10.1111/soin.12007. For a quantitative study that shows that, while many Jewish Israelis prefer to define themselves as Israeli or Jewish, Ashkenazi and Mizrahi identities still play an important role in their identity, see Noah Lewin-Epstein and Yinon Cohen, "Ethnic Origin and Identity in the Jewish Population of Israel," *Journal of Ethnic and Migration Studies*, 45, no. 11 (June 27, 2019): 1–20, https://doi.org/10.1080/1369183X.2018.1492370.
33 Boyarin, *Traveling Homeland*, 54. W. E. B. Du Bois, *The Souls of Black Folk* (London: Penguin, 1996), 5.

Chapter 7

1 Sayed Kashua, "A New Translation of Philip Roth Made My Life a Living Hell," *Haaretz*, March 27, 2010, http://www.haaretz.co.il/misc/1.1194968 [Hebrew].
2 Bernard Avishai, the American-Israeli political scientist and commentator, takes at least partial credit for introducing Kashua to Roth's work: "I once gave a Hebrew translation of *The Human Stain* to an Arab-Israeli friend, the novelist and journalist Sayed Kashua ... He stayed up all night to finish it. *Portnoy's Complaint* had had a similar effect." The context is his book, *Promiscuous: Portnoy's Complaint and Our Doomed Pursuit of Happiness* (New Haven, CT: Yale University Press, 2012), 153.
3 See Karen Grumberg, *Place and Ideology in Contemporary Hebrew Literature* (Syracuse, NY: Syracuse University Press, 2011), 123–57.
4 Ruth Margalit, "Israel's Favorite Palestinian Calls It Quits," *New Yorker*, September 7, 2015, http://www.newyorker.com/magazine/2015/09/07/an-exile-in-the-corn-belt.
5 Incidentally, the decision to leave for the United States took place after I had written the paper on which this chapter is based.

6   Sayed Kashua, *Dancing Arabs*, trans. Miriam Shlesinger (New York: Grove, 2004). Original edition 2002.
7   Sayed Kashua, *Let It Be Morning*, trans. Miriam Shlesinger (New York: Black Cat, 2006). Original edition 2004.
8   Sayed Kashua, *Second Person Singular*, trans. Mitch Ginsburg (New York: Grove, 2012). Original edition 2010. Sayed Kashua, *Exposure*, trans. Mitch Ginsburg (London: Chatto & Windus, 2013).
9   As the literary critic Hanna Herzig argues, Kashua rarely shows himself using his authority directly but uses "tricks" to bring his messages home. See Hanna Herzig, "Sayed Kashua as a Jewish Anti-Hero," *Second Opinion* (2011), http://2nd-ops.com/2ndop/?p=6596 [Hebrew].
10 Sayed Kashua, "Mister Roth and I," *Haaretz*, February 1, 2008, sec. Weekend Supplement, 6 [Hebrew]. Some of Kashua's columns are available in *Haaretz*'s English edition, http://www.haaretz.com/; Sayed Kashua, *Native: Dispatches from an Israeli-Palestinian Life*, trans. Ralph Mandel (New York: Grove, 2016).
11 The best academic account of the Jewish backlash against Roth and his ways of handling it can be found in Alan Cooper's *Philip Roth and the Jews* (Albany: SUNY Press, 1996). For a journalistic yet comprehensive account, see Claudia Roth Pierpont, *Roth Unbound*, chap. "Defenders of the Faith."
12 Mahmoud Kayyal, "'Arabs Dancing in a New Light of Arabesques': Minor Hebrew Works of Palestinian Authors in the Eyes of Critics," *Middle Eastern Literatures* 11, no. 1 (April 2008): 47, https://doi.org/10.1080/14752620801896297.
13 Gil Hochberg, "To Be or Not to Be an Israeli Arab: Sayed Kashua and the Prospect of Minority Speech-Acts," *Comparative Literature* 62, no. 1 (2010): 84.
14 Kashua, "New Translation."
15 Hochberg explains, "Educated in a Jewish boarding school, his mastery of Hebrew far exceeds his knowledge of written Arabic (*fuṣḥā*). Furthermore, his existence and daily experiences, as his writings make clear, have always been in Hebrew, a fact that makes his writing in Hebrew a natural, if not necessary, choice … Writing in Hebrew never represents for Kashua and his narrators simply a movement away from the self (or 'true identity') and towards assimilation into the culture of the colonizer" (82).
16 Kayyal, 36.
17 Roth, *Portnoy's Complaint*, 61.
18 *Portnoy*, 64.
19 *Portnoy*, 73.
20 It needs to be acknowledged that this view suggests that satire is factual exposé and not a writer's construction. This is not what I maintain; rather, Kashua plays with this view in order to make his own point.
21 Adia Mendelson-Maoz and Liat Steir-Livny, "The Jewish Works of Sayed Kashua Subversive or Subordinate?" *Israel Studies Review* 26, no. 1 (June 2011): 107–29,

https://doi.org/10.3167/isr.2011.260111; Batya Shimony, "Shaping Israeli-Arab Identity in Hebrew Words—The Case of Sayed Kashua," *Israel Studies* 18, no. 1 (2013): 146–69.

22 Amir Fox, "Rape by Deception: On the Saber Kashour Case," *The Israeli Democracy Institute*, December 20, 2010, http://www.idi.org.il/ [Hebrew].
23 See Hochberg, "To Be," 71–3, for a brief history of this motif in Palestinian writing.
24 Tamar Mishmar's Hebrew translation of Nella Larsen's *Passing* was published in 2017.
25 Sayed Kashua, "Why I Refuse to Read Books in English," *Haaretz*, November 18, 2010, http://www.haaretz.co.il/misc/1.1230814 [Hebrew].
26 The association is relevant even if Kashua did not mean to insert it. However, there are a number of other parallels (large and small) between the novels that give reason to assume that Kashua was thinking of *The Human Stain* when working on *Second Person Singular*. Three examples should suffice: both use university or college campuses as a setting, both have a jealous husband as an important character, and both feature the use of handwriting experts.

Coda

1 Armin Rosen, "Who Is Julia Salazar? Brooklyn State Senate Candidate's Complex Personal History and Views," *Tablet Magazine*, August 23, 2018, https://www.tabletmag.com/jewish-news-and-politics/269094/who-is-julia-salazar.
2 Rosen.
3 "Their mother, Christine Salazar, indicated in a public September 2012 Facebook post that she planned on attending services at the Brooklyn Tabernacle, a nondenominational evangelical church in downtown Brooklyn" (Rosen).
4 Ben Fractenberg, "Julia Salazar Says Jewish Roots Helped Inspire Her Political Activism," *The Forward*, July 17, 2018, https://forward.com/news/405471/julia-salazar-says-jewish-roots-helped-inspire-her-political-activism/. See also "Julia Salazar," *Lilith Magazine*, Summer 2018, https://www.lilith.org/articles/julia-salazar/. Both of these are quoted by Rosen as an indication of how other reporters accept Salazar's version of her heritage.
5 Mark Washofsky, "How Does Reform Judaism Define Who Is a Jew?," ReformJudaism.org, June 6, 2013, https://reformjudaism.org/practice/ask-rabbi/how-does-reform-judaism-define-who-jew. For instance, the Central Conference of American Rabbis decided to consider a man educated in both Jewish and Christian belief systems as a non-Jew because he never committed to Judaism alone. See "CCAR Responsa on Patrilineal Descent, Apostasy, and Synagogue Honors (No. 5758.11)," Central Conference of American Rabbis, accessed August 5, 2019,

https://www.ccarnet.org/ccar-responsa/nyp-no-5758-11/. Such a man would need to undergo a conversion to be seen as Jewish, as Salazar did (according to her statement).

6 Rosen, "Who Is Julia Salazar?"
7 Rosen.
8 Charles Dunst, "Julia Salazar Forced by Furor to Clarify Her Jewish Background," *The Forward*, August 24, 2018, https://forward.com/news/breaking-news/408944/julia-salazar-forced-by-furor-to-clarify-her-jewish-background/.
9 Arielle Levites, "What Julia Salazar's Jewish Identity Taught Me About My Own," *The Forward*, September 5, 2018, https://forward.com/opinion/409702/what-julia-salazars-jewish-identity-taught-me-about-my-own/.
10 Salazar is sometimes compared to Rachel Dolezal, an academic and activist who presented herself as African American for many years despite her European ancestry. Dolezal was exposed by her parents in 2015 to much uproar.
11 Adam Jaffe, Adina Cooper, Allen Lipson, Eva Kalikoff, Julia Peck, Lizzy Wolozin, Maya Lee Parritz, Noah Schoen, and Tyler Dratch, "We Are Julia Salazar's Former Classmates: We Had To Speak Out," *The Forward*, September 5, 2018, https://forward.com/opinion/letters/409680/we-are-julia-salazars-former-classmates-we-had-to-speak-out/.
12 For a most explicit statement on the position Bitton goes against, see Ilan Stavans, "Think Julia Salazar Isn't 'Jewish Enough'? You're Writing Off All Latin American Jews," *The Forward*, August 28, 2018, https://forward.com/opinion/409157/think-julia-salazar-isnt-jewish-enough-youre-writing-off-all-latin/.
13 Ari Y. Kelman, Tobin Belzer, Ilana Horwitz et al., "Traditional Judaism: The Conceptualization of Jewishness in the Lives of American Jewish Post-Boomers," *Jewish Social Studies* 23, no. 1 (2017): 153, https://doi.org/10.2979/jewisocistud.23.1.05.
14 Regarding the Council, see Josh Lambert, "Since 2000," 632ff.
15 Several friends told me that the image reminds them of a swastika. This association was not our intention. Yet a vague shadow of the Nazi symbol is fitting for a book that had its origins with my fascination with Philip Roth's choice to write about Anne Frank as if she had survived the Holocaust.

Appendix: An Abridged Map of Author Connections

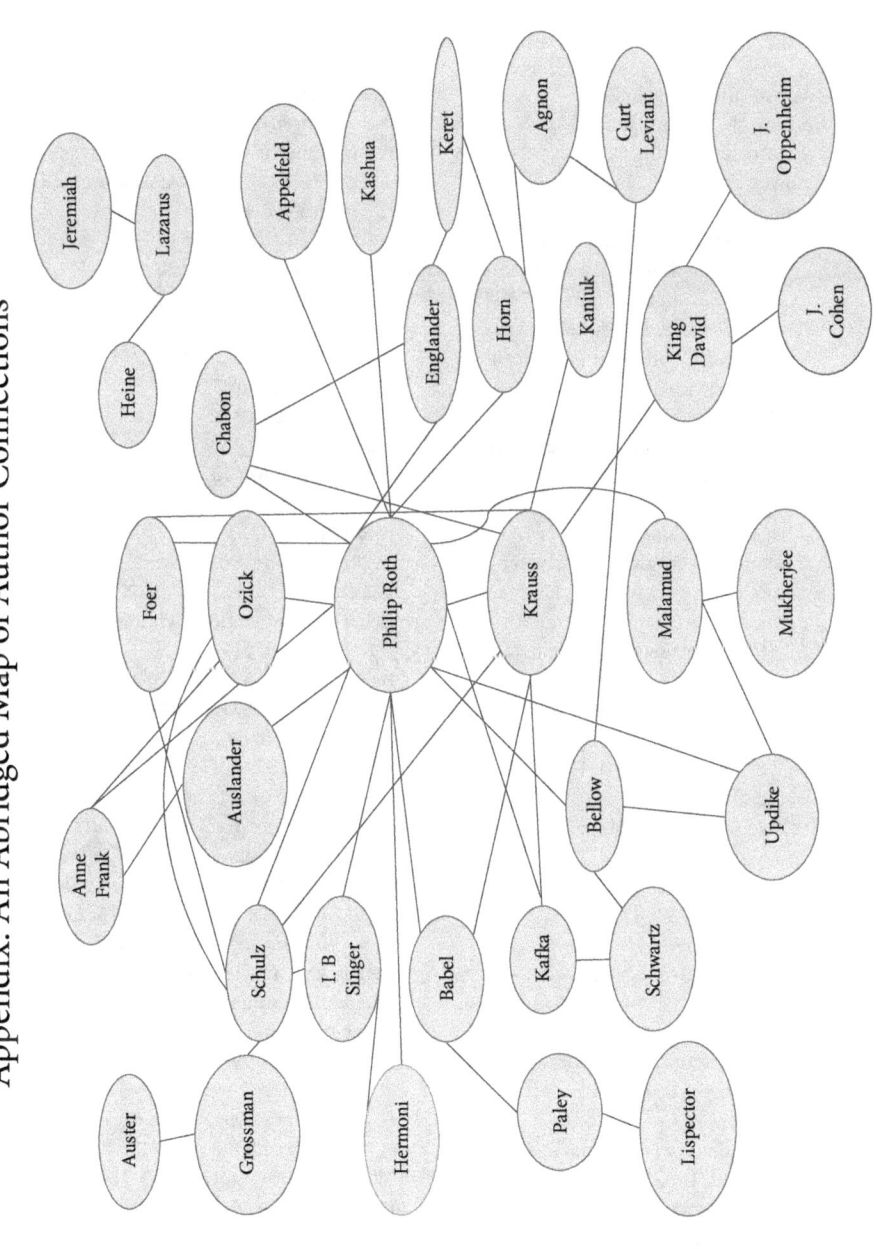

Index

Abraham (the Father) 121–2
Abramovich, Sholem Yankev *see* Mendele Mocher Sforim
acknowledgments 18, 51, 57–8, 116
Adorno, Theodor 86–7
affiliation, literary, between Jewish American and Jews writing in other European languages 71–83, 89–95, 119–24; between Jewish American and other American writers 61; between Jewish American and Yiddish writers 66–71; between American Jewish writers and Biblical author-figures 62–5; between American Jewish writers and Israeli writers 105–53; computer models of 14; effect on literary criticism 9–12; effect on non-literary Jewish identity 161–3; for reintroducing neglected authors 10–11; location of 41–59; vocabulary for describing 2, 23–39
African American writers 35, 49–50
Agnon, Shmuel Yosef 110–11, 113
Akiva, Rabbi 65
Allen, Woody 102–3, 150
Alter, Robert 11
Alvarez, Al 98
Amichai, Yehuda 96, 113
Amis, Martin 139
anti-Semitism 24–5, 63–4, 69–70, 76, 79, 93, 99–102, 108–10, 115, 121, 140, 146, 148
Appelfeld, Aharon 20, 107–10
Appelfeld, Itzak 108–9
Arabic 6, 143, 147
Ashkenazi identity (Ashkenaziness) 110–12, 138, 140, 161, 189 n32
Atwood, Margaret 10, 53–4, 78; *Lady Oracle* 10, 78; *Negotiating with the Dead* 78

Auslander, Shalom 48, 103; *Hope: A Tragedy* 48, 103
Austen, Jane 174 n5
Auster, Paul 116–17, 124; *Man in the Dark* 116–17, 124
author-characters 47–51
autofiction 42, 45, 49, 120
autopoetics 23

Babel, Isaac 1, 11, 27, 76–7, 93, 124
Bakhtin, Mikhail 17
Baraka, Amiri 49
Bar Mitzva 103, 163
Bartana, Ortsion 137
Barthes, Roland 52–3
beards 100, 102–3, 109
Beckett, Samuel 96
Beethoven, Ludwig van 86, 97
Bellette, Amy (fictional character) 24, 28, 31–4, 87, 103
Bellow, Saul 4–5, 8, 10–13, 27, 32–3, 35, 38, 48–50, 56–7, 58–9, 62, 65, 67, 72–3, 76, 96, 107–8, 110, 116, 118, 129, 132–3, 139, 145, 153; *Great Jewish Short Stories* 4, 38, 58–9, 65; *Herzog* 176 n33; *Humboldt's Gift* 49–50; *Mr. Sammler's Planet* 72, 176 n33; *Ravelstein* 49; *To Jerusalem and Back* 107–8, 110, 116, 118; Translating "Gimpel the Fool" 67)
Ben-Ezer, Ehud 138–9
Bernhard, Thomas 96
Berryman, John 50
Bible 37, 63–5, 99, 162; Exodus 113; Ezekiel 62–3; Genesis 121–2; Hebrews 99; Psalms 62, 64–5, 125; Song of Songs 64–5
biblical author figures 62–5, 124–5
bildungsroman 33–4
Binding of Isaac *see* Isaac
biofiction 48

biographical legend 43
biographical reading 43–6
biography 52
biography, fictionalized *see* biofiction
biography, group 13
Bitton, Mijal 159–60
Blanchot, Maurice 78
Bloom, Allan 49
Bloom, Harold 15, 28–9, 37, 58; *Anxiety of Influence* 15, 28–9
blurbs 59
body hair 116
Bolaño, Roberto 96
Borges, Jorge Luis 10, 96
Bourdieu, Pierre 97
Brenner, Yosef Haim 13
bris 72
British Jewish writers 62
Brod, Max 123
Brooks, Mel 102
Brown, Claude 49
Bruce, Lenny 55

Cahan, Abraham 65; *The Rise of David Levinsky* 65; Talmud 65; Yiddish 66–7
Canadian Jewish writers 62
celebrity 3, 17, 41–3, 53, 131, 145
Chabad 102, 162–3
Chabon, Michael 33, 55, 77, 112–13, 135; *Amazing Adventures of Kavalier & Clay* 112; *Kingdom of Olives and Ash: Writers Confront the Occupation* 113; *Yiddish Policemen's Union* 71, 113; *Wonder Boys* 33
Chekhov, Anton 1, 38
circumcision *see* bris
Cleaver, Eldridge 49
Coetzee, J. M. 12, 92, 96
Cohen, Joshua 124–5; *Moving Kings*, 124–5; *Witz* 125
computer models of networks 14
conflation of author with character 45–8
Conrad, Joseph 88; "Shadow-Line" 88
continuity/contiguity of Jewish literature 6–7, 127–8
conversion 38–9, 158–9
Cooley, Charles Horton 9
Creative writing programs 14–15, 33

Dante 54
Danticat, Edwidge 89
David, King of Israel 63–4, 124–5
David, Larry 102–3
Deborah the Prophet 174–5 n5
Declaration of Independence of the State of Israel 120
Dedications (as a location for affiliation) 35, 57, 59, 70, 77, 116–17, 121
Deleuze, Gilles 6, 127–8
DeLillo, Don 92
Diaspora 119, 127–41, 150
Dickens, Charles 102–3; *Oliver Twist* 102–3; *Our Mutual Friend* 102–3
Dolezal, Rachel 192 n10
Doré, Gustave 99–101; *La légende du Juif errant* 99–101
double consciousness 141
Douglass, Fredrick 49
Du Bois, W. E. B 141

editing (as affiliation) 35, 38, 59, 66–7, 77, 83, 113, 123, 134–5
Elijah the Prophet 102
Eliot, T. S. 25, 72
Ellison, Ralph 61
Emerson, Ralph Waldo 61–2
Englander, Nathan 34–5, 53, 55, 59, 107, 112–17, 161; *Dinner at the Center of the Earth* 115; *New American Haggadah* 34–5, 161; *What We Talk about When We Talk about Anne Frank* 59, 115–16
Erpenbeck, Jenny 96
ethos 42–3
Eugenides, Jeffrey 96
Eurydice 81–2
exile *see* diaspora
Ezekiel the prophet 63–5

family (as part of literary network) 29–31
family resemblance 2, 26–7
fathers 12, 26–32, 69–70, 78–9, 95–6, 101–2, 121, 148–9, 156–7, 163
Felski, Rita 8, 43–4, 54
Fitzgerald, F. Scott 41
Flaubert, Gustave 147, 167 n5

Foer, Jonathan Safran 10, 34–5, 45, 55, 77–8, 113, 161; *Everything Is Illuminated* 45; *Here I Am* 113; *New American Haggadah* 34–5, 161
forewords *see* introductions
Forster, E. M. 57
Frank, Anne 1, 16, 24, 26, 28, 32, 37, 48, 76, 79, 87, 103, 124, 161
Franzen, Jonathan 53, 96
Freud, Sigmund 25, 28
friendship (as affiliation) 13–15, 34–5

Gaitskill, Mary 96
Gavron, Assaf 113
gender 12–13
ghostwriting 39
Ginsburg, Allen 65
Glasner, Arik 139–40
Gnessin, Uri Nissan 166 n38
Goffman, Erving 2–3, 8–9, 17, 44
Gogol, Nikolai 1, 38, 51, 75
Gouri, Haim 107
grandparents 29–30, 57, 92, 104, 108, 162–3
Greenberg, Eliezer 67
Grossman, David 77, 96, 116–17, 124
Grossman, Ori 116–17
Guattari, Felix 6, 127–8

Hadary, Amnon 129
Haggadah, Passover *see* Passover
Hareven, Shulamith 132–3
Hebrew 5–6, 33, 38, 49, 56, 62, 69, 110–13, 121, 129–30, 143, 146–8
Hebrew literature 6, 13, 19, 64–5, 105–19, 123, 125, 129, 134–6
Heine, Heinrich 38–9, 71, 77, 124, 161–2
Heller, Joseph 11, 139
Hemon, Aleksandar 53
Herbert, Zbigniew 96
Hermoni Matan 134–6; *Spielvogel, Spielvogel* 135–6; *Hebrew Publishing Company* 134–5
Herzog, Omri 139
Holocaust, the 61, 76–83, 108–9, 111, 121, 140
Holocaust survivors 24, 48, 61, 72, 85, 89, 94–5, 102–4, 108–9

homosociality 31–2, 112, 114–15
Horn, Dara 48, 55, 113; *A Guide to the Perplexed* 48, 113; *The World to Come* 48
Howe, Iriving 66–7, 73–5, 79, 137; "Philip Roth Reconsidered" 73–5, 79, 137; *Treasury of Yiddish Poetry* 67; *Treasury of Yiddish Stories* 67; *World of Our Fathers* 66–7
Hutchins, Robert 33

identity, Israeli *see* Israeliness
identity, Jewish *see* Jewishness
identity, public *see* public identity
illustration *see* visual representation
immigrant writers 57–8, 66–7, 76–7, 123, 180 n26, 184 n23
influence 1–2, 15–16, 26, 28–31, 36, 48, 55, 58, 116–17, 143–4
interpretation (as affiliation) 37–8, 56–7, 65, 67
intertextuality (as a concept) 16–17
interviews (as location for affiliation) 8–9, 10, 24, 34–5, 55–6, 70–1, 91, 92–3, 108–9, 117, 135, 173 n48
introductions (as location for affiliation) 38, 56–9, 65, 76–7
Irving, John 73; *World Acording to Garp* 73
Isaac (biblical figure) 121–2, 162
Islam 148–9
Israel, Land of 63, 119–20, 128
Israel, State of 4–5, 12, 25, 48–9, 62, 71, 105–53
Israeli-Arab Wars 105, 107, 116–17, 132–3
Israeliness (Israeli identity) 110, 114–15, 124, 133–5, 127–41
Israeli-Palestinian conflict 25, 144, 147

Jacobson, Howard 62, 174 n5
James, Henry 14–16, 36–7, 44, 80, 82; *Aspern Papers* 44, 80, 82; "Middle Years," 36–7; *Portrait of a Lady* 16
Jarrell, Randall 50
Jeremiah the prophet 64
Jewishness/Jewish identity, association with old age 85, 99–104; attempts

to define 2, 4–6; binding 121–2,
162–3; defined as tradition 160–1;
defined as/by religion 4, 153, 156–8,
160–1; defined by affiliation 2,
23–39, 67, 75, 77, 121–2, 124, 134,
155–63; defined by anti-Semitism
140; defined by a religious textual
tradition 62–6, 119, 161–3; defined
by language(s) used 5–6, 61–3, 69,
102; defined by race, ethnicity, or
genetics 2, 4–5, 26–7, 153, 160–1;
in non-literary American context
6, 155–62; Israel 105, 113–14,
119, 125, 127, 137; performed and
produced 5–6, 12, 150, 153, 156–7,
159–60; resource in the literary
marketplace 113
Johnson, James Weldon 152; *The
Autobiography of an Ex-Colored
Man* 152
Jong, Erica 11
Joyce, James 24, 72, 147, 167–8 n5;
Finnegans Wake 72; *Portrait of the
Artist as a Young Man* 24, 167–8
n5l; *Ulysses* 167–8 n5

Kafka, Franz 1, 4, 11–12, 14, 17–19, 26,
32–3, 37, 45, 49, 51–3, 55–7, 71–5,
77, 79–81, 93, 96, 119–24, 161;
Americanized 122; as an Israeli
119–24; as a modernist 11–12,
71–2; *Metamorphosis* 75
Kaniuk, Yoram 96, 117–20, 152; *Last Jew*
117–20; *Confessions of a Good Arab*
152
Karr, Mary 96
Kashour, Saber 151–2
Kashua, Sayed 5, 127, 130, 138, 143–53;
accusation of self-hatred 145–7;
Dancing Arabs 145; insisting on
difference from Jews 150–3; *Let
It Be Morning* 145; "Mister Roth
and I" 145–7; "New Translation
of Philip Roth Made My Life a
Living Hell" 143, 147–53; read as
Jewish 5, 150, 153; satirist 147–50;
Second Person Singular (Exposure)
145, 151–2; television series 143,

146; *Track Changes* 145; Writing in
Hebrew 146–7
Kazin, Alfred 11
Kepesh, David (fictional character) 37, 51,
80, 169 n30
Keret, Etgar 59, 113–16
Kesey, Ken 33
King David *see* David, King of Israel
Klima, Ivan 108
Krauss, Nicole 10, 12, 48, 55, 59, 76–7,
85–6, 89–104, 107, 112–13, 117–25,
135, 158, 161; "Born Again," 113,
117–19; *Forest Dark* 59, 91, 99, 107,
119–25, 161; *Great House* 90, 95–6,
98–9; *History of Love* 76–7, 85,
89–104, 118–19, 121–2; Israel 107,
112–13, 117–25; obituary writing
91–4, 113, 117–19, 122; old age 48,
85–6, 89–104; reception 97–9
Kristeva, Julia 16
Kundera, Milan 14, 38

Laor, Yitzhak 133–4, 137
Larsen, Nella 152; *Passing* 152
late style 85–104
Latour, Bruno 7–8, 15, 25, 54, 128
Lazarus, Emma 12, 38–9, 62–4, 71, 158,
161–2; "New Colossus" 174–5 n7
" New Ezekiel" 62–3; as translator
38–9, 63, 71
Lee, Chang-rae 96
Levi, Primo 108
Leviant, Curt 110–12; *Yemenite Girl*
110–12
Levites, Arielle 158–9
Lispector, Clarice 76–7
literary affiliation *see* affiliation, literary
Lonoff E. I. (fictional character) 1–2,
24–39, 49, 76, 86
love 32–3, 36, 44, 82, 104
Lowell, Robert 50
Lubavitcher Rebbe 102

Mailer, Norman 5, 11, 27, 49, 139
Maimonides (Rambam, Moshe ben
Maimon) 48, 161
Malamud, Bernard 4–5, 8, 11–12, 27, 35,
49–50, 56–8, 62, 67, 73, 76, 106,

115, 129, 185 n28; *The Tenants* 35, 49–50
Mandelstam, Osip 93
Mann, Thomas 72, 86; *Doctor Faustus* 86
Mark Twain 107
Markfield, Wallace 10–11
Mason, Jackie 102
Melville, Herman 107
Mencken, H. L. 63–4
Mendele Mocher Sforim 66, 71, 73–4, 131
Mikan Ve'eylakh 130
Mizrachi Jews 12, 129, 140, 189 n32
mothers, 29–30, 37–8, 77, 78, 101, 104, 138
Mukherjee, Bharati 57–8; *Darkness* 57–8
muses 55, 59, 116

Nabokov, Vladimir 46; *Lolita* 46
Nakba *see* Israeli-Palestinian conflict
narratology 42–3
negation of exile 128–35
Netanyahu, Benjamin 140
networks, literary *see* affiliation, literary
New Jew 108–9, 111, 116, 131–2, 139
Nister, Der 48
Nothomb, Amélie 92–3; *Hygiene and the Assassin* 92–3

obituaries 62, 76, 91–4, 97, 117–19, 122
Ocasio-Cortez, Alexandria 155
Oedipus complex 7, 25, 28
old age 85–104
Olmert, Ehud 116
Oppenheim, James 63–4; *Songs for the New Age* 63–4
Orientalism 64
Orpheus 78, 81–2
Oz, Amos 116
Ozick, Cynthia 56, 67–70, 77; as critic 56; "Envy, or Yiddish in America" 67–70; *Messiah of Stockholm* 70, 77; as translator Yiddish poetry 67, 69

painting *see* visual representation
Paley, Grace 30, 76–7; "Goodbye and Good Luck" 30
paratext 1, 4, 41–2, 51–9, 85–6, 88, 96; *see also* biography, blurbs, dedications, interviews, obituaries, photographs, reviews, visual representations
Passing 151–2
Passover 34, 37, 103, 136–7, 161
Peres, Shimon 107
Peretz, I. L. 58, 65–6
Peterson, Bob 53–4
photographs 52–4, 114–15
phylacteries *see* tefillin
Plimpton, George 55
Pound, Ezra 72
public identity 1–4; performed in fiction 41–51; performed in paratexts 51–9
Pynchon, Thomas 117

Rabin, Yitzhak 107
race, Jews as a 5, 27
Raphael 55–6
reading (as affiliation) 33, 35–7, 43–4, 49–50, 51, 56–7, 76, 104, 111–12, 122, 134, 141, 143, 147, 150–1, 161–3
Reed, Lou 58–9
religion, statements against 148–9, 162–3
Rembrandt 90
reviews 46–7, 50–1 57, 70, 73, 85–6, 97–8, 131–40; Rhizome 6, 127–8
Richler, Mordecai 62
Rilke, Rainer Maria 72, 74, 96
rivalry (as affiliation) 35, 67–70
Roethke, Theodore 50
Roman-a-Clef 49
romantic relations (as affiliation) 16, 24, 27–9, 31–2, 81–2, 104, 121, 166 n39
Rosen, Armin 155–60
Rosenfeld, Isaac 35
Rosh Hashana 149
Roth Pierpont, Claudia 52
Roth, Ernst 89
Roth, Henry 57–8, 87
Roth, Philip 1–2, 8, 10–17, 24–39, 41–59, 61–2, 67, 70–83, 85–9, 92, 95–9, 101–3, 105–10, 113, 119, 122, 127–39, 143–53, 162–3; conflated with his characters 45–7; editor of "Writers from the Other Europe" 38, 77; Israel 25, 105–10, 131–2,

138; observer of the literary world 23–4; old age 85–9, 92, 95–9, 101–3; reception in Israel 127–39, 143–53; reception in United States 11–12, 45–7, 58–9, 73–5, 79, 137; retirement 88–9; Yiddish 30–1, 70–1

Roth, Philip, books and short stories by, *American Pastoral* 87; *Breast* 37, 51, 74–5, 135; *Counterlife* 25, 88, 115–16; "Conversion of the Jews" 103; *Deception* 108–10; *Dying Animal* 169 n30; "Eli, the Fanatic" 102, 109; *Everyman* 186–7 n9; *Exit Ghost* 42, 85–9, 98, 113; *Facts* 30; *Ghost Writer* 1–2, 16, 23–39, 42, 46–51, 67, 76, 78–9, 87–8, 103–4, 146–8; *Human Stain* 87, 152–3; *Humbling* 186–7 n9; *I Married a Communist* 26, 28, 87; *Letting Go* 15–16; "Looking at Kafka" 32–3, 37, 47, 57, 122; *My Life as a Man* 47, 135, 168 n23; *Nemeses* 89; *Nemesis* 88, 98; *Operation Shylock* 45, 105–6; *Patrimony* 95–6; *Plot against America* 133, 137; *Portnoy's Complaint* 18–19, 31, 45–7, 51, 53, 55–6, 73–4, 78, 99, 105, 131–9, 134, 145–51; *Prague Orgy* 78–83; *Professor of Desire* 51, 80; *Reading Myself and Others* 35, 56; *Sabbath's Theater* 145; *Shop Talk* 56–7, 108; *Why Write? Collected Nonfiction 1960-2013* 56

Sabra *see* New Jew
Said, Edward 25–7, 86
St. Paul 99
Salazar, Julia 12, 155–61
Salinger, J. D. 5
Sappho 54
Schneerson, Menachem Mendel *see* Mendele Mocher Sforim
Scholem, Gershom 131
Schulz, Bruno 19, 38, 56, 70–1, 77–8, 82–3, 95, 96, 177 n42
Schwartz, Delmore 49–51, 58, 72; "In Dreams Begin Responsibilities" 49; *Shenandoah* 72

Scott, Sir Walter 101; *Ivanhoe* 101
Sebald, W. G. 12, 96
Seder *see* Passover
Sedgwick, Eve Kosofsky 31–2
Sexism 11, 29, 45, 133
Shahar, David 107
Shakespeare, William 86–7, 101; *Merchant of Venice* 101
Sheaffer, Tim 55
Sholem Aleichem 66, 71
Shteyngart, Gary 53, 96, 180 n26
Singer, Isaac Bashevis 5, 49, 56, 67–73, 124, 134, 136; "Gimpel, the Fool," 67, 136
Smith, Zadie 53
sociology 2–3, 7, 9–10, 145
sociology of literature 8–9, 14, 54–5, 97
Socrates 147
Solomon, King 64
Spiegelman, Art 160 n20; *Maus* 160 n20
stand-up comedy 55, 75, 102–3
star text 17
Stegner, Wallace 33
Strauss, Richard 87–9
student-teacher relationships *see* teacher-student relationships
Susann, Jacqueline 45–6

Talmud 6, 37, 58, 64–5, 119, 129
teacher-student relationships (as affiliation) 24, 30, 32–4, 58–9, 69
tefillin 162–3
Tolstoy, Leo 93
Tomaševkij, Boris 43
translation (as affiliation) 38–9, 56, 63, 67, 69–70, 83, 90, 93, 104, 111, 113–15, 130

Updike, John 11, 86, 132–3, 152
Uris, Leon 58–9, 133, 138, 183 n4; *Exodus* 58–9, 133, 138, 183 n4

Vidal, Gore 11
visual representation 54–5, 90, 99–101, 151; *see also* photographs

Waldman, Ayelet 113
Walker, Alice 29

Wallace, David Foster 9, 53
Wandering Jew, The (folkloric figure) 99–101
Wells, H. G. 72
White, Edmund 96
Whitman, Walt 61–4
Wittgenstein, Ludwig 26–8
Wolfe, Thomas 167 n5
Woolf, Virginia 29, 135; *A Room of One's Own* 29; *Orlando* 135
Wright, Richard 49

X, Malcolm 49

Yad Vashem 121
Yeats, William Butler 72, 74–5

Yehoshua A. B. 113
Yezierska, Anzia 66
Yiddish 6, 30–1, 66–71, 102, 112, 140
Yiddish Literature 6, 13, 19, 48, 56, 58, 61–2, 66–71, 73–4, 78, 82, 129, 134–6
Yom Kippur 97–8

Zionism 105, 110, 111, 115–16, 119–20, 122–3, 128–9, 133–5, 137–40
Zuckerman, Nathan (fictional character) 1–2, 16, 23–39, 42, 46–51, 67, 76, 78–83, 85–9, 103–4, 115–16, 146–8

www.ingramcontent.com/pod-product-compliance
Lightning Source LLC
Chambersburg PA
CBHW072236290426
44111CB00012B/2124